DATA TITANS

Data Titans

NAVIGATING THE AI REVOLUTION IN BIG DATA

Dr. Hesham Mohamed Elsherif

ELDONUSA Publishing

Contents

ABOUT THE AUTHOR

DATA TITANS

Navigating the AI Revolution in Big Data
Dr. Hesham Mohamed Elsherif

An expert in Empirical research methodology, Dr. Elsherif specializes particularly in the Qualitative approach and Action research. This specialization has not only strengthened his research endeavors but has also allowed him to contribute invaluable insights and advancements in these areas.

Over the years, Dr. Elsherif has made significant contributions to the academic world not only as a professional researcher but also as an Adjunct Professor. This multifaceted role in the educational landscape has further solidified his reputation as a thought leader and pioneer.

Furthermore, Dr. Elsherif's expertise isn't confined to one region. He has served as a consultant to numerous educational institutions on an international scale, sharing best practices, innovative strategies, and his deep insights into the ever-evolving realms of management and technology.

Combining a passion for education with an unparalleled depth of knowledge, Dr. Elsherif continues to inspire, educate, and lead in both the library and academic communities.

PREFACE

In an era where data is likened to oil for its immense value, the fusion of Artificial Intelligence (AI) and Big Data stands as a beacon of transformative power. This book, "Data Titans: Navigating the AI Revolution in Big Data," is born from a compelling need to dissect and understand this monumental shift. The journey of writing this book has been as enlightening as it is challenging, diving into the intricate webs spun by AI in the vast universe of Big Data.

The genesis of this exploration was a simple question: How is AI reshaping the landscape of Big Data? However, as I delved deeper, this question branched into a myriad of facets - ethical considerations, technological advancements, industry-specific applications, and the very future we are steering towards. This book is a culmination of those explorations, aimed at providing a comprehensive yet accessible guide to anyone intrigued by the interplay of AI and Big Data.

One of the primary motivations behind this book is the demystification of AI in the context of Big Data. The term 'AI' often conjures images of science fiction, yet its real-world applications are both more mundane and more profound. From predicting consumer behavior to revolutionizing healthcare diagnostics, AI's integration with Big Data is reshaping industries and, by extension, our daily lives. This book aims to shine a light on these changes, offering insights into how AI processes, interprets, and leverages vast datasets.

Another key aspect I have endeavored to address is the ethical and privacy concerns surrounding AI and Big Data. As much as these technologies promise unprecedented growth and opportunities, they also pose significant challenges related to data security, privacy, and ethical decision-making. These concerns are not just academic; they have real-world implications for businesses, governments, and individuals alike. Through this book, readers will gain an understanding of these challenges and the evolving frameworks aimed at addressing them.

Furthermore, "Data Titans" does not shy away from the technical complexities inherent in AI and Big Data. However, the technical discourse is balanced with practical insights, making it accessible to a broader audience, including professionals, students, and enthusiasts. The inclusion of case studies, industry-specific applications, and expert opinions provides a real-world anchor to the theoretical discussions.

The book also looks towards the future, offering a glimpse into emerging trends and technologies that are poised to redefine the AI and Big Data landscape. In doing so, it serves as a guide for professionals and students seeking to carve out a career in this dynamic field.

In writing "Data Titans," I have drawn not only from academic research and industry reports but also from conversations with experts, practitioners, and educators in the field of AI and Big Data. Their insights and experiences have been invaluable in shaping the narrative of this book.

As you embark on this journey through the pages of "Data Titans," I invite you to engage with an open mind and a keen sense of curiosity. Whether you are a seasoned professional in the field of AI and Big Data or an intrigued newcomer, this book aims to enrich your understanding and spark a deeper interest in this fascinating and ever-evolving domain.

Welcome to the world of Data Titans, where the future of AI and Big Data unfolds.

Dr. Hesham Mohamed Elsherif

WHO SHOULD READ THIS BOOK?

"Data Titans: Navigating the AI Revolution in Big Data" is designed to resonate with a broad spectrum of readers, ranging from industry professionals to academic scholars, and from curious enthusiasts to forward-thinking policymakers. This book offers valuable insights, practical knowledge, and a forward-looking perspective on AI and Big Data. Below are the key groups who will find this book particularly beneficial:

1. **Data Science and AI Professionals:** For those already immersed in the fields of data science, machine learning, or AI, this book serves as a comprehensive resource to understand the latest trends, challenges, and opportunities presented by Big Data. It offers a deeper dive into specialized AI techniques tailored for handling vast datasets, as well as discussions on ethical considerations and future advancements in the field.

2. **Business Leaders and Managers:** Executives and managers who are responsible for steering their companies through the digital age will find this book invaluable. It provides insights into how AI and Big Data can be leveraged for strategic decision-making, operational efficiency, and customer engagement, along with case studies from various industries.

3. **IT Professionals and Software Developers:** This book is an excellent resource for IT professionals and developers looking to expand their expertise into the realm of AI and Big Data. It covers the technological foundations, integration challenges, and the latest tools and frameworks used in the industry.

4. **Students and Academic Researchers:** Students in fields such as computer science, data science, AI, and related disciplines will find this book a thorough educational resource. It covers both the foundational concepts and the cutting-edge advancements in the field, along with career guidance for those aspiring to enter the industry.

5. **Policy Makers and Regulators:** For those involved in policy-making, regulation, or governance, this book offers a clear understanding of the implications, challenges, and potential of AI in Big Data. The discussions on data privacy, ethical considerations, and regulatory frameworks provide essential insights for informed decision-making.

6. **Tech Enthusiasts and Futurists:** Individuals with a keen interest in technology and its impact on the future will find this book a fascinating read. It not only covers the current state of AI and Big Data but also delves into future trends and predictions, offering a glimpse into how these technologies will shape our world.

7. **Entrepreneurs and Start-up Founders:** This book is a treasure trove for entrepreneurs and start-up founders aiming to leverage AI and Big Data in their ventures. It provides practical insights into how these technologies can be used to gain a competitive edge, understand market dynamics, and drive innovation.

8. **Educators and Trainers:** Educators and trainers in the field of technology, data science, and business management can use this book as a reference to design their curriculum, update their knowledge base, and provide a comprehensive learning experience to their students.

9. **General Readers with Curiosity in AI and Big Data:** Even if you're not a professional in the field, but have a burgeoning curiosity about AI, Big Data, and their impact on society and the future, this book offers an accessible and engaging pathway to understanding these complex but fascinating topics.

In summary, "Data Titans" is a must-read for anyone who wishes to gain a comprehensive understanding of the dynamic and rapidly evolving landscape of AI and Big Data, and their profound impact on industries, economies, and societies.

WHY THIS BOOK IS ESSENTIAL READING?

"Data Titans: Navigating the AI Revolution in Big Data" is not just another book on the shelves of technological discourse; it is a vital compass in a world increasingly driven by data and artificial intelligence. Here are several compelling reasons why this book is essential reading for a wide range of audiences:

1. **Demystifying Complex Concepts:** AI and Big Data are fields riddled with complex concepts and technical jargon. This book breaks down these complexities into understandable language, making it accessible to readers with varying levels of expertise. Whether you are a seasoned professional or a curious novice, you'll find the content both enlightening and engaging.

2. **Comprehensive Coverage:** The book provides a holistic view of the AI and Big Data landscape. From foundational technologies to ethical considerations, and from current applications to future trends, it covers all the essential aspects. This comprehensive approach makes it a one-stop resource for understanding the entire ecosystem of AI and Big Data.

3. **Practical Insights and Real-World Applications:** Beyond theoretical knowledge, this book is rich in practical insights. It includes numerous case studies, examples, and narratives from real-world applications across various industries. These practical

elements illustrate how theories and concepts are being applied in real-world scenarios, making the content more relatable and useful.

4. **Navigating Ethical and Privacy Concerns:** As much as AI and Big Data are about technological advancements, they also raise significant ethical and privacy concerns. This book tackles these issues head-on, providing thoughtful discussions on how to navigate these challenges responsibly. It encourages readers to consider the broader implications of these technologies on society and individuals.

5. **Future-Oriented Perspective:** "Data Titans" doesn't just dwell on current technologies and practices; it also casts an eye to the future. It explores emerging trends, potential future developments, and the likely impact of AI and Big Data on different sectors. This forward-looking perspective is crucial for anyone looking to stay ahead in a rapidly evolving field.

6. **Career Development and Skill Enhancement:** For those looking to develop a career in AI, Big Data, or related fields, this book serves as a valuable guide. It highlights essential skills, educational pathways, and career opportunities, providing a roadmap for professional growth and development in these dynamic industries.

7. **Global and Cross-Industry Relevance:** The insights and discussions in this book are not limited to any single region or industry. AI and Big Data are global phenomena, and this book addresses their impact and applications across various sectors and geographies. This makes it relevant to a global audience and across multiple industries.

8. **Informed Decision-Making for Business Leaders:** For business leaders and decision-makers, understanding AI and Big Data is no longer optional but essential. This book provides the knowledge needed to make informed decisions about adopting and integrating these technologies into business strategies.

9. **Academic and Research Value:** For students and researchers, this book is a treasure trove of information, serving as both a study guide and a research reference. The comprehensive coverage of topics ensures it is a valuable addition to academic libraries and personal collections.

10. **Empowering General Readers:** Even for general readers with a casual interest in technology, this book empowers with knowledge, helping to understand how AI and Big Data are shaping our world, our work, and our future.

In summary, "Data Titans" is essential reading because it not only educates and informs but also inspires and provokes thought. It is a book that equips its readers to navigate the complex and ever-changing landscape of AI and Big Data, making it an indispensable guide for anyone looking to understand and engage with these pivotal technologies of the 21st century.

Introduction

Introduction to AI and Big Data:

The introductory section of "Data Titans: Navigating the AI Revolution in Big Data" sets the stage for a deep and comprehensive exploration into the intertwined worlds of Artificial Intelligence (AI) and Big Data. This chapter aims to provide readers with a foundational understanding of both concepts, their evolution, and their growing significance in the modern world.

Understanding AI and Big Data: Definitions and Evolution

AI refers to the simulation of human intelligence in machines that are programmed to think like humans and mimic their actions (Russell & Norvig, 2016). The term may also be applied to any machine that exhibits traits associated with a human mind, such as learning and problem-solving. Big Data, on the other hand, is characterized by its volume, velocity, variety, and veracity, and refers to the massive sets of data that are collected, processed, and analyzed to uncover patterns, trends, and associations, particularly relating to human behavior and interactions (Mayer-Schönberger & Cukier, 2013).

The intersection of AI and Big Data is particularly powerful. Big Data provides the vast amounts of information needed for AI algorithms to learn and adapt, while AI provides the means to analyze and extract meaningful insights from this data, often in real-time (Jordan & Mitchell, 2015).

The Importance of AI and Big Data in the Modern Context

In today's digital era, the relevance of AI and Big Data cannot be overstated. They drive innovation in diverse sectors, from healthcare, where AI algorithms assist in diagnosing diseases (Esteva et al., 2019), to finance, where Big Data analytics are crucial for risk assessment and decision making (Bholat et al., 2015). The synergy of AI and Big Data is propelling advancements in autonomous vehicles, personalized marketing, smart cities, and much more.

Challenges and Opportunities

While the integration of AI with Big Data offers immense opportunities, it also presents significant challenges. Issues related to data privacy, security, and ethical use of AI are at the forefront of ongoing debates (Tene & Polonetsky, 2012). Moreover, the need for advanced infrastructure and skilled professionals to manage and interpret Big Data and develop AI solutions is increasingly critical (Davenport & Patil, 2012).

This introductory chapter of "Data Titans" aims to provide a clear, concise, and engaging overview of AI and Big Data, setting the stage for more detailed exploration in subsequent chapters. It is designed to be accessible to readers from various backgrounds, offering a balanced view of the possibilities and challenges posed by these technologies.

The Evolution of Big Data and the Rise of AI:

The convergence of Big Data and Artificial Intelligence (AI) marks a pivotal epoch in the annals of technological evolution. In this section of "Data Titans: Navigating the AI Revolution in Big Data," we embark on a journey through the historical progression of Big Data and the ascent of AI, underscoring how these phenomena have become interdependent forces reshaping our world.

The Dawn of Big Data

The term "Big Data" emerged as a way to describe datasets too large and complex for traditional data-processing application software to handle efficiently (Laney, 2001). The genesis of Big Data can be traced back to the early 2000s when industry analyst Doug Laney articulated the now-mainstream definition of big data as the three Vs: Volume, Velocity, and Variety (Laney, 2001). This era witnessed an exponential increase in data volume, fueled by the advent of the internet, social media platforms, and the proliferation of digital devices.

The Advent of AI: From Concept to Reality

While the concept of AI has been around since the mid-20th century, its practical application was limited until recent decades. The term "Artificial Intelligence" was first coined by John McCarthy in 1956, referring to machines capable of performing tasks that typically require human intelligence (McCarthy et al., 2006). However, it wasn't until the 21st century, with the advent of advanced machine learning algorithms and increased computational power, that AI began to realize its full potential (Kaplan & Haenlein, 2019).

The Symbiotic Relationship Between Big Data and AI

he true power of AI comes to the forefront when coupled with Big Data. AI algorithms, particularly in machine learning and deep learning, require vast amounts of data to learn and make informed decisions. The surge in Big Data has provided the necessary fuel for these algorithms to evolve and become more sophisticated (Jordan & Mitchell, 2015). This synergy has been pivotal in advancements such as predictive analytics, natural language processing, and computer vision.

Challenges and Ethical Considerations

As AI continues to advance and Big Data grows ever larger, ethical considerations and challenges such as data privacy, security, and the potential for bias in AI algorithms have become hot-button issues. Scholars have raised concerns about the ethical use of Big Data and the transparency of AI systems (Mittelstadt et al., 2016). Addressing these concerns is crucial for the responsible development and implementation of AI technologies.

The Future Trajectory

The evolution of Big Data and the rise of AI are not just historical phenomena; they are ongoing processes that continue to shape the technological landscape. The future promises even more integration of

AI in various sectors, leveraging Big Data for innovative applications and transforming industries (Sivarajah et al., 2017).

The introduction to the evolution of Big Data and the rise of AI sets the stage for understanding how these technologies have evolved independently and together. This historical context is essential for comprehending their current state and future potential.

Objectives and Scope of the Book:

The primary objective of "Data Titans: Navigating the AI Revolution in Big Data" is to elucidate the intricate dynamics between Artificial Intelligence (AI) and Big Data, providing an in-depth exploration of their confluence and its far-reaching implications. This treatise aims to furnish a comprehensive understanding, addressing both the theoretical underpinnings and practical applications of AI in the realm of Big Data. It endeavors to dissect the complex, multifaceted relationship between these two domains, shedding light on how AI algorithms harness the power of massive datasets and, conversely, how Big Data fuels AI advancements.

In achieving this, the book sets forth several specific goals: firstly, to demystify the technical complexities inherent in AI and Big Data analytics, rendering them accessible to a diverse readership (Hastie, Tibshirani, & Friedman, 2009); secondly, to provide a critical examination of the ethical, legal, and societal challenges that emerge at the intersection of AI and Big Data (Floridi, 2016); and thirdly, to prognosticate the future trajectory of these technologies, contemplating their potential to engender transformative changes across various sectors (Brynjolfsson & McAfee, 2014).

Scope

The scope of this scholarly work is deliberately expansive, yet focused. It traverses a wide array of topics within the domains of AI and Big Data. The book commences with a historical overview, tracing the evolution of Big Data and the ascendancy of AI, thereby setting a contextual backdrop for the ensuing discourse (Mayer-Schönberger

& Cukier, 2013). Subsequent chapters delve into the technical aspects, exploring AI methodologies such as machine learning, deep learning, and their application in processing and analyzing vast datasets (Goodfellow, Bengio, & Courville, 2016).

Furthermore, the book addresses the practical implementation of AI in Big Data across diverse industries, from healthcare to finance, underscoring the transformative impact of these technologies in real-world scenarios (Agrawal, Gans, & Goldfarb, 2018). A critical analysis of ethical, privacy, and regulatory concerns forms an integral part of the narrative, highlighting the need for responsible stewardship of these powerful technologies (O'Neil, 2016).

The final segments of the book are dedicated to envisaging the future, contemplating emerging trends, and predicting how ongoing advancements in AI and Big Data might unfold. This prognostic approach not only provides a glimpse into the future but also serves as a guide for policymakers, industry practitioners, and academics in navigating the evolving landscape (Bostrom, 2014).

Conclusion

In summary, "Data Titans: Navigating the AI Revolution in Big Data" is an ambitious scholarly endeavor that seeks to provide a thorough, nuanced understanding of the interplay between AI and Big Data. Its comprehensive scope, coupled with a commitment to addressing both current realities and future possibilities, renders it an indispensable resource for anyone engaged in or affected by these transformative technologies.

Chapter 1: The Foundations of AI in Big Data

The bedrock of understanding the confluence of Artificial Intelligence (AI) and Big Data lies in comprehending their foundational elements and the mechanisms through which they synergistically operate. This section of "Data Titans: Navigating the AI Revolution in Big Data" delves into the underpinnings of AI within the context of Big Data, elucidating the theoretical and practical frameworks that form the backbone of this integration.

Theoretical Foundations of AI in Big Data

At its core, AI in the context of Big Data is underpinned by complex algorithms and computational theories that enable machines to perform tasks which traditionally require human intelligence. This includes machine learning (ML), a subset of AI, which focuses on developing algorithms that enable computers to learn from and make predictions or decisions based on data (Bishop, 2006). Deep learning, an advanced form of ML, is particularly instrumental in parsing through the intricacies of Big Data, utilizing neural networks to analyze and interpret vast and complex datasets (LeCun, Bengio, & Hinton, 2015).

The theoretical foundations of AI in the realm of Big Data are anchored in a profound understanding of computational algorithms, statistical models, and machine learning techniques. This section of "Data Titans: Navigating the AI Revolution in Big Data" aims to elucidate these foundational theories, providing an academic purview into how AI algorithms function within the expansive and complex landscape of Big Data.

Computational Algorithms and Statistical Models

At the heart of AI's ability to process and analyze Big Data are sophisticated computational algorithms and statistical models. These algorithms are designed to identify patterns, extract features, and make predictions based on large datasets. Statistical models in AI, including Bayesian networks and regression models, enable the quantification of uncertainties and probabilistic reasoning in decision-making processes (Bishop, 2006). The efficiency of these models is crucial in managing the volume and complexity inherent in Big Data.

Computational Algorithms:

Computational algorithms form the backbone of AI in Big Data applications, serving as the engines that process, analyze, and derive meaning from massive datasets. These algorithms are designed to handle the complexity and scale inherent in Big Data, providing efficient and scalable solutions for tasks ranging from data preprocessing to advanced analytics. Key aspects of computational algorithms in this context include:

Scalability: Algorithms must be scalable to handle the volume, velocity, and variety of Big Data. They should efficiently process large datasets distributed across diverse computing environments, such as clusters and cloud platforms.

Parallelism: Many computational algorithms leverage parallel computing paradigms to exploit the inherent parallelism in Big Data processing. Techniques like MapReduce, Spark, and distributed computing frameworks enable efficient parallel execution, enhancing performance and throughput.

Optimization: Optimization techniques are crucial for improving the efficiency and effectiveness of computational algorithms. These include algorithmic optimizations to reduce computational complexity, as well as system-level optimizations to enhance resource utilization and throughput.

Adaptability: Given the dynamic nature of Big Data environments, algorithms must be adaptable to evolving data characteristics and requirements. This necessitates the incorporation of adaptive learning mechanisms, real-time feedback loops, and dynamic resource allocation strategies.

Privacy and Security: With concerns surrounding data privacy and security, computational algorithms in AI must integrate mechanisms for safeguarding sensitive information. Techniques such as differential privacy, homomorphic encryption, and secure multiparty computation are employed to preserve confidentiality while enabling meaningful analysis of Big Data.

Statistical Models:

Statistical models play a pivotal role in extracting insights and making informed decisions from Big Data. These models provide the framework for understanding the underlying patterns, relationships, and uncertainties within datasets, thereby enabling predictive modeling, hypothesis testing, and probabilistic inference. Key components of statistical models in the context of AI in Big Data include:

Descriptive Statistics: Descriptive statistics techniques are employed to summarize and visualize the characteristics of Big Data, facilitating exploratory data analysis and hypothesis generation. Measures such as mean, median, variance, and correlation offer insights into the central tendency, dispersion, and relationships present in the data.

Predictive Modeling: Statistical models enable predictive analytics by capturing the relationships between input variables and target outcomes. Techniques such as regression analysis, time series forecasting, and machine learning algorithms (e.g., decision trees, neural networks) are utilized to build predictive models that generalize from data and make accurate forecasts.

Inferential Statistics: Inferential statistics techniques are employed to draw conclusions and make inferences about populations based on sample data. Methods such as hypothesis testing, confidence intervals, and Bayesian inference facilitate robust statistical inference, allowing researchers to assess the significance of observed effects and quantify uncertainties.

Probabilistic Graphical Models: Probabilistic graphical models provide a formalism for representing and reasoning about uncertainty and dependency structures in Big Data. Models such as Bayesian networks and Markov random fields capture probabilistic relationships among variables, enabling probabilistic inference, anomaly detection, and decision-making under uncertainty.

Model Evaluation and Validation: Rigorous evaluation and validation of statistical models are essential to ensure their reliability and generalization capabilities. Techniques such as cross-validation, bootstrapping, and model selection criteria (e.g., AIC, BIC) are employed to assess model performance, identify overfitting, and optimize model complexity.

Theoretical foundations of AI in Big Data, encompassing computational algorithms and statistical models, form the cornerstone of modern data-driven technologies. By leveraging advanced algorithms and statistical techniques, organizations can unlock the full potential of Big Data to gain actionable insights, drive innovation, and create value across various domains. However, the effective utilization of these foundations requires a holistic understanding of their principles, methodologies, and applications, along with ongoing research and development efforts to address emerging challenges and opportunities in the dynamic landscape of AI and Big Data.

Machine Learning: The Engine of AI in Big Data

Machine Learning (ML), a pivotal branch of AI, is fundamentally about designing and applying algorithms that enable computers to learn from data. The premise of ML is to develop models that can improve their performance at a task with experience, without being explicitly programmed for every contingency (Alpaydin, 2020). Deep learning, a subset of ML, plays a significant role in interpreting Big Data. Utilizing neural networks, deep learning algorithms can process and analyze data with a level of depth and complexity that was previously unattainable (Goodfellow, Bengio, & Courville, 2016).

Machine Learning Paradigms:

Machine learning encompasses a broad spectrum of algorithms and techniques that enable systems to learn from data and improve performance over time. In the realm of Big Data, several key machine learning paradigms emerge as fundamental pillars:

Supervised Learning: Supervised learning algorithms learn from labeled training data, where each input is associated with a corresponding output or target variable. These algorithms aim to generalize from the training data to make predictions on unseen data instances. Common supervised learning tasks include classification (e.g., spam detection, image recognition) and regression (e.g., sales forecasting, price prediction).

Unsupervised Learning: Unsupervised learning algorithms operate on unlabeled data, seeking to uncover hidden patterns or structures within the dataset. Clustering algorithms, such as k-means and hierarchical clustering, segment data into meaningful groups based on similarity metrics, while dimensionality reduction techniques like principal component analysis (PCA) and t-distributed stochastic neighbor embedding (t-SNE) facilitate visualization and feature extraction.

Semi-Supervised Learning: Semi-supervised learning combines elements of supervised and unsupervised learning by leveraging both labeled and unlabeled data. These algorithms exploit the abundance of unlabeled data to improve model performance, particularly in scenarios where labeled data is scarce or expensive to obtain.

Reinforcement Learning: Reinforcement learning involves training agents to interact with an environment and learn optimal decision-making strategies through trial and error. Agents receive feedback in the form of rewards or penalties based on their actions, allowing them to learn from experience and refine their behavior over time.

Reinforcement learning has applications in autonomous systems, robotics, and game playing.

Challenges and Considerations:

Despite its immense potential, applying machine learning to Big Data poses several challenges and considerations:

Scalability: Traditional machine learning algorithms may struggle to scale with the volume and velocity of Big Data. Scalable algorithms and distributed computing frameworks, such as Apache Spark and TensorFlow, are essential for processing massive datasets efficiently.

Complexity and Dimensionality: Big Data often exhibits high dimensionality and complexity, which can lead to overfitting and model degradation. Dimensionality reduction techniques and regularization methods help mitigate these challenges by extracting relevant features and controlling model complexity.

Data Quality and Preprocessing: The quality and cleanliness of data significantly impact the performance of machine learning models. Robust data preprocessing pipelines, including data cleaning, feature engineering, and normalization, are critical for ensuring the integrity and reliability of input data.

Interpretability and Explainability: As AI systems become increasingly pervasive, the interpretability and explainability of machine learning models are gaining importance. Techniques such as model interpretability algorithms and surrogate models facilitate understanding and trust in AI-driven decision-making processes.

Ethical and Societal Implications: The deployment of AI in Big Data raises ethical and societal concerns, including bias in algorithmic decision-making, privacy implications, and potential job displacement. Responsible AI practices, regulatory frameworks, and ethical guidelines are essential for addressing these challenges and ensuring the responsible development and deployment of AI systems.

Future Directions:

The future of AI in Big Data hinges on advancements in machine learning algorithms, methodologies, and applications. Key areas of focus for future research and development include:

Deep Learning and Neural Networks: Deep learning techniques, fueled by advances in neural networks and deep architectures, hold promise for tackling complex problems in Big Data analytics, such as natural language processing, image recognition, and speech synthesis.

Federated Learning and Edge Computing: Federated learning enables collaborative model training across distributed devices and data sources, while edge computing brings computation closer to data sources, reducing latency and privacy concerns. These paradigms have the potential to revolutionize AI in decentralized and resource-constrained environments.

Explainable AI and Fairness: Addressing the interpretability and fairness of machine learning models remains a priority, with research efforts focused on developing explainable AI techniques and mitigating algorithmic biases to ensure transparency and fairness in AI-driven decision-making.

Meta-Learning and AutoML: Meta-learning approaches aim to automate the process of model selection, hyperparameter tuning, and feature engineering, making machine learning more accessible and efficient for non-experts. AutoML platforms and tools streamline the development and deployment of machine learning pipelines, accelerating innovation and democratizing AI.

In conclusion, machine learning serves as the engine of AI in Big Data, enabling systems to extract insights, make predictions, and drive decision-making processes at scale. By advancing machine learning algorithms, methodologies, and applications, researchers and practitioners can unlock the full potential of Big Data to address complex challenges, drive innovation, and create value across diverse domains. However, addressing the inherent challenges and ethical considerations associated with AI in Big Data requires a multidisciplinary approach, encompassing technological advancements, regulatory frameworks, and ethical guidelines to ensure the responsible and equitable development and deployment of AI systems.

Data-Driven Decision Making

The integration of AI in Big Data is largely focused on data-driven decision making. This involves using AI algorithms to process vast datasets, derive insights, and make informed decisions. The theoretical underpinning of this approach is grounded in the concept that data, when properly analyzed, can reveal patterns and insights that are not immediately apparent but are critical for strategic decision making (Provost & Fawcett, 2013).

Data Collection and Integration:

At the core of data-driven decision-making is the collection and integration of diverse datasets from disparate sources. Theoretical frameworks and methodologies for data collection and integration ensure the availability of high-quality, comprehensive datasets for analysis. This involves techniques such as data extraction, transformation, and loading (ETL), data cleansing, and integration of structured and unstructured data sources. Theoretical foundations in this area encompass data management principles, data governance frameworks, and interoperability standards to ensure data quality, consistency, and accessibility.

Data Exploration and Visualization:

Exploratory data analysis (EDA) and data visualization techniques provide insights into the underlying patterns, trends, and relationships within the data. Theoretical foundations in data exploration and visualization encompass statistical methods, visualization techniques, and interactive tools for data exploration. Exploratory data analysis techniques such as descriptive statistics, correlation analysis, and dimensionality reduction enable analysts to gain a deeper understanding of the data, while data visualization techniques such as scatter plots, histograms, and heatmaps facilitate the interpretation and communication of findings.

Predictive Modeling and Forecasting:

Predictive modeling techniques enable organizations to anticipate future trends, outcomes, and behaviors based on historical data. Theoretical foundations in predictive modeling encompass machine learning algorithms, statistical models, and time series analysis techniques. Supervised learning algorithms such as regression analysis and classification models are employed for predictive modeling tasks, while time series analysis techniques such as autoregressive integrated moving average (ARIMA) and exponential smoothing models are used for forecasting future trends and patterns.

Prescriptive Analytics and Optimization:

Prescriptive analytics techniques go beyond descriptive and predictive analytics to recommend optimal courses of action to achieve desired outcomes. Theoretical foundations in prescriptive analytics encompass optimization algorithms, simulation models, and decision theory principles. Optimization algorithms such as linear programming, integer programming, and genetic algorithms are used to identify optimal solutions to complex decision-making problems, while simulation models enable organizations to explore different scenarios and evaluate the impact of alternative strategies.

Real-Time Analytics and Decision Automation:

Real-time analytics techniques enable organizations to analyze and respond to data in near real-time, facilitating agile decision-making processes. Theoretical foundations in real-time analytics encompass stream processing algorithms, event processing systems, and complex event processing (CEP) techniques. Stream processing algorithms such as Apache Kafka and Apache Flink enable the processing of continuous data streams, while event processing systems and CEP techniques facilitate the detection of meaningful patterns and events in real-time data streams.

Ethical and Regulatory Considerations:

Ethical and regulatory considerations play a critical role in data-driven decision-making, particularly in domains such as healthcare, finance, and governance. Theoretical foundations in ethical and regulatory considerations encompass principles of data privacy, security, and fairness, as well as regulatory frameworks such as GDPR, HIPAA, and Basel III. Organizations must adhere to ethical guidelines and regulatory requirements to ensure the responsible and ethical use of data in decision-making processes, safeguarding individual rights and protecting against potential biases and discrimination.

In conclusion, the theoretical foundations of AI in Big Data provide the framework for data-driven decision-making processes, enabling organizations to leverage insights derived from large and complex datasets to inform strategic, operational, and tactical decisions. By embracing theoretical principles and methodologies in data collection, exploration, modeling, and analysis, organizations can harness the power of Big Data to drive innovation, optimize performance, and achieve competitive advantage. However, addressing ethical and regulatory considerations is essential to ensure the responsible and ethical use of data in decision-making processes, fostering trust and accountability in AI-driven decision-making.

Challenges in AI and Big Data Integration

While the theoretical foundations provide a robust framework for the integration of AI in Big Data, they also present challenges. One significant challenge is the 'curse of dimensionality,' which refers to the exponential increase in complexity that arises with the addition of dimensions (features) in a dataset (Bellman, 1961). Another challenge is ensuring the accuracy and reliability of the AI models, particularly in the context of the vast and diverse nature of Big Data (Halevy, Norvig, & Pereira, 2009).

Understanding the theoretical foundations of AI in Big Data is essential for comprehending how these technologies work individually and in tandem. These foundations underscore the sophistication of AI algorithms and the complexity of managing and analyzing Big Data. As AI continues to evolve, these theoretical underpinnings will guide its integration and application in the ever-expanding universe of Big Data.

Data Characteristics and Challenges

The efficacious application of AI in Big Data hinges on understanding the inherent characteristics of Big Data – volume, velocity, variety, and veracity. The sheer volume of data presents computational and storage challenges, while the velocity necessitates algorithms capable of real-time processing. The variety of data, ranging from structured to unstructured formats, requires sophisticated analytical tools for effective interpretation. Lastly, veracity underscores the importance of accuracy and reliability of data in AI applications (Kitchin, 2014).

In the intricate tapestry of Big Data and Artificial Intelligence (AI), understanding the characteristics and challenges of data is paramount. "Data Titans: Navigating the AI Revolution in Big Data" allocates a critical section to dissect the inherent properties of Big Data and the concomitant challenges they pose for AI applications. This analysis is pivotal in comprehending how AI can be effectively harnessed to navigate and exploit the vast seas of data in the digital age.

Inherent Characteristics of Big Data

Big Data is typified by its distinct characteristics, commonly referred to as the 'four Vs': Volume, Velocity, Variety, and Veracity (Laney, 2001). Volume refers to the immense quantities of data generated every second, presenting significant storage and processing challenges. Velocity denotes the rapid rate at which data is produced, collected, and processed, necessitating real-time analysis capabilities. Variety alludes to the diverse types of data, from structured numerical data to unstructured text, images, and video, requiring sophisticated parsing and interpretation methods. Lastly, Veracity concerns the quality and trustworthiness of the data, a critical factor in ensuring the accuracy of AI-driven analyses and decisions.

Challenges in Handling Big Data

The handling of Big Data for AI applications is fraught with challenges. One of the primary issues is the management of its sheer volume. Storing and processing large datasets demand extensive computational resources and efficient data management strategies (Marz & Warren, 2015). Additionally, the velocity of data generation requires AI systems capable of processing information in near real-time, a feat that necessitates advanced algorithms and high-performance computing infrastructures (McAfee & Brynjolfsson, 2012).

The variety of data presents another significant challenge. AI systems must be adept at processing and analyzing diverse data formats, requiring a level of flexibility and adaptability in algorithm design (Fan, Han, & Liu, 2014). This diversity also implies a need for sophisticated data integration techniques to ensure cohesive and comprehensive data analysis.

Moreover, the veracity of data is a crucial concern. AI systems rely on the quality of the input data for their accuracy. Poor data quality can lead to erroneous outcomes and misguided decision-making processes (Wang & Strong, 1996). Ensuring the integrity and reliability of data is therefore a critical aspect of AI applications in Big Data.

The exploration of the characteristics and challenges of Big Data within the realm of AI underscores the complexities involved in effectively harnessing this data. As AI continues to evolve, addressing these challenges will be crucial in maximizing the potential of AI applications in Big Data environments.

Symbiosis of AI and Big Data

The symbiotic relationship between AI and Big Data is predicated on the premise that Big Data provides the necessary raw material (data) for AI algorithms to process and learn from, while AI offers the methodologies and computational prowess to mine insights from Big Data. This reciprocal relationship is central to advancements in areas such as predictive analytics, where AI algorithms predict future trends based on historical data (Provost & Fawcett, 2013).

In the scholarly treatise "Data Titans: Navigating the AI Revolution in Big Data," a pivotal section is devoted to elucidating the symbiotic relationship between Artificial Intelligence (AI) and Big Data. This interdependence is not merely a confluence of two technological phenomena but a synergistic partnership that amplifies the capabilities and potential applications of each. Understanding this symbiosis is essential for comprehending how AI and Big Data are collectively reshaping the landscape of data analytics and decision-making processes in the digital era.

AI as the Analytical Engine for Big Data

The essence of AI's role in this symbiosis lies in its capacity to serve as a sophisticated analytical engine for Big Data. AI, particularly through its subsets of machine learning and deep learning, provides the methodological framework to extract meaningful insights from the vast, complex datasets characteristic of Big Data (Hastie, Tibshirani, & Friedman, 2009). These AI algorithms are adept at identifying patterns, discerning trends, and making predictions, transforming raw data into actionable intelligence.

Advanced Analytics:

AI techniques such as machine learning, natural language processing (NLP), and computer vision form the backbone of advanced analytics in Big Data environments. These techniques enable organizations to uncover patterns, trends, and correlations within massive datasets that may be too complex for traditional analytical approaches. Machine learning algorithms, in particular, excel at tasks such as classification, regression, clustering, and anomaly detection, allowing organizations to derive valuable insights and make data-driven decisions.

Scalability and Performance:

One of the key advantages of AI in Big Data is its ability to scale and perform complex analytics tasks on massive datasets. AI algorithms, when coupled with distributed computing frameworks like Apache Hadoop and Spark, can process and analyze petabytes of data efficiently across distributed computing clusters. This scalability ensures that organizations can derive insights from Big Data in a timely manner, enabling real-time or near-real-time decision-making processes.

Adaptability and Learning:

AI systems exhibit adaptability and learning capabilities, allowing them to continuously improve their analytical performance over time. Through techniques such as supervised learning, unsupervised learning, and reinforcement learning, AI models can adapt to changing data patterns and environments, ensuring that analytical insights remain relevant and accurate. This adaptability is particularly crucial in dynamic and evolving Big Data ecosystems where data characteristics and requirements may change rapidly.

Complex Pattern Recognition:

Big Data often contains intricate patterns and relationships that may not be readily apparent to human analysts. AI excels at complex pattern recognition tasks, such as identifying subtle trends, correlations, and anomalies within large and heterogeneous datasets. Techniques such as deep learning, which leverages neural networks with multiple layers, are particularly effective at uncovering intricate patterns in unstructured data types like text, images, and videos.

Cognitive Insights and Decision Support:

AI systems have the capability to provide cognitive insights and decision support to human decision-makers by analyzing vast amounts of data and presenting actionable recommendations. Through techniques such as predictive modeling, sentiment analysis, and recommendation systems, AI can assist organizations in making informed decisions across various domains, including marketing, finance, healthcare, and cybersecurity. By augmenting human intelligence with AI-driven insights, organizations can enhance decision-making processes and achieve better outcomes.

AI serves as the analytical engine for Big Data, enabling organizations to unlock the full potential of vast and complex datasets. Through advanced analytics, scalability, adaptability, complex pattern recognition, and cognitive insights, AI empowers organizations to derive actionable insights and make data-driven decisions that drive innovation, optimize operations, and create competitive advantage. As AI and Big Data continue to evolve, the symbiotic relationship between the two will play an increasingly pivotal role in shaping the future of data-driven decision-making across industries and domains.

Big Data as the Fuel for AI

Conversely, Big Data acts as the indispensable fuel that powers AI. The efficacy and accuracy of AI algorithms are contingent on the quantity and quality of data available for learning and analysis. Big Data, with its voluminous and diverse datasets, offers a rich training ground for AI models, enabling them to refine their algorithms and enhance their predictive accuracy (Provost & Fawcett, 2013). This abundance of data is crucial for AI systems to learn, adapt, and evolve.

Data Quantity and Variety:

Big Data provides AI systems with a wealth of diverse and voluminous datasets that serve as the raw material for learning and analysis. The sheer quantity and variety of data enable AI algorithms to discover complex patterns, correlations, and trends that may not be apparent in smaller datasets. By processing large volumes of structured and unstructured data from various sources such as social media, sensors, and transaction logs, AI systems gain a comprehensive understanding of the underlying phenomena they aim to model or analyze.

Training Data for Machine Learning:

Machine learning algorithms, a core component of AI systems, rely heavily on training data to learn patterns and relationships. Big Data serves as the training ground for these algorithms, providing ample examples for supervised learning tasks such as classification and regression. The abundance of labeled data in Big Data environments enables machine learning models to generalize effectively and make accurate predictions on unseen data instances. Moreover, Big Data facilitates the creation of diverse and representative training datasets, which helps mitigate issues related to bias and overfitting in machine learning models.

Uncovering Insights and Trends:

Big Data acts as a rich source of insights and trends that drive AI-driven decision-making processes. Through techniques such as data mining, statistical analysis, and predictive modeling, AI systems extract valuable insights from Big Data, enabling organizations to identify emerging trends, forecast future events, and optimize business processes. By analyzing large-scale datasets, AI systems can uncover hidden patterns and correlations that inform strategic decisions, enhance operational efficiency, and drive innovation across various domains.

Real-Time Analytics and Feedback Loops:

The real-time nature of Big Data enables AI systems to operate in dynamic environments and respond rapidly to changing conditions. By processing streaming data and event streams in real-time, AI systems can generate immediate insights and trigger timely actions or alerts. Real-time analytics and feedback loops facilitate continuous learning and adaptation, allowing AI systems to refine their models and strategies based on the most up-to-date information. This iterative process of learning from real-time data ensures that AI systems remain relevant and effective in dynamic and evolving environments.

Challenges and Considerations:

While Big Data serves as a powerful resource for AI, its utilization also presents several challenges and considerations:

Data Quality and Governance: Ensuring the quality, reliability, and integrity of Big Data is essential for the effectiveness of AI algorithms. Organizations must implement robust data governance frameworks and data quality management practices to address issues such as data duplication, inconsistency, and incompleteness.

Scalability and Infrastructure: Processing and analyzing Big Data at scale require scalable infrastructure and computing resources. Organizations must invest in technologies such as distributed computing frameworks, cloud computing platforms, and high-performance computing clusters to handle the volume and velocity of Big Data effectively.

Privacy and Security: Big Data often contains sensitive and confidential information, raising concerns about privacy and security. Organizations must implement stringent data security measures, access controls, and encryption techniques to protect sensitive data from unauthorized access, breaches, and cyber threats.

Ethical and Societal Implications: The use of Big Data in AI-driven applications raises ethical and societal concerns, including issues related to data privacy, bias, fairness, and transparency. Organizations must adopt ethical principles, regulatory compliance, and responsible AI practices to address these concerns and ensure the ethical and responsible use of Big Data in AI applications.

Big Data serves as the fuel that powers AI systems, enabling them to learn, analyze, and generate insights at scale. By providing vast quantities of diverse and rich datasets, Big Data empowers AI algorithms to uncover patterns, trends, and correlations that drive data-driven decision-making processes. However, the effective utilization of Big Data in AI applications requires addressing challenges related to data quality, scalability, privacy, security, and ethical considerations. By overcoming these challenges and leveraging the symbiotic relationship between AI and Big Data, organizations can harness the full potential of data-driven technologies to drive innovation, optimize operations, and create value across various domains.

Mutual Enhancement and Challenges

This mutual enhancement, however, is not without its challenges. The complexity and variety of Big Data demand increasingly sophisticated AI algorithms to process and analyze it effectively. This necessitates continual advancements in AI techniques and computing power (Jordan & Mitchell, 2015). Additionally, the symbiosis must navigate issues of data quality and integrity, ensuring that AI systems are fed accurate and reliable data to produce valid results (Wang & Strong, 1996).

Mutual Enhancement:

Data Enrichment and Contextual Understanding: Big Data provides the raw material for AI algorithms to learn from, while AI techniques enhance the understanding and contextualization of the data. Through machine learning and natural language processing, AI systems can extract meaningful insights, patterns, and sentiments from large and diverse datasets, thereby enriching the understanding of the underlying data.

Scalability and Efficiency: Big Data infrastructure and technologies enable the storage, processing, and analysis of massive datasets at scale. AI algorithms, in turn, leverage these scalable infrastructure components to efficiently process and analyze vast amounts of data, enabling organizations to derive actionable insights and make informed decisions in real-time or near-real-time.

Predictive Analytics and Decision Support: By combining Big Data and AI, organizations can harness the power of predictive analytics and decision support systems to anticipate future trends, forecast outcomes, and optimize decision-making processes. AI techniques such as machine learning models and predictive modeling algorithms leverage historical and real-time data to generate accurate predictions, enabling organizations to proactively address challenges and seize opportunities.

Automation and Optimization: AI-driven automation and optimization techniques streamline and enhance various aspects of Big Data management and analysis. Through techniques such as automated data preprocessing, anomaly detection, and resource optimization, AI systems can automate repetitive tasks, optimize workflows, and improve the efficiency of Big Data processes, thereby reducing costs and enhancing productivity.

<u>**Challenges:**</u>

Data Quality and Governance: Ensuring the quality, reliability, and integrity of Big Data is a significant challenge in AI-driven environments. Poor data quality, data inconsistency, and data governance issues can undermine the effectiveness and reliability of AI algorithms, leading to inaccurate insights and flawed decision-making processes.

Scalability and Performance: Scaling AI algorithms to process and analyze Big Data efficiently remains a technical challenge. While advancements in distributed computing and parallel processing have improved scalability, organizations still face challenges related to optimizing performance, minimizing latency, and managing computational resources effectively.

Privacy and Security: Big Data often contains sensitive and confidential information, raising concerns about data privacy and security. AI-driven applications must adhere to stringent privacy regulations, implement robust data encryption and access controls, and mitigate risks associated with data breaches and cyber threats to safeguard sensitive data and protect individual privacy rights.

Bias and Fairness: AI algorithms trained on biased or incomplete datasets may produce biased outcomes, leading to unfair or discriminatory decision-making processes. Addressing bias and fairness issues in AI-driven environments requires careful data selection, algorithmic transparency, and fairness-aware model development techniques to ensure equitable outcomes for all stakeholders.

The symbiotic relationship between AI and Big Data offers immense opportunities for organizations to derive insights, optimize processes, and drive innovation. By mutually enhancing each other, AI and Big Data enable predictive analytics, decision support, automation, and optimization across various domains. However, addressing challenges related to data quality, scalability, privacy, and bias is essential to realize the full potential of this symbiotic relationship and ensure the ethical and responsible deployment of AI-driven solutions in Big Data environments. Through continuous innovation, collaboration, and ethical governance, organizations can harness the power of AI and Big Data to drive positive societal impact and create value in an increasingly data-driven world.

Ethical and Privacy Considerations

Furthermore, the symbiotic relationship between AI and Big Data brings to the fore critical ethical and privacy considerations. The use of vast amounts of personal and sensitive data raises concerns regarding consent, data protection, and the potential misuse of information. Ensuring ethical AI practices and robust data privacy measures is imperative in maintaining public trust and safeguarding individual rights (Tene & Polonetsky, 2012).

The symbiosis of AI and Big Data is a cornerstone of the modern data-driven world, offering unprecedented opportunities for insights and innovations. This section of "Data Titans" underscores the importance of this relationship in leveraging the full potential of both fields, while also acknowledging the challenges and responsibilities that accompany this powerful alliance.

Ethical Considerations:

Bias and Fairness: AI algorithms trained on biased datasets may perpetuate existing biases and lead to unfair or discriminatory outcomes. Organizations must implement measures to mitigate bias in AI models, such as ensuring diverse representation in training datasets, monitoring algorithmic decisions for fairness, and implementing fairness-aware model development techniques.

Transparency and Accountability: The opacity of AI algorithms poses challenges in understanding how decisions are made and holding accountable for potential errors or biases. Promoting transparency in AI-driven decision-making processes, such as providing explanations for algorithmic decisions and disclosing data sources and model architectures, enhances accountability and fosters trust among stakeholders.

Privacy Preservation: Big Data often contains sensitive personal information, raising concerns about privacy infringement and data misuse. Organizations must prioritize data privacy and implement robust privacy protection measures, such as data anonymization, encryption, and access controls, to safeguard sensitive information and protect individual privacy rights.

Data Ownership and Consent: Clarifying data ownership rights and obtaining informed consent from individuals for data collection and usage are fundamental ethical principles in Big Data environments. Organizations must establish clear data ownership policies, inform individuals about how their data will be used, and obtain explicit consent for data processing activities to ensure respect for individual autonomy and privacy preferences.

Privacy Considerations:

Data Minimization: Adopting principles of data minimization involves collecting and retaining only the minimum amount of data necessary for a specific purpose. By minimizing data collection and storage, organizations can reduce the risk of privacy breaches and limit exposure to potential data misuse or unauthorized access.

Security Safeguards: Implementing robust data security measures, such as encryption, access controls, and secure data transmission protocols, is essential for protecting sensitive information from unauthorized access, breaches, and cyber threats. By prioritizing data security, organizations can mitigate risks and safeguard the confidentiality and integrity of Big Data assets.

Privacy by Design: Integrating privacy considerations into the design and development of AI-driven systems through privacy-enhancing technologies and privacy-preserving techniques promotes privacy by design principles. Techniques such as differential privacy, homomorphic encryption, and federated learning enable organizations to build privacy-preserving AI solutions that minimize privacy risks and enhance user trust.

Regulatory Compliance: Adhering to relevant data protection regulations and privacy laws, such as the General Data Protection Regulation (GDPR) in the European Union and the California Consumer Privacy Act (CCPA) in the United States, is essential for ensuring compliance with legal requirements and avoiding penalties for non-compliance. Organizations must stay abreast of evolving regulatory landscapes and implement measures to address regulatory obligations related to data privacy and protection.

Ethical and privacy considerations are paramount in the symbiosis of AI and Big Data, requiring organizations to adopt responsible practices and ethical frameworks to ensure the ethical and responsible deployment of AI-driven solutions. By addressing bias and fairness, promoting transparency and accountability, safeguarding data privacy, and complying with relevant regulations, organizations can mitigate risks, build trust among stakeholders, and uphold ethical principles in the integration of AI and Big Data. Through ethical governance, collaboration, and continuous monitoring, organizations can harness the transformative potential of AI and Big Data while respecting individual rights and societal values.

Ethical Considerations and Data Privacy

The deployment of AI in Big Data raises pivotal ethical questions, particularly in the realms of data privacy, consent, and algorithmic transparency. The challenge lies in developing AI systems that respect privacy and ethical norms while still being able to harness the full potential of Big Data (Mittelstadt et al., 2016). The ongoing discourse in this area is critical in shaping policies and practices that govern the use of AI in Big Data.

In the critical exposition "Data Titans: Navigating the AI Revolution in Big Data," a section of paramount importance is dedicated to the ethical considerations and data privacy concerns intrinsic to the integration of Artificial Intelligence (AI) and Big Data. This segment scrutinizes the moral and ethical quandaries and data stewardship challenges that emerge at this nexus, reflecting on their implications for society, individuals, and organizations.

Ethical Considerations:

Bias and Fairness: AI algorithms trained on biased datasets may perpetuate existing biases and lead to unfair or discriminatory outcomes. It's essential to mitigate bias by ensuring diverse representation in training data, implementing fairness-aware algorithms, and regularly auditing AI systems for bias.

Transparency and Accountability: The opacity of AI algorithms can erode trust and accountability. Promoting transparency by providing explanations for algorithmic decisions and disclosing data sources enhances accountability and fosters trust among stakeholders.

Human Oversight and Responsibility: While AI systems can automate decision-making processes, human oversight remains crucial to ensure ethical decision-making and intervene in cases of algorithmic errors or ethical violations. Organizations should establish clear lines of responsibility and accountability for AI-driven processes.

Privacy Preservation: Protecting individuals' privacy rights is paramount in AI and Big Data environments. Organizations must prioritize data privacy and implement robust privacy protection measures, such as data anonymization, encryption, and access controls, to safeguard sensitive information from unauthorized access and misuse.

Data Privacy Challenges:

Data Collection and Consent: Obtaining informed consent for data collection and usage is fundamental to respecting individuals' privacy rights. Organizations should clearly communicate data collection practices, purposes, and usage to users and obtain explicit consent for data processing activities.

Data Security and Breach Prevention: Securing Big Data infrastructure and systems against unauthorized access, breaches, and cyber threats is critical to protecting sensitive information. Implementing robust data security measures, such as encryption, access controls, and security audits, helps mitigate the risk of data breaches and unauthorized access.

Data Minimization: Collecting and retaining only the minimum amount of data necessary for a specific purpose reduces the risk of privacy breaches and limits exposure to potential data misuse. Organizations should adopt data minimization principles to minimize the collection and storage of unnecessary or sensitive information.

Regulatory Compliance: Adhering to data protection regulations and privacy laws, such as the GDPR in the EU and the CCPA in the US, is essential for ensuring compliance with legal requirements and protecting individuals' privacy rights. Organizations must stay abreast of evolving regulatory landscapes and implement measures to address regulatory obligations related to data privacy and protection.

Strategies for Addressing Ethical Considerations and Data Privacy Challenges:

Ethical Frameworks and Guidelines: Developing and adhering to ethical frameworks and guidelines for AI and Big Data helps guide ethical decision-making and responsible conduct. Organizations should establish ethical principles and values that prioritize fairness, transparency, accountability, and privacy.

Privacy-Enhancing Technologies: Leveraging privacy-enhancing technologies, such as differential privacy, homomorphic encryption, and federated learning, enables organizations to build privacy-preserving AI solutions that minimize privacy risks and protect sensitive information.

Ethical AI Governance: Implementing robust governance structures and mechanisms for ethical AI ensures that ethical considerations and privacy concerns are integrated into all stages of AI development and deployment. Ethical AI governance frameworks should include mechanisms for ethics reviews, risk assessments, and stakeholder engagement.

Education and Training: Educating employees and stakeholders about ethical principles, data privacy best practices, and regulatory requirements fosters a culture of ethical conduct and privacy awareness within organizations. Training programs should cover topics such as bias mitigation, data privacy, and ethical decision-making in AI and Big Data contexts.

In conclusion, addressing ethical considerations and data privacy challenges is paramount in the symbiosis of AI and Big Data. By prioritizing fairness, transparency, accountability, and privacy, organizations can mitigate risks, build trust among stakeholders, and uphold ethical principles in the integration of AI and Big Data. Through the adoption of ethical frameworks, privacy-enhancing technologies, robust governance structures, and education and training initiatives, organizations can ensure the responsible and ethical deployment of AI-driven solutions while safeguarding individuals' privacy rights and promoting trust in AI and Big Data technologies.

Ethical Considerations in AI and Big Data

The ethical landscape of AI and Big Data is rife with complexities. One prominent issue is the potential for inherent biases in AI algorithms, which can perpetuate and even exacerbate societal inequalities (Barocas & Selbst, 2016). AI systems, being dependent on data for learning, can inadvertently learn and amplify biases present in their training datasets. This necessitates a conscientious approach to algorithm design and dataset selection to mitigate bias and ensure fairness (Mittelstadt et al., 2016).

Another ethical concern is the autonomy of AI systems. As AI increasingly influences critical decisions in sectors like healthcare, criminal justice, and finance, there is a pressing need to ensure that these decisions are transparent and accountable (Bostrom & Yudkowsky, 2014). The 'black box' nature of some AI systems, particularly deep learning models, poses challenges to transparency, making it imperative to develop methodologies to interpret and explain AI decisions (Castelvecchi, 2016).

Data Privacy Concerns

Data privacy is a paramount concern in the era of Big Data and AI. The vast amounts of personal and sensitive data utilized by AI systems raise significant privacy issues (Tene & Polonetsky, 2012). This is exacerbated by the capabilities of AI to extract and infer sensitive information from seemingly innocuous data, potentially leading to privacy invasions.

The General Data Protection Regulation (GDPR) in the European Union represents a significant step in addressing these privacy concerns, providing guidelines and regulations for data protection and privacy (Voigt & Von dem Bussche, 2017). However, ensuring compliance with such regulations, particularly in the context of global data flows and the transnational nature of AI and Big Data operations, remains a complex challenge.

Data Privacy Concerns:

Data Collection and Consent: The collection of vast amounts of personal data in Big Data environments raises concerns about individuals' consent and control over their data. Organizations must obtain informed consent from individuals for data collection and usage, clearly communicating the purposes and scope of data processing activities.

Data Security and Breach Risks: Big Data repositories are prime targets for cyberattacks and data breaches due to the volume and sensitivity of the stored information. Weak security measures, such as inadequate encryption, access controls, and security protocols, can expose sensitive data to unauthorized access, breaches, and misuse.

Data Retention and Storage: Storing large volumes of personal data for extended periods poses risks of data retention and storage. Organizations must establish data retention policies and practices that limit the storage duration of personal data to the minimum necessary for the intended purposes, reducing the risk of unauthorized access and misuse.

Data Sharing and Third-Party Risks: Sharing Big Data with third parties, such as partners, vendors, or service providers, introduces risks of data exposure and misuse. Organizations must carefully evaluate third-party data handling practices, establish data sharing agreements, and implement robust contractual and technical safeguards to protect shared data from unauthorized access and misuse.

Data Anonymization and De-Identification: Anonymizing or de-identifying personal data before processing or sharing it can mitigate privacy risks by removing or obscuring personally identifiable information. However, the effectiveness of anonymization techniques may be limited by the risk of re-identification through data linkage or inference, necessitating careful evaluation and validation of anonymization practices.

Algorithmic Transparency and Accountability: The opacity of AI algorithms raises concerns about the transparency and accountability of algorithmic decision-making processes. Organizations must strive for algorithmic transparency by providing explanations for algorithmic decisions and disclosing data sources, model architectures, and decision-making criteria to ensure accountability and foster trust among stakeholders.

Strategies for Addressing Data Privacy Concerns:

Privacy by Design: Integrating privacy considerations into the design and development of AI and Big Data systems through privacy-by-design principles promotes privacy-conscious practices from the outset. Organizations should adopt privacy-enhancing technologies, such as encryption, differential privacy, and federated learning, to minimize privacy risks and protect sensitive information.

Data Minimization and Purpose Limitation: Collecting and processing only the minimum amount of personal data necessary for specific, legitimate purposes reduces privacy risks and limits exposure to potential data misuse. Organizations should adopt data minimization and purpose limitation principles to restrict data collection, storage, and usage to essential, lawful purposes.

Data Governance and Compliance: Establishing robust data governance frameworks and compliance programs helps ensure adherence to data protection regulations and privacy laws. Organizations should implement data protection policies, conduct privacy impact assessments, and appoint data protection officers to oversee compliance with legal requirements and industry standards.

Ethical AI Governance: Implementing ethical AI governance structures and mechanisms ensures that ethical considerations, including privacy concerns, are integrated into all stages of AI development and deployment. Ethical AI governance frameworks should include mechanisms for ethics reviews, risk assessments, and stakeholder engagement to promote responsible and ethical AI practices.

User Empowerment and Transparency: Empowering individuals with control over their data and providing transparency about data processing practices enhances user trust and confidence in AI and Big Data systems. Organizations should offer users options for managing their data preferences, accessing their data, and obtaining information about data processing activities to promote transparency and accountability.

In conclusion, addressing data privacy concerns is essential in the symbiosis of AI and Big Data to uphold individuals' rights, protect sensitive information, and foster trust in data-driven technologies. By adopting privacy-by-design principles, implementing robust data governance and compliance measures, and promoting ethical AI governance practices, organizations can mitigate privacy risks, safeguard individuals' privacy rights, and uphold ethical standards in the integration of AI and Big Data. Through proactive efforts and responsible data practices, organizations can ensure that AI-driven solutions leverage the transformative power of Big Data while respecting privacy and promoting trust among stakeholders.

Balancing Innovation with Ethical Responsibility

The task at hand is to balance the enormous potential for innovation and advancement offered by AI and Big Data with ethical responsibility and privacy considerations. This involves establishing robust ethical guidelines, ensuring transparent and fair AI processes, and enforcing strict data privacy and protection measures (Jobin, Ienca, & Vayena, 2019). It also requires ongoing dialogue among technologists, ethicists, policymakers, and the public to navigate these challenges effectively.

Balancing Innovation and Ethical Responsibility:

Innovative Applications: AI and Big Data enable innovative applications across various domains, including healthcare, finance, transportation, and cybersecurity. These technologies empower organizations to extract insights, optimize processes, and create value from vast datasets, driving innovation and competitive advantage.

Ethical Implications: The rapid advancement of AI and Big Data also raises ethical concerns related to privacy, fairness, transparency, accountability, and bias. Ethical implications arise from algorithmic decision-making processes, data collection and usage practices, and the societal impact of AI-driven technologies.

Trade-Offs and Considerations: Balancing innovation with ethical responsibility requires careful consideration of the trade-offs between technological advancement and ethical concerns. Organizations must weigh the potential benefits of AI and Big Data innovation against the risks and ethical implications associated with data privacy, fairness, and societal impact.

Proactive Ethical Frameworks: Establishing proactive ethical frameworks and guidelines helps guide responsible conduct and ethical decision-making in AI and Big Data environments. Ethical frameworks should prioritize principles such as fairness, transparency, accountability, privacy, and social responsibility to ensure that innovation aligns with ethical standards and societal values.

Strategies for Balancing Innovation and Ethical Responsibility:

Ethical Design and Development: Integrating ethical considerations into the design and development of AI and Big Data systems ensures that ethical principles are embedded into the technology from the outset. Organizations should adopt ethical design practices, conduct ethics reviews, and involve diverse stakeholders in the development process to identify and mitigate potential ethical risks.

Ethical AI Governance: Implementing robust governance structures and mechanisms for ethical AI governance promotes responsible and ethical AI practices. Ethical AI governance frameworks should include mechanisms for ethics reviews, risk assessments, and stakeholder engagement to ensure that AI-driven innovations adhere to ethical standards and societal values.

Transparency and Accountability: Promoting transparency in AI and Big Data processes enhances accountability and fosters trust among stakeholders. Organizations should provide explanations for algorithmic decisions, disclose data sources and processing practices, and establish mechanisms for auditing and oversight to ensure transparency and accountability in AI-driven technologies.

Ethical Data Practices: Adopting ethical data practices, such as data minimization, purpose limitation, and user empowerment, helps mitigate privacy risks and protect individuals' rights in AI and Big Data environments. Organizations should prioritize data privacy, obtain informed consent for data collection and usage, and empower users with control over their data to uphold ethical data practices.

In conclusion, balancing innovation with ethical responsibility is essential in the symbiosis of AI and Big Data to ensure that technological advancements align with ethical standards and societal values. By establishing proactive ethical frameworks, promoting responsible conduct and ethical decision-making, and prioritizing transparency, accountability, and privacy, organizations can navigate the complexities of AI and Big Data while upholding ethical standards and promoting trust among stakeholders. Through collaborative efforts and ethical governance, organizations can harness the transformative potential of AI and Big Data to drive innovation, optimize processes, and create value while respecting ethical principles and promoting societal well-being.

The exploration of ethical considerations and data privacy in the context of AI and Big Data is crucial for the responsible advancement of these technologies. "Data Titans" addresses these issues comprehensively, underscoring the need for ethical vigilance and robust privacy frameworks in the ever-evolving digital landscape.

The foundational aspects of AI in Big Data are characterized by a complex interplay of theoretical principles, data characteristics, technological challenges, and ethical considerations. Understanding these foundations is imperative for harnessing the potential of AI in Big Data while navigating its challenges responsibly.

Characteristics and Challenges:

A critical exposition is devoted to dissecting the multifaceted nature of Big Data. This segment meticulously delineates the distinctive characteristics of Big Data, while concurrently addressing the plethora of challenges it presents, particularly when interfaced with Artificial

Intelligence (AI) technologies. This discourse is instrumental in cultivating a profound comprehension of the Big Data landscape, a prerequisite for leveraging AI effectively in this domain.

Characteristics of Big Data

Big Data is distinguished by its inherent characteristics, often encapsulated by the four Vs: Volume, Velocity, Variety, and Veracity (Laney, 2001).

1. **Volume**: This refers to the colossal quantities of data generated every moment, emanating from myriad sources including social media, sensors, digital imagery, and transactional systems. The voluminous nature of this data necessitates significant storage capacities and sophisticated processing capabilities.

2. **Velocity**: This aspect highlights the rapid rate at which data is generated, collected, and necessitates processing. The brisk pace of data inflow demands real-time analysis and prompt decision-making, which is often a critical requirement in domains like finance and online services.

3. **Variety**: Big Data encompasses a diverse array of data types – structured numerical data, unstructured text, video, audio, and more. This heterogeneity demands versatile processing tools capable of handling and integrating diverse data formats for comprehensive analysis.

4. **Veracity**: This characteristic underscores the reliability and accuracy of data. In the context of Big Data, ensuring data quality and integrity is paramount, as the decision-making processes heavily rely on the trustworthiness of the data.

Challenges Posed by Big Data

The characteristics of Big Data inherently present a set of challenges, particularly when amalgamated with AI technologies:

1. **Storage and Processing**: The sheer volume of Big Data necessitates advanced solutions for storage and efficient processing. Technologies like cloud computing and new database paradigms like NoSQL have emerged as responses to this challenge (Marz & Warren, 2015).

2. **Real-Time Analysis**: The velocity of data generation requires AI systems capable of performing real-time analysis. This is crucial for applications where timely data processing is vital, such as fraud detection and online customer interactions (McAfee & Brynjolfsson, 2012).

3. **Data Integration and Management**: Given the variety in Big Data, integrating and managing this data in a coherent manner is a significant challenge. This necessitates sophisticated data integration tools and algorithms capable of handling diverse data types (Fan, Han, & Liu, 2014).

4. **Data Quality and Governance**: Ensuring the veracity of Big Data is a major concern. Poor data quality can lead to inaccurate AI model predictions and flawed decision-making. Robust data governance frameworks are essential to maintain the quality and integrity of data (Wang & Strong, 1996).

Understanding the characteristics and challenges of Big Data is fundamental to the deployment of AI in this realm. The "Data Titans" book's exploration of these aspects provides readers with the necessary insights to navigate the complex Big Data landscape, a critical step towards harnessing the full potential of AI in Big Data environments.

AI Basics: From Machine Learning to Deep Learning:

A profound and detailed exposition is presented on the elemental concepts of Artificial Intelligence (AI), specifically delving into the realms of Machine Learning (ML) and Deep Learning (DL). This segment is pivotal in elucidating the foundational principles that underlie the application of AI in the context of Big Data, offering an erudite perspective on the progression from basic machine learning techniques to the more intricate architectures of deep learning.

Machine Learning: The Cornerstone of AI

Machine Learning, a fundamental subset of AI, is predicated on the notion of enabling machines to learn from data, identify patterns, and make decisions with minimal human intervention (Alpaydin, 2020). ML encompasses a range of algorithms and techniques, including supervised learning, where models are trained on labeled data; unsupervised learning, where models discern patterns in unlabeled data; and reinforcement learning, where models learn through trial and error to achieve a specified goal.

The application of ML in Big Data is transformative, enabling the extraction of meaningful insights from large datasets. Techniques such as regression analysis, decision trees, and support vector machines are widely utilized in diverse sectors, from finance to healthcare, demonstrating the versatility and efficacy of ML in handling complex data-driven challenges (Hastie, Tibshirani, & Friedman, 2009).

Deep Learning: Advancing Beyond Traditional Machine Learning

Deep Learning, an advanced subset of ML, represents a paradigm shift in AI's capability to process and analyze data. DL employs neural networks with multiple layers (hence the term "deep") to model complex patterns and relationships in data. This architecture enables the handling of higher-level abstractions and representations, making DL particularly adept at tasks such as image and speech recognition, and natural language processing (LeCun, Bengio, & Hinton, 2015).

The utility of DL in the context of Big Data is significant, given its ability to autonomously learn feature representations from raw data, bypassing the need for manual feature extraction. This attribute makes DL extraordinarily effective in discerning intricate patterns and nuances in vast and complex datasets, a capability that is at the core of many contemporary AI breakthroughs (Goodfellow, Bengio, & Courville, 2016).

Challenges and Considerations in ML and DL

Despite the profound capabilities of ML and DL, there are challenges and considerations that must be acknowledged. One of the primary concerns is the "black box" nature of some deep learning models, where the decision-making process is not transparent or easily interpretable. This raises issues of accountability and trust in AI systems, especially in critical applications (Castelvecchi, 2016).

Moreover, both ML and DL models are heavily reliant on the quality and quantity of data. Biases in training data can lead to skewed or unfair decision-making by AI systems, highlighting the need for rigorous data governance and ethical AI practices (Barocas & Selbst, 2016).

The exploration of ML and DL in "Data Titans" provides a foundational understanding of how these technologies drive AI applications in Big Data. By detailing the progression from basic ML algorithms to sophisticated DL networks, the book offers readers a comprehensive view of the AI landscape, crucial for grasping the full potential and implications of AI in Big Data.

The Symbiosis of AI and Big Data:

A pivotal section elucidates the synergistic interplay between Artificial Intelligence (AI) and Big Data, a confluence that has engendered profound transformations across multiple domains. This discourse delves into the intricacies of this symbiosis, highlighting how the amalgamation of AI's advanced analytical capabilities with the expansive datasets characteristic of Big Data is reshaping the technological landscape.

The Complementarity of AI and Big Data

The essence of the symbiosis between AI and Big Data lies in their complementary nature. AI, particularly in its advanced forms of machine learning and deep learning, thrives on large datasets for training and model refinement. Big Data provides this requisite volume and variety, offering a rich substrate for AI algorithms to extract insights and patterns (Hashem et al., 2015). Conversely, the complexities and vastness of Big Data necessitate the sophisticated analytical prowess of AI to unlock its potential, rendering AI an indispensable tool for Big Data analytics (Chen, Mao, & Liu, 2014).

Enhancing AI with Big Data

Big Data's diverse and voluminous datasets enable AI systems to achieve higher levels of accuracy and efficiency. By training on extensive datasets, AI models can generalize better and make more precise predictions, a phenomenon that is crucial in applications ranging from predictive analytics in business to diagnostic procedures in healthcare (Jordan & Mitchell, 2015). Furthermore, Big Data allows AI to handle real-world complexities, providing a more nuanced understanding of patterns and trends that would be imperceptible in smaller datasets.

Big Data Analytics Powered by AI

The role of AI in Big Data analytics is multifaceted. AI algorithms, especially those in machine learning and deep learning, are adept at identifying complex patterns, trends, and relationships within Big Data, tasks that are beyond the capability of traditional data analysis techniques. This ability is particularly significant in scenarios involving unstructured data, such as text, images, and videos, where AI can provide insights that are not readily apparent (Mayer-Schönberger & Cukier, 2013).

Challenges in the Symbiosis

Despite the clear benefits, the symbiosis of AI and Big Data is not devoid of challenges. Data quality and integrity are paramount; AI models are only as good as the data they are trained on. Issues like data bias, noise, and incompleteness can significantly skew AI outputs, leading to erroneous conclusions (Barocas &

Selbst, 2016). Additionally, the management of Big Data in terms of storage, processing, and privacy protection presents logistical and ethical challenges, necessitating robust data governance frameworks (Kitchin, 2014).

Ethical and Privacy Considerations

The intersection of AI and Big Data raises significant ethical and privacy concerns. The capability of AI to extract sensitive information from large datasets poses risks related to privacy breaches and ethical misuse. Ensuring ethical AI practices and adhering to stringent data privacy laws and regulations is imperative in this symbiosis (Tene & Polonetsky, 2012).

The symbiotic relationship between AI and Big Data is a cornerstone of contemporary data-driven innovation. This section in "Data Titans" not only highlights the mutual enhancement of AI and Big Data but also provides a critical analysis of the challenges and responsibilities inherent in this partnership. Understanding this symbiosis is crucial for leveraging the transformative potential of AI and Big Data while navigating their complexities responsibly.

Chapter 2: AI Technologies Powering Big Data

A segment is meticulously devoted to delineating the diverse array of AI technologies that are instrumental in harnessing the power of Big Data. This discourse navigates through the sophisticated landscape of AI methodologies, underscoring how these technologies are revolutionizing the processing, analysis, and interpretation of Big Data.

Machine Learning Models in Big Data

Machine Learning (ML) stands at the forefront of AI technologies empowering Big Data analytics. These models, particularly supervised and unsupervised learning algorithms, are adept at extracting patterns and insights from large datasets. Supervised learning models, such as neural networks, decision trees, and support vector machines, are utilized for predictive analytics, where they generate predictions based on historical data. Unsupervised learning models, including clustering and principal component analysis, are pivotal in identifying hidden patterns and structures within unlabelled data (James et al., 2013).

Significance of Machine Learning Models:

Pattern Recognition and Prediction: Machine learning models excel at recognizing patterns and making predictions from large and complex datasets. By analyzing vast amounts of data, these models can identify hidden correlations, trends, and anomalies that may not be apparent to human analysts.

Scalability and Efficiency: Machine learning algorithms are designed to scale with the volume and velocity of Big Data. With the advent of distributed computing frameworks like Apache Spark and TensorFlow, organizations can leverage parallel processing and distributed computing to train and deploy machine learning models on massive datasets efficiently.

Automation of Decision-Making: Machine learning models automate decision-making processes by learning from historical data and making predictions or recommendations based on new inputs. This automation streamlines operations, improves efficiency, and enables organizations to make data-driven decisions in real-time or near-real-time.

Personalization and Recommendation Systems: Machine learning powers personalized recommendation systems in e-commerce, content streaming, and social media platforms. By analyzing user behavior and preferences, these models deliver personalized recommendations, product suggestions, and content tailored to individual users' interests and preferences.

Predictive Maintenance and Anomaly Detection: In industrial IoT (Internet of Things) settings, machine learning models enable predictive maintenance by analyzing sensor data to predict equipment failures or maintenance needs before they occur. Additionally, these models can detect anomalies in real-time data streams, enabling organizations to identify and mitigate potential issues promptly.

Key Applications of Machine Learning Models in Big Data:

Natural Language Processing (NLP): NLP techniques enable machines to understand, interpret, and generate human language. In Big Data environments, NLP models analyze unstructured text data from sources such as social media, customer reviews, and emails to extract insights, sentiment analysis, and automate text-based tasks like chatbots and virtual assistants.

Image and Video Analysis: Machine learning models for image and video analysis leverage deep learning techniques to interpret and analyze visual data. These models are used in applications such as facial recognition, object detection, medical imaging analysis, and surveillance systems, enabling organizations to extract valuable insights from visual content at scale.

Predictive Analytics and Forecasting: Machine learning models power predictive analytics and forecasting applications across various domains, including finance, healthcare, marketing, and supply chain management. These models analyze historical data to predict future trends, customer behavior, market demand, and business outcomes, enabling organizations to make informed decisions and mitigate risks proactively.

Fraud Detection and Cybersecurity: In the realm of cybersecurity, machine learning models play a crucial role in detecting and preventing fraud, intrusion, and cyberattacks. These models analyze network traffic, user behavior, and system logs to identify anomalous patterns and potential security threats, enabling organizations to strengthen their defenses and protect against cyber threats.

Challenges and Opportunities:

Data Quality and Bias: Ensuring the quality and representativeness of training data is essential for the effectiveness of machine learning models. Biases in training data can lead to biased outcomes and unfair decision-making, highlighting the importance of data preprocessing, bias mitigation techniques, and diverse representation in training datasets.

Interpretability and Explainability: The opacity of some machine learning models raises concerns about interpretability and explainability. Organizations must prioritize model interpretability techniques, such as feature importance analysis, model visualization, and surrogate models, to provide insights into model predictions and foster trust among stakeholders.

Ethical and Regulatory Considerations: The deployment of machine learning models in Big Data environments raises ethical and regulatory concerns, including issues related to privacy, fairness, accountability, and transparency. Organizations must adhere to ethical guidelines, regulatory frameworks, and industry standards to ensure the responsible and ethical use of machine learning models in Big Data applications.

Continual Learning and Adaptation: Machine learning models must adapt to changing data distributions and environments to maintain their effectiveness over time. Continual learning techniques, such as online learning, transfer learning, and ensemble methods, enable models to adapt to new data and evolving conditions, ensuring their relevance and accuracy in dynamic Big Data ecosystems.

Machine learning models play a central role in harnessing the power of Big Data to drive innovation, make predictions, and derive actionable insights across various domains. From pattern recognition and predictive analytics to personalization and cybersecurity, these models empower organizations to unlock the full potential of Big Data and make informed decisions in real-time. However, addressing challenges such as data quality, interpretability, ethical considerations, and continual learning is essential to maximize the effectiveness and ethical responsibility of machine learning models in Big Data environments. Through continuous innovation, collaboration, and ethical governance, organizations can leverage machine learning models to extract value from Big Data while upholding ethical principles and safeguarding individuals' rights.

Natural Language Processing for Unstructured Data Analysis

Natural Language Processing (NLP), a subfield of AI, plays a crucial role in analyzing and interpreting unstructured data, primarily textual content. NLP algorithms enable machines to understand, interpret, and generate human language, facilitating the extraction of meaningful information from vast repositories of text data. Applications of NLP in Big Data include sentiment analysis, topic modeling, and automated summarization, which are critical in areas such as social media analytics and customer feedback analysis (Indurkhya & Damerau, 2010).

Significance of Natural Language Processing (NLP):

Unstructured Data Analysis: Unstructured textual data, such as social media posts, customer reviews, emails, and documents, constitutes a significant portion of Big Data. NLP enables organizations to analyze and derive insights from this unstructured data, unlocking valuable information that may otherwise remain hidden or underutilized.

Language Understanding and Generation: NLP techniques enable machines to understand, interpret, and generate human language. By processing and analyzing textual data, NLP models can perform tasks such as sentiment analysis, entity recognition, topic modeling, summarization, and translation, facilitating human-like language understanding and generation capabilities.

Decision Support and Automation: NLP powers decision support systems and automation workflows by extracting actionable insights and automating text-based tasks. Organizations leverage NLP for tasks such as customer service automation, content categorization, information retrieval, and sentiment-based decision-making, streamlining operations and improving efficiency.

Personalization and Customer Engagement: NLP drives personalized customer experiences and engagement through applications such as chatbots, virtual assistants, and recommendation systems. By understanding and responding to user queries and preferences in natural language, NLP-powered systems deliver personalized recommendations, product suggestions, and conversational interactions tailored to individual users' needs and preferences.

Key Applications of Natural Language Processing (NLP) in Big Data:

Sentiment Analysis: Sentiment analysis, also known as opinion mining, involves analyzing textual data to determine sentiment polarity (positive, negative, or neutral). Organizations use sentiment analysis to gauge public opinion, monitor brand sentiment, and assess customer feedback, enabling them to make data-driven decisions and enhance customer satisfaction.

Named Entity Recognition (NER): NER is the task of identifying and classifying named entities, such as persons, organizations, locations, dates, and numerical expressions, in unstructured text. NER enables organizations to extract structured information from textual data, automate information extraction tasks, and enhance data organization and search capabilities.

Topic Modeling: Topic modeling algorithms, such as Latent Dirichlet Allocation (LDA) and Non-negative Matrix Factorization (NMF), cluster textual data into topics based on shared semantic themes or concepts. Organizations use topic modeling to uncover latent patterns, trends, and themes within large document collections, enabling them to explore and navigate textual data more effectively.

Text Summarization: Text summarization techniques automatically generate concise summaries of longer documents or articles, distilling key information and insights from textual data.

Organizations leverage text summarization for tasks such as document summarization, news aggregation, and content curation, enabling users to access relevant information quickly and efficiently.

Challenges and Opportunities:

Ambiguity and Context Sensitivity: Natural language is inherently ambiguous and context-sensitive, posing challenges for NLP models in understanding and interpreting textual data accurately. Addressing these challenges requires advanced NLP techniques, such as contextual word embeddings, pre-trained language models, and semantic parsing, to capture nuanced meanings and context-dependent interpretations.

Data Quality and Noise: Unstructured textual data often contains noise, errors, and inconsistencies that can impact the performance of NLP models. Data preprocessing techniques, such as text cleaning, tokenization, and lemmatization, help improve data quality and prepare textual data for analysis by removing irrelevant or noisy information.

Bias and Fairness: NLP models trained on biased datasets may perpetuate existing biases and lead to unfair or discriminatory outcomes. Mitigating bias in NLP models requires careful data selection, algorithmic fairness measures, and bias detection techniques to ensure equitable representation and treatment of diverse demographic groups.

Interpretability and Explainability: The opacity of some NLP models raises concerns about interpretability and explainability. Organizations must prioritize model interpretability techniques, such as attention mechanisms, feature visualization, and model-agnostic explanations, to provide insights into model predictions and foster trust among stakeholders.

Natural Language Processing (NLP) plays a vital role in unlocking the value of unstructured textual data in Big Data environments. From sentiment analysis and named entity recognition to topic modeling and text summarization, NLP enables organizations to extract actionable insights, automate text-based tasks, and enhance decision-making processes. However, addressing challenges such as ambiguity, data quality, bias, and interpretability is essential to maximize the effectiveness and ethical responsibility of NLP models in Big Data applications. Through continuous innovation, collaboration, and ethical governance, organizations can leverage NLP to harness the full potential of textual data and drive innovation, efficiency, and customer engagement in the era of Big Data.

AI-Driven Data Visualization Techniques

Data visualization, enhanced by AI, is an essential aspect of Big Data analytics, enabling the translation of complex data sets into comprehensible and insightful visual representations. AI-driven visualization tools employ algorithms to automatically detect and highlight key patterns, trends, and anomalies in data, facilitating more efficient and effective data interpretation by humans. These tools are particularly important in fields where rapid and accurate interpretation of data is crucial, such as financial market analysis and healthcare diagnostics (Few, 2009).

Significance of AI-Driven Data Visualization:

Insight Extraction and Exploration: AI-driven data visualization techniques enable organizations to uncover hidden patterns, trends, and relationships within large and complex datasets. By transforming raw data into visual representations, these techniques facilitate exploratory analysis and help users gain a deeper understanding of the underlying data.

Decision Support and Communication: Data visualization serves as a powerful tool for decision support and communication, enabling stakeholders to make informed decisions based on data-driven insights. AI-driven visualization techniques enhance decision-making processes by presenting data in intuitive and interactive formats, enabling stakeholders to identify trends, anomalies, and actionable insights at a glance.

Pattern Recognition and Anomaly Detection: AI-powered data visualization techniques leverage machine learning algorithms to identify patterns, outliers, and anomalies in Big Data. By applying advanced analytics and anomaly detection algorithms to visual representations of data, organizations can detect irregularities, outliers, and potential risks in real-time, enabling proactive decision-making and risk mitigation.

Personalization and Interactivity: AI-driven data visualization tools offer personalized and interactive experiences tailored to individual user preferences and needs. By leveraging user interactions and machine learning algorithms, these tools adapt to user preferences, filter data dynamically, and provide personalized recommendations, enhancing user engagement and understanding of complex data.

Key Applications of AI-Driven Data Visualization:

Interactive Dashboards: AI-powered interactive dashboards enable users to explore and analyze data visually through interactive charts, graphs, and maps. These dashboards aggregate and visualize data from multiple sources, enabling users to monitor key performance indicators (KPIs), track trends, and identify insights in real-time.

Predictive Analytics Visualization: AI-driven visualization techniques facilitate the visualization of predictive analytics models and forecasts, enabling users to understand and interpret model predictions effectively. By visualizing predictive insights, organizations can make data-driven decisions, anticipate future trends, and optimize business strategies proactively.

Geospatial Visualization: AI-powered geospatial visualization techniques enable organizations to visualize and analyze spatial data, such as geographic information, satellite imagery, and location-based data. These techniques leverage machine learning algorithms to analyze spatial patterns, identify trends, and visualize insights on interactive maps, enabling organizations to make informed decisions based on spatial data.

Network Visualization: AI-driven network visualization techniques enable organizations to visualize complex networks, such as social networks, supply chains, and transportation networks. These techniques leverage graph analysis and machine learning algorithms to identify network structures, detect anomalies, and visualize network dynamics, enabling organizations to optimize network performance and mitigate risks.

Challenges and Opportunities:

Scalability and Performance: AI-driven data visualization techniques must scale with the volume and complexity of Big Data to ensure optimal performance. Addressing scalability challenges requires leveraging distributed computing frameworks, parallel processing, and optimized rendering techniques to visualize large-scale datasets efficiently.

Interpretability and Explainability: Ensuring the interpretability and explainability of AI-driven visualization techniques is essential for fostering trust and understanding among users. Organizations must prioritize techniques for explaining visualizations, providing contextual information, and enabling users to understand the underlying data and algorithms.

Data Integration and Fusion: Integrating data from heterogeneous sources and formats poses challenges for AI-driven data visualization techniques. Addressing data integration challenges requires adopting data integration platforms, standardizing data formats, and leveraging data fusion techniques to unify disparate data sources and enable comprehensive visualization and analysis.

Ethical Considerations: AI-driven data visualization techniques raise ethical considerations related to data privacy, bias, fairness, and transparency. Organizations must adhere to ethical guidelines, regulatory requirements, and industry standards to ensure the responsible and ethical use of AI-driven visualization techniques in Big Data environments.

AI-driven data visualization techniques play a crucial role in unlocking the value of Big Data by enabling organizations to extract insights, facilitate decision-making, and communicate complex information effectively. From interactive dashboards and predictive analytics visualization to geospatial and network visualization, these techniques empower organizations to leverage the power of AI and Big Data to drive innovation, optimize operations, and achieve business objectives. However, addressing challenges such as scalability, interpretability, data integration, and ethical considerations is essential to maximize the effectiveness and ethical responsibility of AI-driven data visualization techniques in Big Data environments. Through continuous innovation, collaboration, and ethical governance, organizations can harness the transformative potential of AI-driven visualization techniques to derive actionable insights and create value in the era of Big Data.

Predictive Analytics and AI

Predictive analytics, a facet of Big Data analytics powered by AI, involves using historical data to make predictions about future events. AI models, particularly those based on machine learning, are trained on historical data to identify patterns and relationships that can be used to predict future outcomes. This application of AI is invaluable in a myriad of sectors, including finance for risk assessment, retail for customer behavior prediction, and healthcare for disease outbreak forecasting (Han, Pei, & Kamber, 2011).

Significance of Predictive Analytics Powered by AI:

Anticipating Future Trends: Predictive analytics powered by AI enables organizations to anticipate future trends and patterns by analyzing historical data and identifying predictive factors. By leveraging advanced machine learning algorithms, predictive models can forecast future outcomes, such as customer behavior, market demand, and business performance, helping organizations adapt and strategize proactively.

Optimizing Decision-Making: Predictive analytics empowers organizations to optimize decision-making processes by providing actionable insights derived from data-driven predictions. By leveraging predictive models, organizations can identify opportunities, mitigate risks, and make informed decisions based on probabilistic forecasts and scenario analysis, leading to improved operational efficiency and competitive advantage.

Enhancing Customer Experience: Predictive analytics enables organizations to personalize customer experiences and anticipate customer needs by analyzing historical data and predicting future behavior. By leveraging AI-driven predictive models, organizations can tailor products, services, and marketing strategies to individual customer preferences, enhancing customer satisfaction and loyalty.

Improving Resource Allocation: Predictive analytics helps organizations optimize resource allocation by forecasting demand, identifying inefficiencies, and allocating resources effectively. By leveraging predictive models to anticipate future demand and resource requirements, organizations can optimize inventory management, workforce planning, and supply chain operations, reducing costs and maximizing productivity.

Key Applications of Predictive Analytics Powered by AI:

Customer Churn Prediction: Predictive analytics models can forecast customer churn by analyzing historical customer data and identifying factors associated with churn behavior. By predicting which customers are at risk of churning, organizations can implement targeted retention strategies, such as personalized offers and proactive outreach, to mitigate churn and retain valuable customers.

Financial Forecasting: Predictive analytics enables financial institutions to forecast market trends, evaluate investment opportunities, and manage risk effectively. By analyzing historical market data and economic indicators, predictive models can forecast asset prices, identify trading opportunities, and optimize investment portfolios, enabling organizations to make data-driven investment decisions.

Predictive Maintenance: In industrial settings, predictive analytics enables organizations to implement predictive maintenance strategies by forecasting equipment failures before they occur. By analyzing sensor data, equipment performance metrics, and maintenance logs, predictive models can predict when equipment is likely to fail, enabling organizations to schedule maintenance proactively, minimize downtime, and reduce maintenance costs.

Healthcare Outcome Prediction: Predictive analytics plays a crucial role in healthcare by enabling organizations to predict patient outcomes, diagnose diseases, and personalize treatment plans. By analyzing electronic health records, medical imaging data, and genetic information, predictive models can forecast patient outcomes, identify at-risk populations, and recommend personalized treatment options, leading to improved patient care and outcomes.

Challenges and Opportunities:

Data Quality and Availability: Ensuring the quality and availability of data is essential for the effectiveness of predictive analytics models. Organizations must address challenges related to data quality, data integration, and data governance to ensure that predictive models are trained on reliable, representative, and up-to-date data.

Model Interpretability and Transparency: The opacity of some predictive analytics models raises concerns about model interpretability and transparency. Organizations must prioritize techniques for explaining model predictions, providing interpretability, and ensuring transparency to foster trust and understanding among users and stakeholders.

Ethical and Bias Considerations: Predictive analytics models trained on biased data may produce biased outcomes and perpetuate existing inequalities. Organizations must address ethical considerations and mitigate bias in predictive models by implementing fairness-aware algorithms, bias detection techniques, and diversity-aware model evaluation methods.

Scalability and Performance: Scalability and performance are critical considerations for deploying predictive analytics models in Big Data environments. Organizations must leverage distributed computing frameworks, parallel processing, and optimized algorithms to ensure that predictive models can scale with the volume and velocity of Big Data and deliver real-time or near-real-time predictions efficiently.

Predictive analytics powered by AI represents a transformative capability within Big Data environments, enabling organizations to anticipate future trends, optimize decision-making, and drive innovation. From customer churn prediction and financial forecasting to predictive maintenance and healthcare outcome prediction, predictive analytics offers a wide range of applications across various domains. However, addressing challenges such as data quality, model interpretability, ethical considerations, and scalability is essential to maximize the effectiveness and ethical responsibility of predictive analytics powered by AI in Big Data environments. Through continuous innovation, collaboration, and ethical governance, organizations can harness the transformative potential of predictive analytics to derive actionable insights, mitigate risks, and create value in the era of Big Data.

Challenges in AI-Powered Big Data Analytics

While AI technologies offer transformative potential in Big Data analytics, they also present challenges. Ensuring the accuracy and reliability of AI models, especially in the context of the diverse and complex nature of Big Data, is paramount. Furthermore, the interpretability of AI models, particularly deep learning models, remains a challenge, raising concerns about the transparency and explainability of AI-driven decisions (Castelvecchi, 2016).

1.Data Quality and Integration:

Challenge: Ensuring the quality, completeness, and consistency of data is essential for the accuracy and reliability of AI-powered analytics. Integrating data from disparate sources with varying formats and structures poses challenges in data integration.

Solution: Organizations should implement data quality management processes, including data cleansing, normalization, and validation, to ensure that data is accurate and consistent. Adopting data integration platforms and technologies can facilitate the seamless integration of data from multiple sources.

2. Scalability and Performance:

Challenge: Processing and analyzing large volumes of data in real-time or near-real-time can strain computational resources and affect the performance of AI algorithms. Scalability becomes crucial as data volumes continue to grow exponentially.

Solution: Leveraging distributed computing frameworks, such as Apache Hadoop and Spark, enables parallel processing and distributed data storage, enhancing scalability and performance. Adopting cloud-based solutions and infrastructure-as-a-service (IaaS) platforms can provide elastic scalability and on-demand resources for handling fluctuating workloads.

3. Model Interpretability and Explainability:

Challenge: Many AI models, particularly deep learning models, are often considered "black boxes," making it challenging to interpret their decisions and predictions. Lack of interpretability and explainability can hinder trust and adoption.

Solution: Organizations should prioritize model interpretability techniques, such as feature importance analysis, model visualization, and surrogate models. Explainable AI (XAI) techniques, including LIME (Local Interpretable Model-agnostic Explanations) and SHAP (SHapley Additive exPlanations), provide insights into model predictions and foster trust among users.

4. Ethical and Bias Considerations:

Challenge: AI-powered analytics may perpetuate biases present in training data, leading to unfair or discriminatory outcomes. Ensuring fairness, transparency, and accountability in AI models is essential for ethical deployment.

Solution: Organizations should implement fairness-aware AI techniques, including bias detection, fairness metrics, and algorithmic fairness constraints, to mitigate biases in AI models. Ethical guidelines and frameworks, such as the AI Ethics Guidelines from organizations like IEEE and ACM, provide principles for responsible AI development and deployment.

5. **Privacy and Security:**

Challenge: Analyzing sensitive data in Big Data environments raises concerns about privacy infringement, data breaches, and unauthorized access. Protecting sensitive information while ensuring data accessibility for analysis is critical.

Solution: Implementing robust data privacy and security measures, such as data anonymization, encryption, access controls, and secure data transmission protocols, helps safeguard sensitive information from unauthorized access and misuse. Compliance with data protection regulations, such as GDPR and CCPA, is essential for protecting individuals' privacy rights.

6. **Talent and Skill Gap:**

Challenge: Building and maintaining AI-powered Big Data analytics capabilities require a skilled workforce with expertise in data science, machine learning, and Big Data technologies. However, there is a shortage of talent with these specialized skills.

Solution: Organizations should invest in training and upskilling programs to develop talent internally and bridge the skill gap. Collaborating with academic institutions, participating in industry partnerships, and fostering a culture of continuous learning can help attract and retain top talent in AI and Big Data analytics.

7. **Regulatory Compliance:**

Chapter 2: AI Technologies Powering Big Data

A segment is meticulously devoted to delineating the diverse array of AI technologies that are instrumental in harnessing the power of Big Data. This discourse navigates through the sophisticated landscape of AI methodologies, underscoring how these technologies are revolutionizing the processing, analysis, and interpretation of Big Data.

Machine Learning Models in Big Data

Machine Learning (ML) stands at the forefront of AI technologies empowering Big Data analytics. These models, particularly supervised and unsupervised learning algorithms, are adept at extracting patterns and insights from large datasets. Supervised learning models, such as neural networks, decision trees, and support vector machines, are utilized for predictive analytics, where they generate predictions based on historical data. Unsupervised learning models, including clustering and principal component analysis, are pivotal in identifying hidden patterns and structures within unlabelled data (James et al., 2013).

Significance of Machine Learning Models:

Pattern Recognition and Prediction: Machine learning models excel at recognizing patterns and making predictions from large and complex datasets. By analyzing vast amounts of data, these models can identify hidden correlations, trends, and anomalies that may not be apparent to human analysts.

Scalability and Efficiency: Machine learning algorithms are designed to scale with the volume and velocity of Big Data. With the advent of distributed computing frameworks like Apache Spark and TensorFlow, organizations can leverage parallel processing and distributed computing to train and deploy machine learning models on massive datasets efficiently.

Automation of Decision-Making: Machine learning models automate decision-making processes by learning from historical data and making predictions or recommendations based on new inputs. This automation streamlines operations, improves efficiency, and enables organizations to make data-driven decisions in real-time or near-real-time.

Personalization and Recommendation Systems: Machine learning powers personalized recommendation systems in e-commerce, content streaming, and social media platforms. By analyzing user behavior and preferences, these models deliver personalized recommendations, product suggestions, and content tailored to individual users' interests and preferences.

Predictive Maintenance and Anomaly Detection: In industrial IoT (Internet of Things) settings, machine learning models enable predictive maintenance by analyzing sensor data to predict equipment failures or maintenance needs before they occur. Additionally, these models can detect anomalies in real-time data streams, enabling organizations to identify and mitigate potential issues promptly.

Key Applications of Machine Learning Models in Big Data:

Natural Language Processing (NLP): NLP techniques enable machines to understand, interpret, and generate human language. In Big Data environments, NLP models analyze unstructured text data from sources such as social media, customer reviews, and emails to extract insights, sentiment analysis, and automate text-based tasks like chatbots and virtual assistants.

Image and Video Analysis: Machine learning models for image and video analysis leverage deep learning techniques to interpret and analyze visual data. These models are used in applications such as facial recognition, object detection, medical imaging analysis, and surveillance systems, enabling organizations to extract valuable insights from visual content at scale.

Predictive Analytics and Forecasting: Machine learning models power predictive analytics and forecasting applications across various domains, including finance, healthcare, marketing, and supply chain management. These models analyze historical data to predict future trends, customer behavior, market demand, and business outcomes, enabling organizations to make informed decisions and mitigate risks proactively.

Fraud Detection and Cybersecurity: In the realm of cybersecurity, machine learning models play a crucial role in detecting and preventing fraud, intrusion, and cyberattacks. These models analyze network traffic, user behavior, and system logs to identify anomalous patterns and potential security threats, enabling organizations to strengthen their defenses and protect against cyber threats.

Challenges and Opportunities:

Data Quality and Bias: Ensuring the quality and representativeness of training data is essential for the effectiveness of machine learning models. Biases in training data can lead to biased outcomes and unfair decision-making, highlighting the importance of data pre-processing, bias mitigation techniques, and diverse representation in training datasets.

Interpretability and Explainability: The opacity of some machine learning models raises concerns about interpretability and explainability. Organizations must prioritize model interpretability techniques, such as feature importance analysis, model visualization, and surrogate models, to provide insights into model predictions and foster trust among stakeholders.

Ethical and Regulatory Considerations: The deployment of machine learning models in Big Data environments raises ethical and regulatory concerns, including issues related to privacy, fairness, accountability, and transparency. Organizations must adhere to ethical guidelines, regulatory frameworks, and industry standards to ensure the responsible and ethical use of machine learning models in Big Data applications.

Continual Learning and Adaptation: Machine learning models must adapt to changing data distributions and environments to maintain their effectiveness over time. Continual learning techniques, such as online learning, transfer learning, and ensemble methods, enable models to adapt to new data and evolving conditions, ensuring their relevance and accuracy in dynamic Big Data ecosystems.

Machine learning models play a central role in harnessing the power of Big Data to drive innovation, make predictions, and derive actionable insights across various domains. From pattern recognition and predictive analytics to personalization and cybersecurity, these models empower organizations to unlock the full potential of Big Data and make informed decisions in real-time. However, addressing challenges such as data quality, interpretability, ethical considerations, and continual learning is essential to maximize the effectiveness and ethical responsibility of machine learning models in Big Data environments. Through continuous innovation, collaboration, and ethical governance, organizations can leverage machine learning models to extract value from Big Data while upholding ethical principles and safeguarding individuals' rights.

Natural Language Processing for Unstructured Data Analysis

Natural Language Processing (NLP), a subfield of AI, plays a crucial role in analyzing and interpreting unstructured data, primarily textual content. NLP algorithms enable machines to understand, interpret, and generate human language, facilitating the extraction of meaningful information from vast repositories of text data. Applications of NLP in Big Data include sentiment analysis, topic modeling, and automated summarization, which are critical in areas such as social media analytics and customer feedback analysis (Indurkhya & Damerau, 2010).

Significance of Natural Language Processing (NLP):

Unstructured Data Analysis: Unstructured textual data, such as social media posts, customer reviews, emails, and documents, constitutes a significant portion of Big Data. NLP enables organizations to analyze and derive insights from this unstructured data, unlocking valuable information that may otherwise remain hidden or underutilized.

Language Understanding and Generation: NLP techniques enable machines to understand, interpret, and generate human language. By processing and analyzing textual data, NLP models can perform tasks such as sentiment analysis, entity recognition, topic modeling, summarization, and translation, facilitating human-like language understanding and generation capabilities.

Decision Support and Automation: NLP powers decision support systems and automation workflows by extracting actionable insights and automating text-based tasks. Organizations leverage NLP for tasks such as customer service automation, content categorization, information retrieval, and sentiment-based decision-making, streamlining operations and improving efficiency.

Personalization and Customer Engagement: NLP drives personalized customer experiences and engagement through applications such as chatbots, virtual assistants, and recommendation systems. By understanding and responding to user queries and preferences in natural language, NLP-powered systems deliver personalized recommendations, product suggestions, and conversational interactions tailored to individual users' needs and preferences.

Key Applications of Natural Language Processing (NLP) in Big Data:

Sentiment Analysis: Sentiment analysis, also known as opinion mining, involves analyzing textual data to determine sentiment polarity (positive, negative, or neutral). Organizations use sentiment analysis to gauge public opinion, monitor brand sentiment, and assess customer feedback, enabling them to make data-driven decisions and enhance customer satisfaction.

Named Entity Recognition (NER): NER is the task of identifying and classifying named entities, such as persons, organizations, locations, dates, and numerical expressions, in unstructured text. NER enables organizations to extract structured information from textual data, automate information extraction tasks, and enhance data organization and search capabilities.

Topic Modeling: Topic modeling algorithms, such as Latent Dirichlet Allocation (LDA) and Non-negative Matrix Factorization (NMF), cluster textual data into topics based on shared semantic themes or concepts. Organizations use topic modeling to uncover latent patterns, trends, and themes within large document collections, enabling them to explore and navigate textual data more effectively.

Text Summarization: Text summarization techniques automatically generate concise summaries of longer documents or articles, distilling key information and insights from textual data. Organizations leverage text summarization for tasks such as document summarization, news aggregation, and content curation, enabling users to access relevant information quickly and efficiently.

Challenges and Opportunities:

Ambiguity and Context Sensitivity: Natural language is inherently ambiguous and context-sensitive, posing challenges for NLP models in understanding and interpreting textual data accurately. Addressing these challenges requires advanced NLP techniques, such as contextual word embeddings, pre-trained language models, and semantic parsing, to capture nuanced meanings and context-dependent interpretations.

Data Quality and Noise: Unstructured textual data often contains noise, errors, and inconsistencies that can impact the performance of NLP models. Data preprocessing techniques, such as text cleaning, tokenization, and lemmatization, help improve data quality and prepare textual data for analysis by removing irrelevant or noisy information.

Bias and Fairness: NLP models trained on biased datasets may perpetuate existing biases and lead to unfair or discriminatory outcomes. Mitigating bias in NLP models requires careful data selection, algorithmic fairness measures, and bias detection techniques to ensure equitable representation and treatment of diverse demographic groups.

Interpretability and Explainability: The opacity of some NLP models raises concerns about interpretability and explainability. Organizations must prioritize model interpretability techniques, such as attention mechanisms, feature visualization, and model-agnostic explanations, to provide insights into model predictions and foster trust among stakeholders.

Natural Language Processing (NLP) plays a vital role in unlocking the value of unstructured textual data in Big Data environments. From sentiment analysis and named entity recognition to topic modeling and text summarization, NLP enables organizations to extract actionable insights, automate text-based tasks, and enhance decision-making processes. However, addressing challenges such as ambiguity, data quality, bias, and interpretability is essential to maximize the effectiveness and ethical responsibility of NLP models in Big Data applications. Through continuous innovation, collaboration, and ethical governance, organizations can leverage NLP to harness the full potential of textual data and drive innovation, efficiency, and customer engagement in the era of Big Data.

AI-Driven Data Visualization Techniques

Data visualization, enhanced by AI, is an essential aspect of Big Data analytics, enabling the translation of complex data sets into comprehensible and insightful visual representations. AI-driven visualization tools employ algorithms to automatically detect and highlight key patterns, trends, and anomalies in data, facilitating more efficient and effective data interpretation by humans. These tools are particularly important in fields where rapid and accurate interpretation of data is crucial, such as financial market analysis and healthcare diagnostics (Few, 2009).

Significance of AI-Driven Data Visualization:

Insight Extraction and Exploration: AI-driven data visualization techniques enable organizations to uncover hidden patterns, trends, and relationships within large and complex datasets. By transforming raw data into visual representations, these techniques facilitate exploratory analysis and help users gain a deeper understanding of the underlying data.

Decision Support and Communication: Data visualization serves as a powerful tool for decision support and communication, enabling stakeholders to make informed decisions based on data-driven insights. AI-driven visualization techniques enhance decision-making processes by presenting data in intuitive and interactive formats, enabling stakeholders to identify trends, anomalies, and actionable insights at a glance.

Pattern Recognition and Anomaly Detection: AI-powered data visualization techniques leverage machine learning algorithms to identify patterns, outliers, and anomalies in Big Data. By applying advanced analytics and anomaly detection algorithms to visual representations of data, organizations can detect irregularities, outliers, and potential risks in real-time, enabling proactive decision-making and risk mitigation.

Personalization and Interactivity: AI-driven data visualization tools offer personalized and interactive experiences tailored to individual user preferences and needs. By leveraging user interactions and machine learning algorithms, these tools adapt to user preferences, filter data dynamically, and provide personalized recommendations, enhancing user engagement and understanding of complex data.

Key Applications of AI-Driven Data Visualization:

Interactive Dashboards: AI-powered interactive dashboards enable users to explore and analyze data visually through interactive charts, graphs, and maps. These dashboards aggregate and visualize data from multiple sources, enabling users to monitor key performance indicators (KPIs), track trends, and identify insights in real-time.

Predictive Analytics Visualization: AI-driven visualization techniques facilitate the visualization of predictive analytics models and forecasts, enabling users to understand and interpret model predictions effectively. By visualizing predictive insights, organizations can make data-driven decisions, anticipate future trends, and optimize business strategies proactively.

Geospatial Visualization: AI-powered geospatial visualization techniques enable organizations to visualize and analyze spatial data, such as geographic information, satellite imagery, and location-based data. These techniques leverage machine learning algorithms to analyze spatial patterns, identify trends, and visualize insights on interactive maps, enabling organizations to make informed decisions based on spatial data.

Network Visualization: AI-driven network visualization techniques enable organizations to visualize complex networks, such as social networks, supply chains, and transportation networks. These techniques leverage graph analysis and machine learning algorithms to identify network structures, detect anomalies, and visualize network dynamics, enabling organizations to optimize network performance and mitigate risks.

Challenges and Opportunities:

Scalability and Performance: AI-driven data visualization techniques must scale with the volume and complexity of Big Data to ensure optimal performance. Addressing scalability challenges requires leveraging distributed computing frameworks, parallel processing, and optimized rendering techniques to visualize large-scale datasets efficiently.

Interpretability and Explainability: Ensuring the interpretability and explainability of AI-driven visualization techniques is essential for fostering trust and understanding among users. Organizations must prioritize techniques for explaining visualizations, providing contextual information, and enabling users to understand the underlying data and algorithms.

Data Integration and Fusion: Integrating data from heterogeneous sources and formats poses challenges for AI-driven data visualization techniques. Addressing data integration challenges requires adopting data integration platforms, standardizing data formats, and leveraging data fusion techniques to unify disparate data sources and enable comprehensive visualization and analysis.

Ethical Considerations: AI-driven data visualization techniques raise ethical considerations related to data privacy, bias, fairness, and transparency. Organizations must adhere to ethical guidelines, regulatory requirements, and industry standards to ensure the responsible and ethical use of AI-driven visualization techniques in Big Data environments.

AI-driven data visualization techniques play a crucial role in unlocking the value of Big Data by enabling organizations to extract insights, facilitate decision-making, and communicate complex information effectively. From interactive dashboards and predictive analytics visualization to geospatial and network visualization, these techniques empower organizations to leverage the power of AI and Big Data to drive innovation, optimize operations, and achieve business objectives. However, addressing challenges such as scalability, interpretability, data integration, and ethical considerations is essential to maximize the effectiveness and ethical responsibility of AI-driven data visualization techniques in Big Data environments. Through continuous innovation, collaboration, and ethical governance, organizations can harness the transformative potential of AI-driven visualization techniques to derive actionable insights and create value in the era of Big Data.

Predictive Analytics and AI

Predictive analytics, a facet of Big Data analytics powered by AI, involves using historical data to make predictions about future events. AI models, particularly those based on machine learning, are trained on historical data to identify patterns and relationships that can be used to predict future outcomes. This application of AI is invaluable in a myriad of sectors, including finance for risk assessment, retail for customer behavior prediction, and healthcare for disease outbreak forecasting (Han, Pei, & Kamber, 2011).

Significance of Predictive Analytics Powered by AI:

Anticipating Future Trends: Predictive analytics powered by AI enables organizations to anticipate future trends and patterns by analyzing historical data and identifying predictive factors. By leveraging advanced machine learning algorithms, predictive models can forecast future outcomes, such as customer behavior, market demand, and business performance, helping organizations adapt and strategize proactively.

Optimizing Decision-Making: Predictive analytics empowers organizations to optimize decision-making processes by providing actionable insights derived from data-driven predictions. By leveraging predictive models, organizations can identify opportunities, mitigate risks, and make informed decisions based on probabilistic forecasts and scenario analysis, leading to improved operational efficiency and competitive advantage.

Enhancing Customer Experience: Predictive analytics enables organizations to personalize customer experiences and anticipate customer needs by analyzing historical data and predicting future behavior. By leveraging AI-driven predictive models, organizations can tailor products, services, and marketing strategies to individual customer preferences, enhancing customer satisfaction and loyalty.

Improving Resource Allocation: Predictive analytics helps organizations optimize resource allocation by forecasting demand, identifying inefficiencies, and allocating resources effectively. By leveraging predictive models to anticipate future demand and resource requirements, organizations can optimize inventory management, workforce planning, and supply chain operations, reducing costs and maximizing productivity.

Key Applications of Predictive Analytics Powered by AI:

Customer Churn Prediction: Predictive analytics models can forecast customer churn by analyzing historical customer data and identifying factors associated with churn behavior. By predicting which customers are at risk of churning, organizations can implement targeted retention strategies, such as personalized offers and proactive outreach, to mitigate churn and retain valuable customers.

Financial Forecasting: Predictive analytics enables financial institutions to forecast market trends, evaluate investment opportunities, and manage risk effectively. By analyzing historical market data and economic indicators, predictive models can forecast asset prices, identify trading opportunities, and optimize investment portfolios, enabling organizations to make data-driven investment decisions.

Predictive Maintenance: In industrial settings, predictive analytics enables organizations to implement predictive maintenance strategies by forecasting equipment failures before they occur. By analyzing sensor data, equipment performance metrics, and maintenance logs, predictive models can predict when equipment is likely to fail, enabling organizations to schedule maintenance proactively, minimize downtime, and reduce maintenance costs.

Healthcare Outcome Prediction: Predictive analytics plays a crucial role in healthcare by enabling organizations to predict patient outcomes, diagnose diseases, and personalize treatment plans. By analyzing electronic health records, medical imaging data, and genetic information, predictive models can forecast patient outcomes, identify at-risk populations, and recommend personalized treatment options, leading to improved patient care and outcomes.

Challenges and Opportunities:

Data Quality and Availability: Ensuring the quality and availability of data is essential for the effectiveness of predictive analytics models. Organizations must address challenges related to data quality, data integration, and data governance to ensure that predictive models are trained on reliable, representative, and up-to-date data.

Model Interpretability and Transparency: The opacity of some predictive analytics models raises concerns about model interpretability and transparency. Organizations must prioritize techniques for explaining model predictions, providing interpretability, and ensuring transparency to foster trust and understanding among users and stakeholders.

Ethical and Bias Considerations: Predictive analytics models trained on biased data may produce biased outcomes and perpetuate existing inequalities. Organizations must address ethical considerations and mitigate bias in predictive models by implementing fairness-aware algorithms, bias detection techniques, and diversity-aware model evaluation methods.

Scalability and Performance: Scalability and performance are critical considerations for deploying predictive analytics models in Big Data environments. Organizations must leverage distributed computing frameworks, parallel processing, and optimized algorithms to ensure that predictive models can scale with the volume and velocity of Big Data and deliver real-time or near-real-time predictions efficiently.

Predictive analytics powered by AI represents a transformative capability within Big Data environments, enabling organizations to anticipate future trends, optimize decision-making, and drive innovation. From customer churn prediction and financial forecasting to predictive maintenance and healthcare outcome prediction, predictive analytics offers a wide range of applications across various domains. However, addressing challenges such as data quality, model interpretability, ethical considerations, and scalability is essential to maximize the effectiveness and ethical responsibility of predictive analytics powered by AI in Big Data environments. Through continuous innovation, collaboration, and ethical governance, organizations can harness the transformative potential of predictive analytics to derive actionable insights, mitigate risks, and create value in the era of Big Data.

Challenges in AI-Powered Big Data Analytics

While AI technologies offer transformative potential in Big Data analytics, they also present challenges. Ensuring the accuracy and reliability of AI models, especially in the context of the diverse and complex nature of Big Data, is paramount. Furthermore, the interpretability of AI models, particularly deep learning models, remains a challenge, raising concerns about the transparency and explainability of AI-driven decisions (Castelvecchi, 2016).

1.Data Quality and Integration:

Challenge: Ensuring the quality, completeness, and consistency of data is essential for the accuracy and reliability of AI-powered analytics. Integrating data from disparate sources with varying formats and structures poses challenges in data integration.

Solution: Organizations should implement data quality management processes, including data cleansing, normalization, and validation, to ensure that data is accurate and consistent. Adopting data integration platforms and technologies can facilitate the seamless integration of data from multiple sources.

1. **Scalability and Performance:**

Challenge: Processing and analyzing large volumes of data in real-time or near-real-time can strain computational resources and affect the performance of AI algorithms. Scalability becomes crucial as data volumes continue to grow exponentially.

Solution: Leveraging distributed computing frameworks, such as Apache Hadoop and Spark, enables parallel processing and distributed data storage, enhancing scalability and performance. Adopting cloud-based solutions and infrastructure-as-a-service (IaaS) platforms can provide elastic scalability and on-demand resources for handling fluctuating workloads.

1. **Model Interpretability and Explainability:**

Challenge: Many AI models, particularly deep learning models, are often considered "black boxes," making it challenging to interpret their decisions and predictions. Lack of interpretability and explainability can hinder trust and adoption.

Solution: Organizations should prioritize model interpretability techniques, such as feature importance analysis, model visualization, and surrogate models. Explainable AI (XAI) techniques, including LIME (Local Interpretable Model-agnostic Explanations) and SHAP (SHapley Additive exPlanations), provide insights into model predictions and foster trust among users.

1. Ethical and Bias Considerations:

Challenge: AI-powered analytics may perpetuate biases present in training data, leading to unfair or discriminatory outcomes. Ensuring fairness, transparency, and accountability in AI models is essential for ethical deployment.

Solution: Organizations should implement fairness-aware AI techniques, including bias detection, fairness metrics, and algorithmic fairness constraints, to mitigate biases in AI models. Ethical guidelines and frameworks, such as the AI Ethics Guidelines from organizations like IEEE and ACM, provide principles for responsible AI development and deployment.

1. Privacy and Security:

Challenge: Analyzing sensitive data in Big Data environments raises concerns about privacy infringement, data breaches, and unauthorized access. Protecting sensitive information while ensuring data accessibility for analysis is critical.

Solution: Implementing robust data privacy and security measures, such as data anonymization, encryption, access controls, and secure data transmission protocols, helps safeguard sensitive information from unauthorized access and misuse. Compliance with data protection regulations, such as GDPR and CCPA, is essential for protecting individuals' privacy rights.

1. **Talent and Skill Gap:**

Challenge: Building and maintaining AI-powered Big Data analytics capabilities require a skilled workforce with expertise in data science, machine learning, and Big Data technologies. However, there is a shortage of talent with these specialized skills.

Solution: Organizations should invest in training and upskilling programs to develop talent internally and bridge the skill gap. Collaborating with academic institutions, participating in industry partnerships, and fostering a culture of continuous learning can help attract and retain top talent in AI and Big Data analytics.

1. **Regulatory Compliance:**

Challenge: Adhering to regulatory requirements and compliance standards, such as GDPR, HIPAA, and PCI-DSS, presents challenges in AI-powered Big Data analytics. Non-compliance can lead to legal and financial consequences.

Solution: Organizations must stay abreast of regulatory developments and ensure compliance with relevant data protection regulations and industry standards. Implementing governance frameworks, conducting regular audits, and appointing data protection officers can help mitigate regulatory risks and ensure responsible data practices.

AI-powered Big Data analytics offer unprecedented opportunities for organizations to derive insights, drive innovation, and gain competitive advantages. However, addressing challenges such as data quality, scalability, model interpretability, ethical considerations, privacy, talent shortage, and regulatory compliance is essential for successful implementation and adoption. By adopting best practices, leveraging emerging technologies, and fostering a culture of responsible data stewardship, organizations can overcome these challenges and harness the transformative power of AI in Big Data analytics to achieve their strategic objectives.

Conclusion

The integration of AI technologies in Big Data analytics represents a monumental shift in our ability to process and derive value from vast datasets. The section in "Data Titans" dedicated to AI technologies powering Big Data provides a comprehensive overview of the current state of these technologies, their applications, and the challenges they entail, thereby equipping readers with a nuanced understanding of this dynamic field.

Machine Learning Models in Big Data:

A substantial focus is placed on explicating the role of Machine Learning (ML) models in the context of Big Data. This segment meticulously explores how ML models, as quintessential components of AI, are ingeniously leveraged to decipher, analyze, and derive actionable insights from the vast troves of data that characterize the Big Data paradigm.

Intricacies of Machine Learning Models in Big Data

Machine Learning, a pivotal cog in the wheel of AI, manifests its prowess predominantly through its ability to learn from and make predictions or decisions based on data. In the realm of Big Data, this involves training ML algorithms on large datasets, enabling these models to uncover hidden patterns, trends, and correlations (Hastie, Tibshirani, & Friedman, 2009). The crux of ML in Big Data lies in its diverse methodologies, each suited to specific types of data and analytical objectives.

1. Supervised Learning in Big Data:

Supervised learning models, which operate on labeled data, are extensively employed in Big Data for predictive analytics. These models include algorithms like linear and logistic regression, support vector machines, and neural networks. They are adept at tasks such as customer churn prediction, fraud detection, and market trend analysis, where historical data is used to predict future outcomes (James et al., 2013).

A segment of profound analytical depth focuses on the intricacies of Supervised Learning within the realm of Big Data. This section delves into the nuanced dynamics of how Supervised Learning, a cornerstone methodology in Machine Learning (ML), is adeptly employed to decipher and make predictive inferences from the voluminous datasets characteristic of Big Data.

Conceptual Framework of Supervised Learning in Big Data

Supervised Learning, a paradigm where ML models are trained using labeled datasets, is instrumental in Big Data analytics. This training involves providing the ML algorithm with input-output pairs, where the desired output (label) is known, enabling the model to learn a mapping from inputs to outputs. Post-training, the model can predict the output for new, unseen data, a capability that is invaluable in a myriad of Big Data applications (Bishop, 2006).

Applications and Implementations

In the context of Big Data, Supervised Learning finds diverse applications:

1. **Predictive Analytics**: Supervised Learning algorithms like regression models and decision trees are widely employed for predictive analytics in Big Data. They are used to forecast future trends based on historical data, such as predicting customer churn, stock prices, or demand for products (James et al., 2013).
2. **Classification Tasks**: For classification tasks, where the objective is to categorize data into predefined classes, algorithms such as Support Vector Machines (SVM) and Neural Networks are extensively utilized. Applications include email spam detection, image recognition, and medical diagnosis where each instance needs to be classified into specific categories (Hastie, Tibshirani, & Friedman, 2009).

Challenges in Supervised Learning for Big Data

The application of Supervised Learning in Big Data, however, confronts several challenges:

1. **Data Quality and Volume**: The efficacy of Supervised Learning models is contingent on the quality and quantity of training data. In Big Data, ensuring the accuracy and representativeness of large datasets is critical, as poor data quality can lead to erroneous model training and predictions (García, Luengo, & Herrera, 2015).
2. **Model Complexity and Overfitting**: A major challenge in Supervised Learning is balancing model complexity with the risk of overfitting. Overfitting occurs when a model learns the training data too well, including its noise and outliers, leading to poor performance on new, unseen data. This is particularly pertinent in Big Data, where the vastness of data can amplify the risk of overfitting (Goodfellow, Bengio, & Courville, 2016).
3. **Scalability**: Another significant challenge is scalability. Big Data environments demand that Supervised Learning algorithms efficiently handle massive datasets, necessitating algorithms that are not only accurate but also scalable and computationally efficient (Jordan & Mitchell, 2015).

In sum, the exploration of Supervised Learning in the context of Big Data, as articulated in "Data Titans," underscores its critical role in extracting insights and making predictions from large datasets. While presenting immense opportunities, it also highlights the challenges that need to be addressed to fully harness the potential of Supervised Learning in Big Data. This analysis provides a nuanced understanding, essential for practitioners and researchers navigating the complex landscape of AI in Big Data.

1. **Unsupervised Learning in Big Data**:

Unsupervised learning models thrive on unlabeled data, discerning inherent structures within the data. Clustering algorithms like k-means and hierarchical clustering, and dimensionality reduction techniques like principal component analysis, are pivotal in segmenting customer markets, identifying anomalies, and reducing the complexity of Big Data for more efficient processing (Bishop, 2006).

A significant focus is accorded to Unsupervised Learning within the sphere of Machine Learning (ML) as applied to Big Data. This segment delves into the complexities and nuances of Unsupervised Learning, elucidating how it plays a pivotal role in extracting insights from the vast, often unstructured datasets characteristic of Big Data environments.

Conceptual Framework of Unsupervised Learning in Big Data

Unsupervised Learning, distinct from its supervised counterpart, involves ML models that are trained on data without predefined labels. The primary objective of these models is to uncover hidden patterns, structures, and relationships within the data, independent of external guidance or annotation. This form of learning is particularly valuable in Big Data scenarios where the sheer volume and complexity of data render manual labeling impracticable or where the potential insights to be gained are not preconceived (Hastie, Tibshirani, & Friedman, 2009).

Applications and Implementations

Unsupervised Learning finds robust applications in the realm of Big Data:

1. **Clustering**: Algorithms like k-means and hierarchical clustering are widely used for segmenting large datasets into meaningful clusters based on inherent similarities within the data. This is invaluable in market segmentation, social network analysis, and genetic clustering where discovering natural groupings in data is crucial (James et al., 2013).

2. **Dimensionality Reduction**: Techniques such as principal component analysis (PCA) and t-distributed Stochastic Neighbor

Embedding (t-SNE) are employed to reduce the number of variables in Big Data, facilitating easier visualization and analysis without significant loss of information. This is essential in fields like bioinformatics and text analytics where high-dimensional data is prevalent (Cunningham & Ghahramani, 2015).

Challenges in Unsupervised Learning for Big Data

The deployment of Unsupervised Learning in Big Data, while promising, confronts several challenges:

1. **Interpretation of Results**: Unlike supervised learning where the outcomes are often clear and quantifiable, the results from unsupervised learning can be more subjective and harder to interpret. This poses a challenge in ensuring that the insights derived are meaningful and actionable (Murphy, 2012).

2. **Scalability and Computational Complexity**: Many unsupervised learning algorithms face challenges in scaling to very large datasets, requiring significant computational resources. Addressing these challenges involves developing more efficient algorithms and leveraging advances in computational hardware (Bengio, Courville, & Vincent, 2013).

3. **Quality of Data**: The quality of insights derived from unsupervised learning is heavily dependent on the quality of the input data. Issues like missing values, noise, and irrelevant features can significantly impact the effectiveness of these models (García, Luengo, & Herrera, 2015).

In "Data Titans," the examination of Unsupervised Learning in Big Data offers an insightful perspective into its capabilities and limitations. This analysis is crucial for practitioners and researchers to leverage the full potential of Unsupervised Learning in uncovering latent patterns and insights from the expansive datasets characteristic of Big Data.

1. **Reinforcement Learning in Big Data:**

Reinforcement learning, a paradigm of ML where models learn to make decisions by receiving rewards or penalties, is increasingly being applied to Big Data. Its applications span from optimizing recommendation systems to automating trading strategies in finance, where the model learns optimal actions through continuous interaction with data (Sutton & Barto, 2018).

A considerable attention is accorded to Reinforcement Learning (RL) within the ambit of Machine Learning (ML) as it pertains to Big Data. This section proffers a deep dive into the intricacies of RL, elucidating its unique position in the ML spectrum and its pivotal role in extracting value from the immense and complex datasets synonymous with Big Data.

Conceptual Framework of Reinforcement Learning in Big Data

Reinforcement Learning, a paradigm of ML distinct from supervised and unsupervised learning, involves training models to make a sequence of decisions. By interacting with a dynamic environment in which it operates, the RL model learns to achieve a defined objective, receiving feedback in the form of rewards or penalties. This method is particularly germane to Big Data scenarios where decision-making processes are complex and the data involved is vast and multifaceted (Sutton & Barto, 2018).

Applications and Implementations

Reinforcement Learning has found significant applications in the context of Big Data:

1. **Dynamic Decision-Making**: RL is adept at handling problems that require a series of decisions, such as in autonomous vehicles, robotics, and in-game strategies, where the model learns optimal actions based on real-time data inputs and feedback (Mnih et al., 2015).

2. **Personalization and Recommendation Systems**: In e-commerce and content streaming services, RL algorithms are employed to personalize user experiences by continually adapting recommendations based on user interactions, leveraging vast amounts of user data to optimize engagement and satisfaction (Zheng et al., 2018).

Challenges in Reinforcement Learning for Big Data

The integration of RL in Big Data is not without its challenges:

1. **Complexity in Training and Computation**: RL models, particularly those dealing with high-dimensional state spaces typical in Big Data, require significant computational resources for training. This complexity is further compounded in environments where feedback is delayed or sparse (Dulac-Arnold et al., 2015).

2. **Balancing Exploration and Exploitation**: One of the central challenges in RL is the trade-off between exploration (trying new things) and exploitation (leveraging known information). In Big Data environments, this balance is critical to ensure that the model does not become trapped in suboptimal policies (Kaelbling, Littman, & Moore, 1996).

3. **Data Quality and Diversity**: The effectiveness of RL algorithms is contingent on the diversity and quality of the data they interact with. Biased or poor-quality data can lead to suboptimal or biased decision-making processes (Osband et al., 2016).

In "Data Titans," the exploration of RL in the context of Big Data offers a comprehensive understanding of how this AI methodology can be employed to navigate complex decision-making scenarios inherent in large datasets. This analysis is instrumental for AI practitioners and researchers, providing insights into the potential and challenges of implementing RL in Big Data environments.

Challenges of Applying ML to Big Data

While ML models are indispensable tools in Big Data analytics, their application is not devoid of challenges:

1. Scalability and Computational Efficiency:

The sheer volume of Big Data demands ML models that are not only accurate but also scalable and computationally efficient. This necessitates ongoing advancements in algorithmic efficiency and computational architectures (Jordan & Mitchell, 2015).

A crucial discourse revolves around the challenges posed by the application of Machine Learning (ML) models to Big Data, with a particular focus on scalability and computational efficiency. This segment delves into the complexities and hurdles faced when scaling ML models to accommodate the vast and growing expanse of Big Data, underscoring the need for advanced computational strategies and innovations.

Scalability Challenges in ML for Big Data

The scalability of ML models in the context of Big Data refers to their ability to effectively process and analyze data volumes that are continually expanding. Big Data, characterized by its enormous volume, variety, and velocity, presents a unique set of challenges:

1. **Handling Vast Datasets**: As data volumes grow exponentially, traditional ML algorithms that perform well on smaller datasets may struggle to maintain their accuracy and efficiency. The challenge lies in adapting these algorithms to handle terabytes or petabytes of data without a significant compromise in performance (Jordan & Mitchell, 2015).

2. **Distributed Computing**: To manage the sheer volume of Big Data, ML models often require distributed computing frameworks that can process data across multiple servers or nodes. This necessitates sophisticated algorithms capable of parallel

processing and handling data partitioning effectively (Dean & Ghemawat, 2008).

3. **Data Streaming and Real-Time Analysis**: In many Big Data applications, data is generated in a continuous stream, necessitating ML models that can learn and adapt in real-time. This presents challenges in terms of developing algorithms that can quickly update their parameters in response to new data (Zaharia et al., 2013).

Computational Efficiency in ML for Big Data

Computational efficiency pertains to the ability of ML models to process and analyze data swiftly and with minimal resource utilization:

1. **Algorithmic Efficiency**: Some ML algorithms, especially complex models like deep learning networks, are computationally intensive. Optimizing these algorithms to reduce their computational load without sacrificing accuracy is a significant challenge (LeCun, Bengio, & Hinton, 2015).

2. **Hardware Limitations**: The computational demands of ML in Big Data often exceed the capacities of conventional hardware. Leveraging advanced technologies such as GPUs (Graphics Processing Units) and TPUs (Tensor Processing Units) has been pivotal in addressing these limitations (Jouppi et al., 2017).

3. **Energy Consumption**: The energy consumption associated with running large-scale ML models on massive datasets is another concern, particularly in the context of environmental sustainability. Developing energy-efficient algorithms and data centers is therefore an ongoing area of research (Strubell, Ganesh, & McCallum, 2019).

The exploration of scalability and computational efficiency challenges in applying ML to Big Data provides crucial insights into the hurdles that need to be overcome. This understanding is vital for researchers and practitioners in AI and Big Data, guiding them in developing more robust, scalable, and efficient ML models suited for the vast and dynamic landscape of Big Data.

1. **Data Quality and Preprocessing**:

The efficacy of ML models is heavily contingent on the quality of the data. In Big Data, issues such as missing values, noise, and inconsistencies pose significant challenges, requiring robust data preprocessing techniques (García, Luengo, & Herrera, 2015).

An insightful examination is dedicated to the challenges associated with data quality and preprocessing in the realm of Machine Learning (ML) applied to Big Data. This critical discourse articulates the complexities and nuances involved in ensuring the integrity and suitability of vast datasets for ML applications, underscoring the importance of meticulous preprocessing and data quality assurance.

Data Quality Challenges in ML for Big Data

Data quality is a fundamental determinant of the efficacy of ML models. In the context of Big Data, where data is often sourced from a multitude of origins and formats, maintaining high data quality presents several challenges:

1. **Inconsistencies and Inaccuracies**: Big Data is susceptible to inconsistencies and inaccuracies, stemming from errors in data collection, transcription errors, or misalignment among different data sources. These inaccuracies can significantly distort the outcomes of ML models (Fan, Lau, & Vojnovic, 2014).

2. **Missing Values and Imputation**: Another prevalent issue in Big Data is missing data. The absence of critical information can lead to biased or inaccurate ML predictions. Imputation methods are often employed to handle missing data, but selecting appropriate imputation techniques is crucial to maintain data integrity (García-Laencina, Sancho-Gómez, & Figueiras-Vidal, 2010).

3. **Noise and Outliers**: Big Data often contains noise and outliers that can skew the performance of ML models. Identifying and mitigating the impact of these anomalies is crucial to ensure that ML models learn the underlying patterns in the data, rather than being influenced by irrelevant variations (Hodge & Austin, 2004).

Preprocessing Challenges in ML for Big Data

Preprocessing is a critical step in preparing data for ML models, especially in Big Data environments:

1. **Feature Selection and Dimensionality Reduction**: Big Data often involves high-dimensional data, which can lead to the curse of dimensionality. Effective feature selection and dimensionality reduction techniques are vital to reduce the number of input variables and focus on the most informative features (Guyon & Elisseeff, 2003).

2. **Data Transformation and Normalization**: Transforming and normalizing data to a suitable scale or format is essential for many ML algorithms. This includes tasks such as scaling features to a uniform range, encoding categorical variables, or transforming skewed data distributions (Jain, Nandakumar, & Ross, 2005).

3. **Handling Imbalanced Data**: In many real-world Big Data scenarios, datasets are imbalanced, meaning some classes are underrepresented. Techniques like oversampling the minority class or undersampling the majority class are often necessary to prevent ML models from being biased towards the majority class (Chawla et al., 2002).

The analysis in "Data Titans" of the challenges of data quality and preprocessing in ML for Big Data offers a nuanced understanding of the critical steps necessary to prepare vast datasets for effective ML applications. Addressing these challenges is indispensable for harnessing the full potential of ML in Big Data, ensuring that the insights derived are accurate, reliable, and actionable.

1. Overfitting and Generalization:

In Big Data, there is a risk that ML models become overfitted, performing well on training data but poorly on unseen data. Ensuring that these models generalize effectively to new data is a critical aspect of ML model development (Goodfellow, Bengio, & Courville, 2016).

The exploration of ML models provides a comprehensive understanding of how these algorithms transform raw data into insightful, actionable knowledge. This examination not only highlights the potential of ML in Big Data but also addresses the inherent challenges, offering a balanced perspective on the application of these advanced technologies in the vast and evolving landscape of Big Data.

A significant analysis is dedicated to addressing the challenges of overfitting and generalization in the application of Machine Learning (ML) models to Big Data. This discussion is critical, as it highlights the intricate balance required to develop ML models that are not only adept at learning from vast datasets but also capable of generalizing their learnings to new, unseen data.

Overfitting in ML Models for Big Data

Overfitting occurs when an ML model learns the training data too well, including its noise and idiosyncrasies, to the detriment of its performance on new data. This phenomenon is particularly pertinent in Big Data environments, where the complexity and diversity of data can exacerbate the tendency of ML models to overfit:

1. **High-Dimensional Data**: Big Data often involves high-dimensional feature spaces, increasing the risk of overfitting, as models have more parameters to adjust to the training data, potentially capturing noise rather than underlying patterns (Hawkins, 2004).

2. **Complex Models and Data Sparsity**: The use of complex models like deep neural networks in Big Data can lead to overfitting, especially in cases of data sparsity where the number of parameters in the model far exceeds the number of observations in some dimensions of the dataset (Zhang et al., 2016).

Generalization in ML Models for Big Data

Generalization refers to the ability of an ML model to perform well on new, unseen data. Ensuring that ML models generalize effectively in Big Data is a key challenge:

1. **Balancing Model Complexity and Simplicity**: Achieving the right balance between model complexity (to capture underlying patterns in data) and simplicity (to avoid overfitting) is crucial. Techniques like regularization and cross-validation are commonly employed to find this balance (James et al., 2013).
2. **Diverse and Representative Training Data**: Ensuring that the training data is diverse and representative of the problem space is essential for generalization. In Big Data, this can be challenging due to the inherent biases in data collection and sampling methods (Bishop, 2006).

Mitigating Overfitting and Enhancing Generalization

To address these challenges, several strategies are employed:

1. **Regularization Techniques**: Regularization methods such as L1 and L2 regularization are used to penalize overly complex models, thus preventing overfitting while allowing the model to capture the essential trends in the data (Tibshirani, 1996).
2. **Cross-Validation**: Cross-validation techniques, particularly k-fold cross-validation, are employed to assess how well a model generalizes to independent data sets, providing insights into the model's performance on unseen data (Kohavi, 1995).

3. **Model Selection and Hyperparameter Tuning**: Careful model selection and hyperparameter tuning, often through grid search or randomized search methods, are crucial in developing models that generalize well (Bergstra & Bengio, 2012).

Conclusion

In the context of Big Data, as elaborated in "Data Titans," the challenges of overfitting and generalization are paramount in the development of effective ML models. Addressing these challenges requires a combination of methodological rigor, sophisticated model evaluation techniques, and a deep understanding of the data's inherent characteristics.

Natural Language Processing for Unstructured Data Analysis:

In the seminal volume "Data Titans: Navigating the AI Revolution in Big Data," a substantial section is devoted to exploring the role of Natural Language Processing (NLP) in the analysis of unstructured data within the vast expanse of Big Data. This discourse delves into the intricacies of NLP, a subfield of AI, demonstrating its pivotal role in deciphering, interpreting, and extracting meaningful insights from unstructured textual data, which forms a significant component of Big Data.

NLP in Unstructured Data Analysis

NLP encompasses a suite of algorithms and techniques designed to enable computers to understand, interpret, and manipulate human language. In the context of Big Data, NLP is instrumental in managing and making sense of unstructured textual data, which is often complex and voluminous:

1. **Text Mining and Information Extraction**: NLP facilitates the extraction of valuable information from large text corpora.

This includes tasks like identifying key phrases, entities (such as names, locations, and dates), and relationships between entities, which are essential for various applications including sentiment analysis, topic modeling, and summarization (Manning & Schütze, 1999).

2. **Sentiment Analysis and Opinion Mining**: NLP algorithms are adept at analyzing sentiments and opinions expressed in text, enabling businesses and organizations to gauge public sentiment towards products, services, or policies. This analysis is crucial for market research, brand monitoring, and social media analytics (Liu, 2012).

Challenges in NLP for Big Data

The application of NLP in Big Data is fraught with challenges:

1. **Handling Ambiguity and Contextual Nuances**: Natural language is inherently ambiguous and context-dependent. NLP algorithms must contend with these ambiguities and the subtleties of language, including idioms, sarcasm, and context-specific meanings (Jurafsky & Martin, 2014).

2. **Scalability and Efficiency**: Processing and analyzing large volumes of text data require NLP algorithms that are not only accurate but also scalable and computationally efficient. This necessitates optimization of algorithms and leveraging distributed computing frameworks (Bird, Klein, & Loper, 2009).

3. **Language Diversity and Adaptability**: With the plethora of languages and dialects globally, developing NLP algorithms that can adapt to different linguistic rules and structures is a significant challenge. This is further complicated by the evolving nature of language and the emergence of internet-based slang and shorthand (Koehn, 2009).

Advancements in NLP for Big Data

To address these challenges, significant advancements have been made in NLP:

Deep Learning in NLP: The integration of deep learning techniques has led to significant improvements in NLP tasks. Neural network-based models, such as transformers and BERT (Bidirectional Encoder Representations from Transformers), have demonstrated remarkable abilities in capturing contextual nuances and complexities of language (Devlin et al., 2018).

Distributed Text Processing: Frameworks like Apache Hadoop and Apache Spark have been instrumental in enabling the distributed processing of text data, enhancing the scalability of NLP applications in Big Data scenarios (Zaharia et al., 2010).

The exploration of NLP in the context of Big Data, as elucidated in "Data Titans," highlights the transformative impact of NLP in managing and extracting insights from unstructured data. By navigating the challenges and leveraging the latest advancements in the field, NLP stands as a critical tool in the Big Data toolkit, unlocking the vast potential hidden in unstructured textual data.

AI-Driven Data Visualization Techniques:

In "Data Titans: Navigating the AI Revolution in Big Data," an insightful segment is dedicated to AI-driven data visualization techniques. This section elucidates how Artificial Intelligence (AI), particularly Machine Learning (ML) and advanced analytical methods, enhances the realm of data visualization in the context of Big Data. This intersection of AI and visualization technology plays a pivotal role in translating complex data sets into more comprehensible, insightful visual representations, facilitating better understanding and decision-making.

AI-Enhanced Data Visualization

The integration of AI into data visualization involves the application of ML algorithms to automatically identify patterns, trends, and anomalies in large data sets, which are then translated into visual formats. This process not only accelerates the visualization of complex data but also uncovers insights that might not be apparent through traditional analysis methods.

1. **Automated Pattern Recognition**: AI algorithms, especially those in unsupervised learning, can identify patterns and correlations within Big Data that might be missed by human analysts. These patterns can then be visually represented, providing an immediate and intuitive understanding of the data (Keim, Qu, & Ma, 2013).

2. **Predictive Visualization**: AI-driven visualization tools can project future trends based on historical data. This predictive capability is particularly valuable in fields like finance, where forecasting market trends is crucial, and in meteorology, for weather prediction (Aigner, Miksch, Schumann, & Tominski, 2011).

Challenges in AI-Driven Data Visualization

The implementation of AI in data visualization, while offering significant advantages, also presents unique challenges:

1. **Complexity of Interpretation**: As AI algorithms become more sophisticated, the interpretation of the visualizations they produce can become more complex, requiring users to have a certain level of expertise to understand and derive actionable insights (Few, 2009).

2. **Bias and Misrepresentation**: There is a risk that AI algorithms may incorporate biases present in the training data, leading to visualizations that misrepresent the underlying reality. Ensuring the neutrality and accuracy of AI-driven visualizations is a significant challenge (Díaz, Hogan, & Lau, 2019).

3. **Scalability and Real-Time Visualization**: In Big Data environments, providing real-time visualization of rapidly changing

data sets is a challenge. Scalable and efficient algorithms are needed to ensure that visualizations are both timely and relevant (Liu, Nersessian, & Stasko, 2008).

Advancements in AI-Driven Data Visualization

Advancements in AI technology are continually addressing these challenges:

1. **Interactive Visualizations**: The development of interactive visualization tools allows users to explore data more deeply, adjusting parameters to view data from different perspectives, thus providing a more comprehensive understanding of complex datasets (Thomas & Cook, 2005).
2. **Integration with Augmented Reality (AR) and Virtual Reality (VR)**: The integration of AR and VR technologies with AI-driven data visualization offers immersive and intuitive ways to interact with and understand complex data structures (Donalek et al., 2014).

In "Data Titans," the discussion on AI-driven data visualization techniques underscores their importance in the Big Data landscape. By transforming complex datasets into accessible and insightful visual formats, these techniques empower decision-makers across various domains, enabling a more nuanced understanding of large-scale data.

Predictive Analytics and AI:

A significant emphasis is placed on the intersection of Predictive Analytics and Artificial Intelligence (AI) within the vast domain of Big Data. This section rigorously examines how AI, especially advanced Machine Learning (ML) algorithms, is revolutionizing the field of predictive analytics by enhancing its capability to extract foresightful insights from extensive data collections.

Enhancing Predictive Analytics with AI

Predictive analytics, traditionally grounded in statistical methods and machine learning, has been transformed by the integration of AI. AI enhances predictive models' ability to analyze vast amounts of data, identify complex patterns, and make accurate predictions about future events or behaviors.

1. **Machine Learning Models in Predictive Analytics**: Advanced ML models, including both supervised learning techniques like regression and classification and unsupervised methods like clustering, have become integral to predictive analytics in Big Data. These models can handle large, diverse datasets and learn from them to make predictions or identify trends (Hastie, Tibshirani, & Friedman, 2009).

2. **Deep Learning for Complex Predictions**: Deep learning, a subset of ML characterized by deep neural networks, has significantly improved the predictive capabilities in complex areas such as image and speech recognition, natural language processing, and sophisticated pattern recognition tasks (LeCun, Bengio, & Hinton, 2015).

Challenges in AI-Driven Predictive Analytics

The application of AI in predictive analytics within Big Data contexts presents several challenges:

1. **Data Quality and Relevance**: The accuracy of predictions made by AI models is heavily contingent on the quality and relevance of the training data. Incomplete or biased data can lead to inaccurate predictions, a phenomenon known as "garbage in, garbage out" (Kelleher & Tierney, 2018).

2. **Model Interpretability and Transparency**: Many AI models, especially complex neural networks, are often seen as "black boxes." Ensuring that these models are interpretable and their

decision-making processes transparent is critical for gaining trust and actionable insights (Molnar, 2020).

3. **Ethical and Privacy Concerns**: Predictive analytics in AI must navigate ethical considerations and privacy concerns, particularly when predictions are based on personal or sensitive data. Adherence to privacy laws and ethical guidelines is paramount to prevent misuse of predictive insights (Shmueli & Koppius, 2011).

Advancements and Innovations in AI-Driven Predictive Analytics

Advancements in AI technologies are continually addressing the challenges in predictive analytics:

1. **Explainable AI (XAI)**: Developments in XAI are focused on making AI models more interpretable and their predictions more understandable to humans. This is crucial for sensitive applications like healthcare and finance, where understanding the rationale behind predictions is as important as the predictions themselves (Gunning, 2017).

2. **Integrating Multiple Data Sources**: AI models in predictive analytics are increasingly capable of integrating and analyzing data from multiple sources, enhancing the richness and accuracy of predictions. This integration includes structured data, unstructured text, images, and even sensor data in IoT (Internet of Things) applications (Zheng et al., 2018).

Conclusion

The exploration of Predictive Analytics and AI in "Data Titans" provides an in-depth understanding of how AI technologies are reshaping the predictive analytics landscape within Big Data. This analysis is crucial for businesses, researchers, and policymakers aiming to leverage the predictive power of AI while addressing its challenges and ensuring ethical and responsible use.

Chapter 3: Big Data Sources and AI Integration

In the insightful compendium, considerable emphasis is placed on the integration of Artificial Intelligence (AI) with various Big Data sources. This segment explores the multifaceted nature of Big Data sources and the complexities involved in integrating these diverse data streams with AI technologies. It highlights how AI can be harnessed to extract, process, and analyze data from myriad sources, thereby transforming raw data into valuable insights.

Diversity of Big Data Sources

Big Data is characterized by its enormous volume, velocity, variety, and veracity, emanating from an array of sources:

1. **Structured Data**:

This includes data from traditional databases, spreadsheets, and ERP systems. AI integration in this context often involves utilizing machine learning algorithms for predictive analytics and trend analysis (Russom, 2011).

The authors meticulously dissect the multifaceted nature of Big Data sources, focusing specifically on the role and integration of structured data within AI paradigms. Structured data, often seen as the bedrock of conventional data analysis, forms a critical component of the Big Data ecosystem and presents unique opportunities and challenges when integrated with Artificial Intelligence (AI) technologies.

Characteristics and Importance of Structured Data in Big Data

Structured data refers to highly organized information that resides in fixed fields within a record or file, typically found in relational databases and spreadsheets. It includes data types like dates, numbers, and strings, which are easily searchable due to their predictable and uniform nature (Russom, 2011).

The integration of AI with structured data is fundamental in numerous Big Data applications. Due to its organized format, structured data is particularly amenable to traditional database operations and straightforward to use in AI and machine learning algorithms. It serves as a valuable source for various predictive analytics, trend analysis, and decision-making processes in fields ranging from finance to healthcare.

Challenges in Integrating AI with Structured Data

Despite its organized nature, integrating AI with structured data in a Big Data context involves specific challenges:

1. **Scalability and Storage**: The vast volumes of structured data generated and collected in Big Data scenarios necessitate scalable storage solutions and efficient database management systems to ensure rapid access and processing (Kambatla et al., 2014).

2. **Data Integration and Aggregation**: In Big Data environments, structured data often needs to be integrated with unstructured and semi-structured data from various sources. This integration process poses challenges in data aggregation, normalization, and ensuring data consistency (Saha & Srivastava, 2014).

3. **Real-Time Processing**: In many applications, there is a need for real-time analysis of structured data. Developing AI models that can process and analyze data in real-time, especially for time-sensitive applications, presents significant computational and algorithmic challenges (Zaharia et al., 2013).

AI Technologies Leveraging Structured Data

To effectively utilize structured data in Big Data analytics, several AI technologies and methodologies are employed:

1. **Machine Learning Models**: Structured data is particularly suitable for supervised machine learning models, such as regression and classification algorithms, which require well-defined feature sets for training and prediction (Hastie, Tibshirani, & Friedman, 2009).
2. **Data Warehousing and Mining**: Advanced data warehousing techniques, combined with data mining, play a crucial role in organizing, storing, and extracting valuable insights from structured data sets at scale (Inmon, 2005).
3. **Predictive Analytics**: Predictive models built using AI algorithms extensively utilize structured data for forecasting and trend analysis, enabling businesses and organizations to make data-driven decisions (Shmueli & Koppius, 2011).

The exploration of structured data in the context of AI and Big Data, as elucidated in "Data Titans," highlights its critical role and the intricacies involved in its integration with AI technologies. Understanding these dynamics is essential for practitioners and researchers in leveraging structured data effectively in the ever-expanding domain of Big Data.

1. **Unstructured Data**:

A significant portion of Big Data is unstructured, coming from sources like social media, emails, and multimedia content. AI, particularly natural language processing and computer vision, plays a crucial role in interpreting and analyzing this data (Fan, Lau, & Vojnovic, 2014).

An in-depth analysis is conducted on the integration of Artificial Intelligence (AI) with unstructured data, a predominant and burgeoning source within the Big Data landscape. Unstructured data, characterized by its non-conformity to a predefined data model, presents distinct challenges and opportunities in the realm of Big Data and AI integration.

Nature and Significance of Unstructured Data in Big Data

Unstructured data encompasses a wide variety of data forms, including text, images, videos, and audio. This type of data does not adhere to a specific format or structure, making it more complex and nuanced compared to structured data. Estimates suggest that a significant majority of Big Data is unstructured, emanating from diverse sources like social media posts, digital images, sensor outputs, and other forms of media (Gandomi & Haider, 2015).

Challenges in Integrating AI with Unstructured Data

The integration of AI with unstructured data involves several nuanced challenges:

1. **Complexity in Processing and Analysis**: Unlike structured data, unstructured data requires more sophisticated processing techniques for extraction, classification, and analysis. Techniques such as Natural Language Processing (NLP) for text, and computer vision for images and videos, are necessary to decode the complexities inherent in unstructured data (Manning & Schütze, 1999).

2. **Data Quality and Standardization**: The quality of unstructured data can be highly variable. Additionally, standardizing this data to make it suitable for analysis is a complex process, involving tasks like data cleansing, normalization, and feature extraction (Fan, Lau, & Vojnovic, 2014).

3. **Storage and Management**: The storage and management of large volumes of unstructured data pose significant challenges due to its size and the lack of uniformity. Efficient data storage

solutions and data management systems are essential to handle this diversity and volume (Sakr et al., 2013).

AI Techniques for Unstructured Data Analysis

To effectively harness unstructured data, various AI techniques and methodologies are employed:

1. **Natural Language Processing (NLP)**: NLP is used extensively for processing and analyzing text data, enabling machines to understand, interpret, and generate human language. This includes tasks like sentiment analysis, topic modeling, and text classification (Jurafsky & Martin, 2014).
2. **Computer Vision**: AI-driven computer vision techniques are employed for processing and analyzing image and video data. This includes applications in facial recognition, object detection, and image classification (Krishna et al., 2016).
3. **Deep Learning**: Deep learning models, particularly convolutional neural networks (CNNs) and recurrent neural networks (RNNs), are highly effective in handling the intricacies of unstructured data, providing advanced capabilities in feature extraction and pattern recognition (LeCun, Bengio, & Hinton, 2015).

The exploration of unstructured data in the context of Big Data and AI underscores its critical importance and the complexities involved in its integration and analysis. Understanding these dynamics is pivotal for practitioners and researchers to effectively leverage unstructured data, unlocking the vast potential it holds in the Big Data arena.

1. **IoT and Sensor Data:**

The Internet of Things (IoT) contributes significantly to Big Data through a multitude of connected devices and sensors. AI integration in this domain often involves real-time processing and analysis for applications like smart cities, health monitoring, and industrial automation (Gubbi et al., 2013).

A segment of the discourse is dedicated to the integration of Artificial Intelligence (AI) with Internet of Things (IoT) and sensor data, a rapidly growing source in the Big Data ecosystem. This analysis elucidates the complexities and potentials of IoT and sensor data as significant contributors to Big Data, highlighting how AI methodologies are instrumental in extracting, processing, and deriving valuable insights from this data.

IoT and Sensor Data in the Big Data Framework

IoT and sensor data are characterized by their real-time, continuous, and often complex nature. This data is generated by a myriad of devices and sensors embedded in various environments, ranging from industrial machinery and urban infrastructure to personal devices and home appliances. It includes a wide array of metrics such as temperature readings, motion data, GPS signals, and much more (Gubbi et al., 2013).

Challenges in Integrating AI with IoT and Sensor Data

The integration of AI with IoT and sensor data presents several unique challenges:

1. **Volume and Velocity**: The sheer volume and high velocity at which IoT and sensor data is generated pose significant challenges in terms of data storage, processing, and real-time analysis (Zheng et al., 2014).

2. **Heterogeneity and Complexity**: IoT and sensor data often come in various formats and standards, adding layers of complexity to data integration, normalization, and analysis. Making sense of this heterogeneous data requires sophisticated AI algorithms capable of handling such diversity (Atzori et al., 2010).

3. **Data Quality and Reliability**: Ensuring the quality and reliability of sensor data is critical, as inaccuracies or noise in the data

can lead to incorrect conclusions. AI models must be designed to account for potential data quality issues (Ray, 2016).

AI Techniques for IoT and Sensor Data Analysis

Several AI techniques and methodologies are employed to harness IoT and sensor data effectively:

1. **Machine Learning for Pattern Recognition**: Machine learning algorithms, especially unsupervised learning techniques, are widely used to identify patterns and anomalies in sensor data, which is crucial for applications like predictive maintenance and anomaly detection (Hodge & Austin, 2004).

2. **Deep Learning for Complex Data Analysis**: Deep learning models, particularly recurrent neural networks (RNNs) and convolutional neural networks (CNNs), are effective in analyzing complex sensor data sequences and spatial-temporal data for applications in areas such as environmental monitoring and smart cities (LeCun, Bengio, & Hinton, 2015).

3. **Edge Computing for Real-Time Analysis**: Edge computing, where data processing occurs close to the data source, is increasingly utilized in conjunction with AI to enable real-time data analysis and reduce latency in decision-making processes (Shi et al., 2016).

In "Data Titans," the exploration of IoT and sensor data within the context of AI and Big Data underscores the significant role of these data sources in the current Big Data landscape. The integration of AI with IoT and sensor data not only addresses the inherent challenges but also unlocks the vast potential of this data, leading to innovative solutions and advancements across various domains.

Challenges in Integrating AI with Big Data Sources

The integration of AI with these varied data sources is not without challenges:

1. **Data Heterogeneity**:

The diversity of data types and formats requires sophisticated pre-processing and transformation techniques to make the data amenable to AI analysis (Kambatla et al., 2014).

A segment is dedicated to dissecting the challenges inherent in integrating Artificial Intelligence (AI) with heterogeneous Big Data sources. This analysis delves into the intricacies of data heterogeneity, a defining characteristic of Big Data that poses significant challenges for AI integration. Data heterogeneity refers to the diversity in data types, structures, and sources, encompassing a range of formats from structured numerical data to unstructured text, images, and beyond.

Complexities of Data Heterogeneity in AI Integration

The heterogeneity of Big Data sources presents a multifaceted challenge for AI systems:

1. **Diverse Data Types and Structures**: Big Data encompasses varied data types, including structured, unstructured, and semi-structured data. Each type necessitates different processing and analysis techniques, making it challenging for AI systems to uniformly handle this diversity (Fan, Lau, & Vojnovic, 2014).

2. **Inconsistencies and Integration Issues**: Data collected from different sources often varies in format and quality, leading to inconsistencies. Integrating this disparate data into a coherent format that can be effectively processed by AI systems is a complex task (Halevy, Rajaraman, & Ordille, 2006).

3. **Semantic Understanding**: The varied nature of data sources also implies semantic differences. Understanding and interpreting the meaning and context of different data types is a significant challenge for AI, particularly in applications involving natural language processing and image recognition (Bizer, Heath, & Berners-Lee, 2009).

Strategies for Addressing Data Heterogeneity in AI

Several strategies are employed to manage the challenges posed by data heterogeneity:

1. **Advanced Data Preprocessing**: Effective data preprocessing methods, including data cleansing, normalization, transformation, and feature extraction, are crucial to handle heterogeneous data. These methods help in standardizing and preparing data for analysis by AI systems (García, Luengo, & Herrera, 2015).
2. **Sophisticated Integration Techniques**: Employing advanced data integration techniques, such as data warehousing and federated databases, can aid in amalgamating heterogeneous data from multiple sources into a unified and consistent format (Lenzerini, 2002).
3. **Use of Ontologies in Semantic Integration**: Ontologies, which provide a framework for representing and sharing domain knowledge, can be instrumental in addressing semantic heterogeneity. They enable AI systems to understand and process the context and relationships within the data (Gruber, 1993).

The exploration of data heterogeneity and its challenges in the context of AI integration with Big Data, as discussed in "Data Titans," underscores the complexity and necessity of developing sophisticated AI tools and techniques to effectively harness the potential of diverse data sources. Addressing these challenges is paramount for leveraging AI in the realm of Big Data, ensuring that insights drawn are comprehensive, accurate, and reflective of the rich diversity inherent in the data.

1. Data Quality and Cleansing:

Ensuring the quality of data from disparate sources and performing necessary cleansing operations is critical. AI models are highly sensitive to the quality of input data (Saha & Srivastava, 2014).

A critical examination is devoted to the challenges of data quality and cleansing in the integration of Artificial Intelligence (AI) with Big Data sources. This segment elucidates the complexities associated with ensuring the high quality and cleanliness of data, which are paramount for the effective application of AI techniques in Big Data analytics.

The Imperative of Data Quality in AI-Driven Big Data Analytics

Data quality is a crucial factor in the success of AI applications within Big Data frameworks. The AI algorithms' ability to learn, predict, and make intelligent decisions is heavily reliant on the quality of the input data. Data quality issues can range from incomplete, inconsistent, and erroneous data to outdated information, which can significantly impair the performance of AI models (Pipino, Lee, & Wang, 2002).

Challenges in Ensuring Data Quality

1. **Identifying and Handling Incomplete Data**: One of the primary challenges is dealing with incomplete datasets. Missing data can skew the results of AI models, leading to inaccurate predictions or analyses. Identifying and imputing missing values or deciding when to exclude incomplete records are critical steps in data preprocessing (Schafer & Graham, 2002).

2. **Addressing Inconsistencies and Errors**: Data collected from various sources often contains inconsistencies and errors. Rectifying these discrepancies, which may involve standardizing data formats, correcting values, or reconciling data from different sources, is essential for maintaining data integrity (Rahm & Do, 2000).

3. **Managing Outliers and Noise**: Detecting and handling outliers and noise in data is another significant challenge. Outliers can be indicative of data quality issues or may represent valuable, albeit rare, occurrences. Determining the appropriate treatment of outliers requires careful consideration to avoid misleading AI analysis outcomes (Hodge & Austin, 2004).

Data Cleansing Strategies for AI Integration

To address these data quality challenges, various data cleansing strategies are employed:

1. **Data Imputation Techniques**: For handling missing data, imputation techniques such as mean imputation, regression imputation, or more advanced methods like multiple imputation can be utilized to fill in missing values (Little & Rubin, 2002).
2. **Automated Data Cleansing Tools**: Utilizing automated data cleansing tools can efficiently identify and correct errors in large datasets. These tools often employ algorithms to detect anomalies, duplicate entries, and inconsistencies in the data (Kim, Choi, Hong, Lee, & Kim, 2003).
3. **Advanced Outlier Detection Methods**: Employing advanced statistical and machine learning techniques for outlier detection helps in identifying and treating outliers appropriately. Methods like standard deviation, clustering, or unsupervised learning algorithms can be effective in outlier detection and treatment (Aggarwal, 2013).

The discourse on data quality and cleansing in "Data Titans" underscores the critical importance of these aspects in the context of AI and Big Data integration. Addressing data quality issues through effective cleansing and preprocessing strategies is fundamental to harnessing the full potential of AI in Big Data analytics, ensuring the reliability and accuracy of derived insights.

1. **Scalability and Performance**:

The sheer volume of data necessitates AI solutions that are scalable and efficient. Distributed computing frameworks and parallel processing are often employed to address these issues (Zaharia et al., 2013).

A segment is dedicated to addressing the challenges of scalability and performance in the integration of Artificial Intelligence (AI) with Big Data sources. This critical examination focuses on the complexities of scaling AI models to handle the enormous volumes and high velocity of data characteristic of Big Data, while maintaining optimal performance.

Scalability Challenges in AI and Big Data Integration

Scalability in the context of AI and Big Data refers to the ability of AI systems to efficiently handle increasing volumes of data and computational complexity. Big Data's inherent attributes of volume, variety, and velocity necessitate AI systems that can scale both horizontally (across more machines) and vertically (more powerful computing resources) to manage the growing data demands:

1. **Handling Massive Data Volumes**: One of the primary challenges is processing and analyzing the vast amounts of data generated daily. Traditional AI algorithms may struggle with such scale, necessitating the development of more scalable machine learning models and data processing techniques (Dean & Ghemawat, 2008).

2. **Distributed Computing and Parallel Processing**: To manage large-scale data processing, AI systems often rely on distributed computing frameworks, such as Apache Hadoop and Apache Spark. These frameworks enable parallel processing of data across clusters of computers, which is essential for handling Big Data (Zaharia et al., 2010).

3. **Real-Time Data Processing**: Many Big Data applications require real-time data analysis. Scaling AI systems to provide real-time insights, especially in scenarios with continuous data streams, presents significant computational and algorithmic challenges (Stonebraker et al., 2010).

Performance Optimization in AI and Big Data

Optimizing the performance of AI systems in Big Data environments involves enhancing the speed, accuracy, and efficiency of these systems:

1. **Algorithmic Efficiency**: Improving the efficiency of AI algorithms is crucial for performance optimization. This involves developing algorithms that can process and analyze data more quickly and with greater accuracy, even as the data scales (Bottou & Bousquet, 2008).

2. **Resource Management and Optimization**: Efficient management of computing resources, such as memory and processing power, is vital. Techniques like data sampling, model compression, and efficient memory management can help optimize resource usage in AI applications (Chen et al., 2014).

3. **Balancing Accuracy with Computational Cost**: In AI models, particularly in deep learning, there is often a trade-off between accuracy and computational cost. Techniques like transfer learning, model pruning, and quantization are used to balance this trade-off, ensuring efficient performance without significantly compromising accuracy (Howard et al., 2017).

The discourse on scalability and performance challenges in "Data Titans" provides a comprehensive understanding of the critical issues faced in integrating AI with Big Data sources. Addressing these challenges is essential for harnessing the power of AI in Big Data analytics, ensuring that AI systems are not only scalable but also perform efficiently as data volumes continue to grow exponentially.

Strategies for Effective AI and Big Data Integration

To effectively integrate AI with Big Data sources, several strategies are employed:

1. **Advanced Analytics and Machine Learning Models:**

Employing advanced analytics and ML models that are capable of handling high-dimensional data and extracting meaningful patterns is essential (Chen et al., 2014).

Considerable attention is devoted to the strategies for effective integration of Artificial Intelligence (AI) with Big Data, particularly focusing on advanced analytics and Machine Learning (ML) models. This discourse sheds light on how sophisticated analytical techniques and ML models are pivotal in distilling valuable insights from the vast and varied reservoirs of Big Data.

Utilization of Advanced Analytics in Big Data

Advanced analytics encompasses a suite of techniques and methodologies that go beyond traditional data analysis and business intelligence. It involves the use of sophisticated tools and algorithms to perform predictive and prescriptive analytics, offering deeper insights and foresight into trends, patterns, and behaviors:

1. **Predictive Analytics**: Predictive analytics utilizes statistical models and machine learning techniques to forecast future events based on historical data. In the Big Data context, this involves analyzing large datasets to predict trends, customer behavior, market movements, and other future occurrences with a degree of certainty (Shmueli & Koppius, 2011).

2. **Prescriptive Analytics**: Prescriptive analytics extends beyond predicting future outcomes to suggesting actions and strategies. It involves the use of optimization and simulation algorithms to advise on possible outcomes and answer "what should be done" questions, considering the implications of each decision (Bertsimas & Kallus, 2020).

Integration of Machine Learning Models with Big Data

Machine Learning models are at the heart of AI's role in Big Data, enabling the automation of analytical model building and offering the ability to scale up to handle vast amounts of complex data:

1. **Supervised Learning for Pattern Recognition and Prediction**: Supervised learning algorithms, such as regression and classification models, are extensively used in Big Data for identifying patterns and making predictions. These models are trained on historical data labeled with the outcome variable and are used for applications like customer segmentation, fraud detection, and demand forecasting (Hastie, Tibshirani, & Friedman, 2009).

2. **Unsupervised Learning for Data Exploration**: Unsupervised learning algorithms, including clustering and dimensionality reduction techniques, are used in Big Data for exploring data patterns, detecting anomalies, and discovering the intrinsic structure of data without pre-labeled outcomes. These techniques are crucial in scenarios where the relationships within data are not known a priori (Bishop, 2006).

3. **Deep Learning for Complex Data Analysis**: Deep learning, a subset of ML, excels in working with large and complex data structures. Deep neural networks, particularly convolutional neural networks (CNNs) and recurrent neural networks (RNNs), are effective for unstructured data analysis, such as image and speech recognition, and natural language processing (LeCun, Bengio, & Hinton, 2015).

Challenges and Considerations

While advanced analytics and ML models offer immense potential in Big Data analytics, they present challenges, including the need for large and diverse training datasets, computational resource requirements, and ensuring model interpretability and ethical use of AI (Molnar, 2020). Additionally, the integration of these models with Big Data requires careful consideration of data privacy and security, particularly when handling sensitive information.

The integration of advanced analytics and ML models with Big Data, as outlined in "Data Titans," represents a transformative approach in extracting, analyzing, and interpreting the vast array of data available in the modern world. This integration is crucial for turning Big Data into actionable insights, driving decision-making processes, and fostering innovations across various sectors. However, it is essential to navigate these integrations thoughtfully, addressing the challenges and ensuring ethical and responsible use of AI and Big Data.

1. **Distributed Data Processing Architectures**:

Utilizing distributed data processing architectures like Apache Hadoop and Spark to handle the volume and velocity of Big Data is crucial for efficient AI integration (White, 2012).

A pivotal focus is placed on the role of distributed data processing architectures in facilitating effective integration of Artificial Intelligence (AI) with Big Data sources. This segment comprehensively discusses how distributed computing frameworks are instrumental in managing the scale and complexity of Big Data, thereby enabling efficient AI processing and analysis.

The Necessity of Distributed Data Processing in Big Data and AI

The advent of Big Data, characterized by its enormous volume, velocity, and variety, necessitates robust data processing architectures capable of handling vast datasets efficiently. Distributed data processing architectures are designed to address this need by dividing the data processing workload across multiple computing nodes, thereby enhancing performance and scalability (Zaharia et al., 2013).

Key Components of Distributed Data Processing Architectures

1. **Parallel Processing**: Fundamental to distributed architectures is the concept of parallel processing, where large datasets are partitioned and processed concurrently across multiple machines. This approach significantly reduces processing times and is essential for real-time analytics (Dean & Ghemawat, 2008).

2. **Scalability and Fault Tolerance**: Distributed architectures are designed to scale horizontally, meaning they can handle increased loads by adding more nodes to the network. They also incorporate fault tolerance, ensuring that the failure of a single node does not compromise the entire system (Thusoo et al., 2010).

3. **Resource Management and Optimization**: Efficient resource management is critical in distributed systems. Technologies like Apache Hadoop and Apache Spark come equipped with resource management capabilities, optimizing the distribution and utilization of computational resources across the network (Zaharia et al., 2010).

Integration of AI with Distributed Data Architectures

The integration of AI with distributed data architectures involves several strategies:

1. **Distributed Machine Learning Algorithms**: Developing and utilizing machine learning algorithms that are specifically designed for distributed environments. These algorithms can process data across different nodes, aggregating insights to form a cohesive analytical output (Chen et al., 2014).

2. **Data Streaming and Real-time Analysis**: Leveraging distributed architectures for streaming data allows for real-time data analysis. This is particularly important for AI applications requiring immediate insights, such as fraud detection and social media monitoring (Kreps et al., 2011).

3. **Big Data Analytics Frameworks**: Utilizing big data analytics frameworks like Apache Hadoop for batch processing and Apache Spark for in-memory processing, which are designed for distributed computing environments. These frameworks are capable of handling both structured and unstructured data, making them suitable for a variety of AI applications (Zaharia et al., 2010).

Challenges in Distributed Data Processing

While distributed data processing architectures offer significant advantages, they also present challenges such as data security and privacy concerns, the complexity of data synchronization across nodes, and the need for specialized skills to manage and operate these systems (Marz & Warren, 2015).

The exploration of distributed data processing architectures in "Data Titans" highlights their critical role in enabling the effective integration of AI with Big Data. By leveraging these architectures, organizations can harness the power of AI toanalyze vast and diverse data sets, unlocking new opportunities for insights and innovation. However, successfully implementing these systems requires careful consideration of their design, deployment, and ongoing management to ensure they meet the demands of Big Data and AI integration.

1. **Data Governance and Ethics**:

Implementing robust data governance frameworks to ensure data security, privacy, and ethical use of AI is imperative, especially given the sensitivity of certain types of data (Kitchin, 2014).

In the critical analysis presented in "Data Titans: Navigating the AI Revolution in Big Data," the book devotes significant attention to the strategic imperatives of data governance and ethics in the integration of Artificial Intelligence (AI) with Big Data. This exploration underscores the necessity of establishing robust governance frameworks and ethical guidelines to navigate the complex interplay between AI technologies and the vast reservoirs of Big Data.

Importance of Data Governance in AI and Big Data Integration

Data governance encompasses the policies, standards, and practices employed to ensure the effective management, quality, and security of data within an organization. In the context of AI and Big Data, effective data governance is crucial for several reasons:

1. **Ensuring Data Quality and Integrity**: High-quality and accurate data is foundational for the effectiveness of AI systems. Data governance policies help in maintaining the accuracy, completeness, and reliability of data, which is essential for AI models to make precise and unbiased predictions and decisions (Otto, 2011).

2. **Data Security and Privacy Compliance**: With the increasing volume and variety of data, especially personal and sensitive information, data governance plays a critical role in ensuring compliance with data protection regulations such as GDPR (General Data Protection Regulation). It helps in implementing appropriate data security measures to safeguard data against breaches and misuse (Langley, 2020).

3. **Standardization and Interoperability**: Effective data governance facilitates the standardization of data formats and promotes interoperability across different systems and platforms. This is particularly important in Big Data environments where data integration from multiple sources is a common occurrence (Khatri & Brown, 2010).

Ethical Considerations in AI and Big Data

The integration of AI with Big Data raises significant ethical considerations that must be addressed:

1. **Bias and Fairness**: AI systems can inadvertently perpetuate and amplify biases present in the training data. Ethical considerations involve ensuring that AI algorithms are fair and do not discriminate against any individual or group (Mittelstadt, Allo, Taddeo, Wachter, & Floridi, 2016).

2. **Transparency and Accountability**: There is a growing demand for transparency in AI decision-making processes. Ethical integration involves creating AI systems whose decisions can be

explained and understood by humans, ensuring accountability in their operations (Wachter, Mittelstadt, & Floridi, 2017).

3. **Responsible Use of AI**: Ethical guidelines are necessary to ensure that AI is used responsibly, particularly in sensitive areas such as surveillance, healthcare, and law enforcement. These guidelines should address issues like consent, individual rights, and societal impact (Jobin, Ienca, & Vayena, 2019).

Strategies for Implementing Data Governance and Ethics in AI and Big Data

Implementing robust data governance and adhering to ethical standards in AI and Big Data requires a multifaceted approach:

1. **Developing Comprehensive Data Policies**: Organizations should develop comprehensive data policies that cover aspects such as data collection, storage, access, and usage, along with compliance with legal and regulatory requirements.
2. **Establishing Ethical AI Frameworks**: Creating ethical frameworks and guidelines for AI development and deployment, which include principles of fairness, transparency, accountability, and respect for privacy.
3. **Continuous Monitoring and Auditing**: Regular monitoring and auditing of AI systems and data processes to ensure adherence to governance policies and ethical standards, and to address any issues proactively.

The discourse in "Data Titans" on data governance and ethics emphasizes their critical importance in the AI and Big Data domain. Effective integration of AI with Big Data sources necessitates a conscientious approach to governance and a commitment to upholding ethical standards, ensuring that AI technologies are used responsibly and for the greater good.

Conclusion

The exploration of Big Data sources and AI integration in "Data Titans" provides a comprehensive understanding of the opportunities and challenges inherent in harnessing AI for Big Data analytics. This examination is crucial for stakeholders in various sectors looking to leverage the synergy between AI and Big Data to drive innovation and gain competitive advantages.

Traditional and Emerging Sources of Big Data:

In the analytical tome "Data Titans: Navigating the AI Revolution in Big Data," there is a profound exploration of both traditional and emerging sources of Big Data and their integration with Artificial Intelligence (AI). This comprehensive section delineates how the landscape of Big Data sources has evolved and expanded, presenting both opportunities and challenges for AI integration.

Traditional Sources of Big Data

Traditional sources of Big Data have predominantly been structured data emanating from conventional databases and information systems. These include:

1. **Enterprise Resource Planning (ERP) Systems**: These systems generate vast amounts of data through business operations, encompassing financial transactions, supply chain activities, and customer relationship management (Davenport, 2013).

2. **Transactional Databases**: This includes data from sales transactions, billing systems, and customer interactions. These databases are critical for business operations and form a significant portion of traditional Big Data sources (Chaudhuri, Dayal, & Narasayya, 2011).

3. **Web Logs and Clickstreams**: Websites and online platforms generate large volumes of log data that track user interactions, such as page views, clicks, and search queries. This data is

instrumental in understanding user behavior and preferences (Kaushik, 2009).

Emerging Sources of Big Data

The advent of digital technology and the Internet of Things (IoT) has led to the emergence of new and diverse sources of Big Data:

1. **Social Media Platforms**: Platforms like Facebook, Twitter, and Instagram generate massive amounts of unstructured data in the form of text, images, and videos. This data is rich in user-generated content, offering valuable insights into public opinion and trends (Kaplan & Haenlein, 2010).

2. **Sensor Data and IoT Devices**: IoT devices and sensors, used in everything from smart homes to industrial equipment, produce large streams of real-time data. This includes data on environmental conditions, user interactions with devices, and machine performance (Gubbi et al., 2013).

3. **Biometric and Health Data**: With the proliferation of wearable technology and digital health records, there is a surge in biometric and health-related data. This includes data from fitness trackers, medical devices, and electronic health records, which are critical for healthcare and wellness applications (Swan, 2013).

Integrating AI with Diverse Big Data Sources

The integration of AI with these diverse data sources requires sophisticated techniques and algorithms:

1. **Data Preprocessing and Standardization**: Given the variety of data formats and structures, preprocessing and standardizing data for AI analysis is essential. This includes data cleansing, normalization, and transformation to ensure data compatibility and quality (García, Luengo, & Herrera, 2015).

2. **Advanced Machine Learning Techniques**: Machine learning models, particularly those capable of handling unstructured data like deep learning algorithms, are crucial for extracting insights from diverse Big Data sources. These models can identify patterns, predict trends, and perform classification tasks across various types of data (LeCun, Bengio, & Hinton, 2015).

3. **Real-Time Data Processing and Analytics**: Emerging Big Data sources, especially from IoT devices, often require real-time processing and analysis. Distributed computing frameworks and stream processing technologies are employed to handle this high-velocity data (Kreps et al., 2011).

The discussion in "Data Titans" on the traditional and emerging sources of Big Data provides a comprehensive view of the evolving Big Data landscape. It highlights how AI integration needs to adapt and evolve to leverage these diverse data sources effectively, transforming raw data into actionable insights and knowledge.

Integrating AI into Big Data Infrastructures:

In the seminal work "Data Titans: Navigating the AI Revolution in Big Data," a profound exploration is dedicated to the integration of Artificial Intelligence (AI) into Big Data infrastructures. This comprehensive analysis delves into the methodologies and technological advancements necessary for embedding AI capabilities within Big Data ecosystems, an integration that is pivotal for transforming massive datasets into actionable insights.

Strategies for AI Integration into Big Data Infrastructures

The seamless integration of AI into Big Data infrastructures involves a multifaceted approach, encompassing both technological and methodological aspects:

1. **Infrastructure Scalability and Elasticity**: AI integration requires Big Data infrastructures that are both scalable and elastic. Scalability ensures that the infrastructure can handle the increasing volumes of data, while elasticity allows it to adapt to varying workloads, especially important for AI applications that involve complex computations and real-time data processing (Marz & Warren, 2015).

2. **Distributed Computing Systems**: AI algorithms, particularly those involving machine learning and deep learning, often require substantial computational resources. Distributed computing systems like Apache Hadoop and Apache Spark provide the necessary framework for processing large-scale data across clusters of computers, making them integral to AI integration in Big Data (Zaharia et al., 2010).

3. **Data Lakes for Unstructured Data**: AI integration in Big Data also involves dealing with unstructured data, which constitutes a significant portion of Big Data. Data lakes, which allow the storage of data in its native format, are crucial for storing and processing unstructured data, providing AI models with the necessary diversity of data for effective learning and analysis (Dixon, 2010).

4. **Advanced Analytics and Machine Learning Platforms**: Integrating AI into Big Data infrastructures also involves the deployment of advanced analytics and machine learning platforms. These platforms provide tools and environments for data scientists and analysts to build, train, and deploy AI models effectively within Big Data ecosystems (Chen et al., 2014).

Challenges in AI and Big Data Integration

Integrating AI into Big Data infrastructures is not without its challenges:

1. **Data Privacy and Security**: The integration of AI in Big Data raises significant privacy and security concerns, especially when dealing with sensitive and personal data. Ensuring robust data security measures and adhering to data privacy regulations are essential (Langley, 2020).
2. **Data Quality and Management**: AI models are only as good as the data they are trained on. Ensuring high data quality and effective data management, including data cleansing and pre-processing, is crucial for the success of AI integration in Big Data (Saha & Srivastava, 2014).
3. **Interoperability and Standardization**: The integration of AI requires interoperability between various data sources and systems. Standardization of data formats and protocols is key to facilitating smooth integration and data exchange between AI models and Big Data infrastructures (Kambatla et al., 2014).

The discourse on integrating AI into Big Data infrastructures in "Data Titans" offers an in-depth understanding of the complexities and necessities of this integration. As the volume and variety of Big Data continue to grow, the strategic integration of AI is crucial for harnessing the potential of this data, driving innovations, and creating value across various sectors.

Case Studies: Successful AI and Big Data Integrations:

In "Data Titans: Navigating the AI Revolution in Big Data," several case studies are examined to illustrate the successful integration of Artificial Intelligence (AI) with Big Data sources. These case studies demonstrate how various industries have harnessed the synergy of AI and Big Data to drive innovation, efficiency, and decision-making.

1. **Healthcare: Predictive Analytics for Patient Care**

   One notable case study involves the use of AI and Big Data in healthcare, particularly in predictive analytics for patient care. A leading example is the application of machine learning models to electronic health records (EHRs) to predict patient outcomes and tailor treatment plans. For instance, Google's DeepMind Health project developed AI algorithms that analyze medical images to detect eye diseases in their early stages (De Fauw et al., 2018). This integration allows for early intervention, potentially saving sight and improving patient outcomes.

2. **Retail: Enhancing Customer Experience and Inventory Management**

   In the retail sector, AI integrated with Big Data has revolutionized customer experience and inventory management. A prime example is Amazon's use of AI in its recommendation systems, which analyze vast amounts of customer data to personalize shopping experiences. Furthermore, AI-driven predictive analytics are employed for efficient inventory management and forecasting demand, ensuring optimal stock levels and reducing wastage (Smith & Linden, 2017).

3. **Finance: Fraud Detection and Risk Management**

   The finance industry has also seen significant advancements through AI and Big Data integration. Financial institutions use AI algorithms to analyze transaction data in real time, enabling the early detection of fraudulent activities. For instance, Mastercard employs AI-driven systems to analyze transaction data across its network, identifying and preventing fraud (Bhattacharyya et al., 2011). Additionally, AI models are utilized for risk management, analyzing market data to predict trends and inform investment strategies.

4. **Transportation: Optimizing Traffic Flow and Public Transport**

   In transportation, AI and Big Data have been used to optimize traffic flow and improve public transport systems. For example, the city of Stockholm implemented an AI-based traffic management system that analyzes traffic data in real time, reducing congestion and improving overall traffic flow (Ekman et al., 2018). Additionally, public transport systems utilize AI to optimize routes and schedules based on passenger data, enhancing efficiency and rider experience.

5. **Environmental Monitoring: Climate Change and Conservation Efforts**

AI and Big Data play a crucial role in environmental monitoring and conservation. NASA uses AI algorithms to analyze satellite data for climate change research, tracking changes in Earth's environment over time (Lary et al., 2016). In conservation, AI-driven image recognition is used to analyze camera trap images for wildlife monitoring, aiding in biodiversity conservation efforts.

Chapter 4: Ethical Considerations and Data Privacy

In the scholarly landscape delineated by "Data Titans: Navigating the AI Revolution in Big Data," ethical considerations and data privacy emerge as critical areas of discourse, particularly in the context of Artificial Intelligence (AI) and Big Data. The intersection of AI and Big Data raises complex ethical questions and significant privacy concerns, necessitating a rigorous and thoughtful approach to these issues.

1. Ethical Considerations in AI and Big Data

The integration of AI with Big Data brings to the forefront several ethical considerations:

Bias and Fairness:

AI systems, if not properly designed and monitored, can perpetuate and even amplify biases present in the training data. This raises ethical concerns about fairness and equality, especially in applications related to social justice, law enforcement, and hiring practices (Barocas & Selbst, 2016).

The burgeoning utilization of Artificial Intelligence (AI) and Big Data in contemporary society necessitates a meticulous examination of ethical considerations, particularly concerning bias and fairness. AI systems, fuelled by vast datasets, have the potential to inadvertently perpetuate and amplify existing societal biases, thus raising profound ethical concerns (Zou & Schiebinger, 2018). This issue is further compounded in the context of data privacy, where the integrity and representativeness of data are paramount.

Bias in AI and Big Data can manifest in multifarious forms, fundamentally stemming from the data upon which these systems are trained. The concept of 'algorithmic bias' arises when AI systems generate outputs that systematically and unfairly discriminate against certain individuals or groups (Barocas, Hardt, & Narayanan, 2019). This phenomenon is not merely a technical anomaly but a reflection of deeper societal disparities. For example, facial recognition technologies have been criticized for their lower accuracy rates in identifying individuals from certain racial and ethnic groups (Buolamwini & Gebru, 2018), thus raising significant ethical concerns regarding fairness and equality.

Fairness in AI, however, is not a monolithic concept but a multifaceted one, encompassing various dimensions such as procedural fairness, distributive fairness, and interactional fairness (Mehrabi et al., 2019). Procedural fairness pertains to the transparency and accountability of the algorithms, while distributive fairness relates to the equitable distribution of benefits and risks of AI technologies. Interactional fairness, on the other hand, addresses the respect and dignity afforded to individuals in the decision-making processes of AI.

Data privacy intersects with these concerns, as the quality and nature of data used in AI systems directly impact the fairness of their outcomes. Inaccurate, incomplete, or biased data can lead to unfair or discriminatory results, thus violating ethical principles of justice and equality (Taylor, Floridi, & van der Sloot, 2017). Furthermore, the collection and use of personal data in AI systems raise critical questions about consent, autonomy, and the right to privacy. The General Data Protection Regulation (GDPR) in the European Union, for instance, provides a legal framework addressing these concerns, emphasizing the importance of informed consent and the rights of individuals to control their personal data (Voigt & von dem Bussche, 2017).

In conclusion, ensuring fairness and mitigating bias in AI and Big Data are not merely technical challenges but fundamentally ethical imperatives. This requires a holistic approach, encompassing not only algorithmic modifications but also broader societal and policy interventions. Continuous dialogue among technologists, ethicists, policymakers, and the public is essential to navigate these complex ethical terrains and foster AI technologies that are both innovative and ethically responsible.

Transparency and Explainability:

AI systems, particularly those employing complex algorithms like deep learning, are often seen as opaque 'black boxes.' Ethical AI requires transparency and explainability, ensuring that stakeholders understand how decisions are made and can trust the outcomes of AI systems (Burrell, 2016).

In the critical discourse on AI and Big Data ethics, a paramount focus is accorded to the twin pillars of transparency and explainability. These concepts are increasingly recognized as essential in the ethical deployment of AI technologies, especially when interfaced with the complex and often opaque realms of Big Data.

Transparency in AI and Big Data

Transparency in the context of AI and Big Data refers to the clarity and openness with which data is collected, processed, and utilized in AI systems. This involves clear communication about how data is used, what algorithms are deployed, and the decision-making processes of AI models.

1. **Building Trust with Transparency**: Transparent practices in AI and Big Data are crucial for building trust among users and stakeholders. In environments where AI decisions significantly impact individuals or groups, understanding the mechanics of these decisions is imperative (Diakopoulos, 2016).

2. **Regulatory Compliance**: Transparency is not just an ethical imperative but also a regulatory requirement in many jurisdictions. For instance, the European Union's General Data Protection Regulation (GDPR) mandates certain levels of transparency in data processing activities (Goodman & Flaxman, 2017).

Explainability in AI and Big Data

Explainability pertains to the ability of AI systems to articulate and justify their decisions in a manner that is understandable to humans. It is particularly vital in contexts where decisions have significant consequences, such as in healthcare, finance, or legal domains.

1. **The Challenge of Complex Models**: Advanced AI models, particularly those based on deep learning, can be highly effective yet inherently complex and opaque. This complexity poses a significant challenge to explainability, as it can be difficult to discern how these models process inputs to arrive at specific outputs (Castelvecchi, 2016).
2. **Balancing Accuracy and Interpretability**: In many cases, there is a trade-off between the accuracy of an AI model and its interpretability. More complex models may offer higher accuracy but less interpretability, which is a challenge when explainability is required (Lipton, 2018).
1. **Tools and Techniques for Enhancing Explainability**: Various methods are being developed to enhance the explainability of AI systems. Techniques like Local Interpretable Model-Agnostic Explanations (LIME) and SHapley Additive exPlanations (SHAP) aim to provide insights into the decision-making processes of complex AI models (Ribeiro et al., 2016).

Ethical and Practical Implications

The ethical and practical implications of transparency and explainability in AI and Big Data are profound:

1. **Ethical Decision-Making**: Transparency and explainability are foundational for ethical decision-making in AI. They enable scrutiny of AI decisions, helping to ensure they are fair, non-discriminatory, and justifiable (Doshi-Velez & Kim, 2017).
2. **Empowering Users and Stakeholders**: By making AI systems more transparent and explainable, users and stakeholders are better equipped to understand, trust, and effectively interact with these systems. This empowerment is crucial for the responsible adoption and use of AI technologies (Wachter, Mittelstadt, & Floridi, 2017).
3. **Facilitating Governance and Oversight**: Enhanced transparency and explainability aid in governance and oversight, allowing regulators, auditors, and other oversight bodies to assess compliance with legal and ethical standards. This is essential for maintaining public trust and ensuring responsible AI deployment (Jobin, Ienca, & Vayena, 2019).

In the landscape of AI and Big Data, as expounded in "Data Titans," transparency and explainability emerge as critical ethical considerations. Their importance lies not only in fostering trust and understanding but also in ensuring the accountability and ethical integrity of AI systems. As AI continues to evolve and permeate various sectors, these considerations will remain central to the discourse on responsible AI development and deployment.

Accountability:

With AI systems making decisions or assisting in decision-making, questions arise about accountability. It is crucial to establish clear guidelines on who is responsible for the decisions made by AI systems, particularly in critical areas like healthcare and finance (Doshi-Velez et al., 2017).

A crucial exploration is dedicated to the theme of accountability in the realm of Artificial Intelligence (AI) and Big Data. This detailed discourse underscores the imperative of establishing clear lines of accountability in AI systems, especially given the complex and often opaque nature of Big Data analytics.

The Significance of Accountability in AI and Big Data

Accountability in AI and Big Data refers to the attribution of responsibility for the decisions and outcomes produced by AI systems. This concept is increasingly vital in scenarios where AI-driven decisions have significant impacts, such as in healthcare, finance, and criminal justice.

1. **Ensuring Responsible AI Practices**: Accountability is key to ensuring that AI practices are responsible and ethical. When AI systems make decisions or take actions that affect individuals or communities, it's crucial to have mechanisms in place that can identify and address any issues or harms that arise (Kroll et al., 2017).

2. **Building Trust in AI Systems**: Transparent accountability structures are essential for building public trust in AI technologies. When users understand who is accountable for AI decisions, they are more likely to trust and accept these technologies (Turilli & Floridi, 2009).

Challenges in Establishing Accountability in AI

Establishing accountability in AI, particularly in the context of Big Data, involves navigating several challenges:

1. **Complexity of AI Systems**: The intricate and often 'black box' nature of certain AI algorithms, especially deep learning models, makes it difficult to pinpoint how specific decisions are made. This complexity poses a challenge in attributing responsibility for those decisions (Burrell, 2016).

2. **Distributed Nature of AI Development**: AI systems are typically the result of contributions from multiple entities, including developers, data scientists, and end-users. This distributed nature

can dilute accountability, making it challenging to identify who is responsible for specific outcomes (Hagendorff, 2020).

3. **Legal and Regulatory Ambiguities**: The current legal and regulatory frameworks may not adequately address the novel scenarios presented by AI and Big Data. This ambiguity can create gaps in accountability, particularly when AI-driven decisions have unforeseen negative consequences (Pagallo, 2018).

Strategies for Enhancing Accountability in AI and Big Data

To address these challenges, several strategies can be employed:

1. **Developing Clear Governance Frameworks**: Establishing robust governance frameworks that delineate roles and responsibilities is essential. These frameworks should define who is accountable at each stage of AI system development and deployment (Martin, 2019).
2. **Implementing Audit Trails and Decision Logs**: Maintaining comprehensive audit trails and decision logs can help in tracing the decision-making process of AI systems. This transparency aids in establishing accountability by providing a record of how and why decisions were made (Ananny & Crawford, 2018).
3. **AI Ethics Boards and Review Processes**: Instituting ethics boards and review processes for AI projects can provide oversight and ensure that ethical and accountability standards are met. These boards can assess AI systems for potential risks and ethical implications (Mittelstadt, 2019).

Accountability in AI and Big Data, as elucidated in "Data Titans," is a cornerstone of ethical AI practice. As AI systems become increasingly integrated into various aspects of society, ensuring accountability is not only a matter of ethical responsibility but also of sustaining public trust and mitigating potential harms. Effective accountability mechanisms are crucial for the responsible development and deployment of AI technologies, ensuring that they serve the public good while respecting individual rights and societal values.

II. Data Privacy Concerns

Data privacy is a paramount concern in the era of Big Data and AI:

Consent and Data Usage:

Issues of consent for data collection and usage are central to data privacy. Users must be informed about how their data is being used, and consent should be obtained, especially for sensitive personal data (Taylor, Floridi, & van der Sloot, 2017).

A significant focus is placed on data privacy concerns, specifically regarding issues of consent and data usage in the context of Artificial Intelligence (AI) and Big Data. This segment delves into the ethical intricacies and challenges associated with obtaining consent for data collection and usage, highlighting the paramount importance of these considerations in maintaining user privacy and trust.

Consent in Data Collection and Usage

1. **Informed Consent:** At the core of data privacy is the principle of informed consent, which requires that individuals are fully aware of and agree to how their data will be used before it is collected. This is especially pertinent in AI and Big Data, where data is often used in complex and sometimes non-transparent ways. Informed consent involves clearly communicating the purpose of data collection, how the data will be processed, and the potential risks and benefits (Mayer-Schönberger & Cukier, 2013).

2. **Challenges with Obtaining Informed Consent:** In the era of Big Data, obtaining genuine informed consent is increasingly challenging. The complexity of AI algorithms and the vast scope of data usage often make it difficult for individuals to fully comprehend what they are consenting to. Moreover, the ubiquity of data collection practices, often embedded in the terms of service agreements that users habitually accept without thorough examination, complicates the issue (Nissenbaum, 2011).

Data Usage: Ethical Considerations and Obligations

1. **Responsible Data Usage**: Ethical data usage goes beyond legal compliance, involving the responsible handling of personal data. This includes using data in ways that are consistent with the context in which it was collected and respecting the intentions and expectations of the individuals to whom the data pertains. It also involves minimizing data collection to what is necessary and avoiding misuse or unauthorized access (Martin, 2016).

2. **Transparency in Data Usage**: Transparency is vital in data usage. Organizations should clearly disclose their data processing practices, including what data is being collected, how it is being used, and with whom it is being shared. This transparency is essential not only for ethical reasons but also for building and maintaining public trust (Tene & Polonetsky, 2012).

1. **Safeguarding Against Data Misuse**: With the increasing capabilities of AI to analyze and infer from large datasets, there is a risk of data being used in ways that can infringe on individual privacy or lead to discriminatory outcomes. Implementing robust data governance frameworks and ethical guidelines is crucial to safeguard against such misuse (Barocas & Selbst, 2016).

The discussion on consent and data usage in "Data Titans" elucidates the complex ethical landscape surrounding data privacy in the context of AI and Big Data. Addressing these concerns requires a concerted effort to establish clear, understandable consent mechanisms and responsible data usage practices. Upholding these ethical standards is critical for ensuring the protection of individual privacy rights and for fostering an environment of trust in the digital age.

Data Protection and Security:

Protecting personal and sensitive data against unauthorized access and breaches is crucial. This involves implementing robust data security measures and adhering to regulatory requirements like GDPR (General Data Protection Regulation) (Malgieri & Custers, 2018).

In the realm of AI and Big Data, data protection and security emerge as critical components under the umbrella of ethical considerations and data privacy. The integration of Artificial Intelligence (AI) with vast troves of data accentuates the need for stringent data protection and robust security measures. This section delves into the intricate dynamics of data protection and security in the context of AI and Big Data, highlighting the ethical imperatives and challenges associated with safeguarding sensitive information.

The Imperative of Data Protection in AI and Big Data

Data protection in AI and Big Data involves implementing measures to ensure the confidentiality, integrity, and availability of data. It is pivotal for several reasons:

1. **Safeguarding Sensitive Information**: With AI systems frequently processing personal and sensitive data, robust data protection mechanisms are essential to prevent unauthorized access and misuse of such information (Romanosky, 2016).
2. **Maintaining User Trust**: User trust in AI systems is contingent on the assurance that their data is protected. Breaches in data security can lead to a loss of trust and reluctance to use AI-driven services (Martin, 2019).
3. **Regulatory Compliance**: Adherence to data protection laws, such as the General Data Protection Regulation (GDPR) in the European Union, is a legal requirement. These regulations mandate stringent data security practices and impose penalties for non-compliance (Voigt & Von dem Bussche, 2017).

Challenges in Ensuring Data Protection and Security

Ensuring data protection and security in AI and Big Data is fraught with challenges:

1. **Complexity of AI Systems**: The complexity of AI algorithms and the vastness of Big Data can make it challenging to implement traditional data security measures. AI systems often require access to large datasets, increasing the potential attack surface for data breaches (Russell, Dewey, & Tegmark, 2015).

2. **Dynamic Nature of Threats**: The landscape of cybersecurity threats is constantly evolving, with new vulnerabilities emerging regularly. Keeping pace with these threats and adapting security measures accordingly is a significant challenge (Taddeo & Floridi, 2018).

3. **Balancing Data Utility and Security**: There is often a tension between maximizing the utility of data for AI applications and ensuring its security. Overly stringent security measures can impede the ability of AI systems to access and learn from data effectively (Borgman, 2012).

Strategies for Enhancing Data Protection and Security

To address these challenges, several strategies can be employed:

1. **Advanced Encryption Techniques**: Implementing state-of-the-art encryption technologies can secure data both at rest and in transit. This includes techniques like homomorphic encryption, which allows data to be processed in its encrypted form (Gentry, 2009).

2. **Regular Security Audits and Compliance Checks**: Conducting regular security audits and ensuring compliance with data protection regulations is crucial. This includes assessing the security of AI systems, data storage infrastructures, and data processing protocols (Kesan, Hayes, & Bashir, 2013).

3. **Developing Robust Access Control Mechanisms**: Establishing stringent access controls ensures that only authorized personnel and systems have access to sensitive data. This includes the use of multi-factor authentication, role-based access control,

and continuous monitoring of access patterns (Sandhu, Coyne, Feinstein, & Youman, 1996).

4. **Incorporating Privacy by Design Principles**: Integrating privacy by design principles in the development of AI systems ensures that data protection is considered at every stage of the system's lifecycle, from design to deployment and beyond (Cavoukian, 2009).

In the landscape of AI and Big Data, as highlighted in "Data Titans," data protection and security are not mere regulatory checkboxes but fundamental ethical imperatives. Effective strategies to safeguard data are integral to the responsible development and deployment of AI technologies, underpinning the trust and reliability essential for their societal acceptance and success.

Data Anonymization:

Anonymizing data to protect individual privacy is often necessary, especially in fields like healthcare. However, the challenge lies in effectively anonymizing data without losing its utility for analysis and insights (Rocher, Hendrickx, & de Montjoye, 2019).

In the comprehensive discourse on AI and Big Data ethics, significant attention is devoted to the subject of data anonymization. This section elucidates the ethical nuances and challenges surrounding data anonymization, a process crucial for safeguarding privacy in the vast landscapes of Big Data and AI.

The Role and Importance of Data Anonymization

Data anonymization involves altering personal data in such a way that the individual subjects cannot be identified, either directly or indirectly, by removing or encrypting personally identifiable information. In the context of Big Data and AI, where vast amounts of personal data are processed, anonymization serves several critical purposes:

1. **Protecting Individual Privacy**: Anonymization is a key tool for protecting individual privacy, a fundamental ethical concern

in data handling. It allows for the utilization of valuable data for analysis and AI model training while safeguarding individual identity (Narayanan & Shmatikov, 2010).

2. **Regulatory Compliance**: Data anonymization is often a requirement under privacy laws such as the General Data Protection Regulation (GDPR) in the EU, which mandates the protection of personal data. Anonymization helps in compliance with such regulations, thus avoiding legal repercussions (Voigt & Von dem Bussche, 2017).

Challenges in Data Anonymization

Despite its importance, data anonymization is fraught with challenges, particularly in the age of AI and Big Data:

1. **Balance Between Utility and Privacy**: Striking a balancebetween maintaining the utility of data for analysis and ensuring privacy through anonymization is complex. Overly aggressive anonymization can strip data of its usefulness, while inadequate anonymization can leave individuals vulnerable to re-identification (Sweeney, 2002).

2. **Risk of Re-identification**: With advances in AI and data analytics, the risk of re-identification, even from anonymized datasets, has increased. Techniques like data linkage and pattern recognition can potentially re-identify individuals by correlating anonymized data with other available datasets (de Montjoye et al., 2015).

1. **Evolving Techniques and Standards**: The field of data anonymization is continuously evolving, with new techniques and challenges emerging regularly. Keeping abreast of these developments and implementing state-of-the-art anonymization methods is essential but challenging (Machanavajjhala et al., 2007).

Strategies for Effective Data Anonymization

To address these challenges, several strategies and best practices can be adopted:

1. **Implementing Robust Anonymization Techniques**: Utilizing advanced anonymization techniques such as differential privacy, which adds 'noise' to data to prevent identification of individuals, can provide robust privacy guarantees while retaining data utility (Dwork, 2008).

2. **Regular Assessment and Testing for Re-identification Risks**: Regularly assessing anonymized datasets for vulnerabilities to re-identification attacks is crucial. This can involve testing datasets against known re-identification techniques and updating anonymization methods as necessary (El Emam & Dankar, 2008).

3. **Maintaining Transparency and Ethical Standards**: Transparency in how data is anonymized and used, coupled with adherence to ethical standards, is essential. Organizations should be clear about their data anonymization practices and ensure that they align with ethical guidelines and privacy laws (Cavoukian, 2009).

4. **Continuous Monitoring and Updating of Anonymization Protocols**: Given the dynamic nature of technology and threats, it is crucial to continuously monitor and update anonymization protocols. This includes staying informed about the latest research, technological advancements, and emerging threats in data privacy (Rubinstein & Hartzog, 2016).

Data anonymization in the context of AI and Big Data, as articulated in "Data Titans," plays a critical role in navigating the ethical landscape of data privacy. It requires a nuanced approach that balances the privacy of individuals with the utility of data. Effective anonymization strategies, grounded in robust techniques and continuous assessment, are paramount in ensuring ethical compliance and maintaining the trust of individuals whose data is being utilized.

III. Balancing Innovation with Ethical and Privacy Concerns

Balancing the potential for innovation that AI and Big Data offer, with ethical and privacy concerns, is a delicate task:

Developing Ethical Guidelines:

Establishing ethical guidelines for AI and Big Data practices is essential. This includes guidelines on data collection, analysis, and usage, ensuring ethical standards are maintained (Jobin, Ienca, & Vayena, 2019).

A pivotal aspect explored is the balance between innovation and the ethical and privacy concerns inherent in AI and Big Data. This balance is crucial, as it directly influences the sustainable and responsible development of technology. An integral component in maintaining this equilibrium is the development of ethical guidelines that govern the use of AI and Big Data.

The Role of Ethical Guidelines in AI and Big Data

Ethical guidelines serve as a framework to guide the development and deployment of AI and Big Data technologies. They are instrumental in:

1. **Ensuring Responsible Use of Technology**: Ethical guidelines help in delineating the boundaries of responsible technology use, ensuring that AI and Big Data applications do not infringe on individual rights or lead to societal harm (Jobin, Ienca, & Vayena, 2019).

2. **Building Trust and Credibility**: Clear ethical standards contribute to building trust among users and stakeholders. They demonstrate a commitment to upholding high ethical standards, which is essential for the credibility and acceptance of AI and Big Data technologies (Hagendorff, 2020).

3. **Navigating Complex Ethical Landscapes**: AI and Big Data often involve complex ethical considerations, such as data privacy,

consent, and bias. Ethical guidelines provide a roadmap for navigating these intricate issues (Mittelstadt et al., 2016).

Challenges in Developing Ethical Guidelines

Creating effective ethical guidelines for AI and Big Data is not without challenges:

1. **Diverse Stakeholder Interests**: Balancing the interests of various stakeholders, including technologists, businesses, policymakers, and the public, can be challenging. Different stakeholders may have conflicting priorities and perspectives on what constitutes ethical use (Whittlestone et al., 2019).
2. **Evolving Technological Landscape**: The rapid pace of technological advancement in AI and Big Data means that ethical guidelines need to be adaptable and responsive to new developments and unforeseen challenges (Floridi & Cowls, 2019).
1. **Global and Cultural Considerations**: Ethical norms and privacy concerns can vary significantly across different cultural and geographical contexts. Developing guidelines that are globally applicable and sensitive to these differences is a complex task (Taddeo & Floridi, 2018).

Strategies for Developing Effective Ethical Guidelines

To address these challenges, several strategies can be employed in the development of ethical guidelines:

1. **Inclusive and Collaborative Approach**: Involving a diverse range of stakeholders in the development process ensures that multiple perspectives are considered. This collaborative approach can lead to more comprehensive and widely accepted guidelines (Fjeld et al., 2020).
2. **Principles-Based Frameworks**: Adopting a principles-based approach to ethical guidelines, focusing on broad ethical

principles such as fairness, transparency, and accountability, can provide flexibility and adaptability in their application (Floridi et al., 2018).

3. **Regular Review and Adaptation**: Ethical guidelines should be viewed as dynamic documents that require regular review and adaptation in response to new developments in technology and evolving societal values (Cath et al., 2018).

4. **Global Consensus and Localization**: While striving for global consensus on core ethical principles, it is also important to allow for localization of guidelines to address regional and cultural specificities (Zeng et al., 2018).

In the context of "Data Titans," the development of ethical guidelines is highlighted as a critical step in balancing innovation with ethical and privacy concerns in AI and Big Data. These guidelines are not just theoretical constructs but practical tools that shape the trajectory of technological development, ensuring that it aligns with societal values and ethical norms.

Privacy by Design:

Integrating privacy into the design of AI systems and Big Data processes, known as Privacy by Design, is crucial. This approach ensures that privacy considerations are embedded at every stage of the development process (Cavoukian, 2012).

In the contemporary context, a critical aspect of balancing innovation with ethical and privacy concerns is the concept of 'Privacy by Design'. This approach emphasizes the integration of privacy and data protection principles from the inception of technological development, rather than as an afterthought.

Privacy by Design in AI and Big Data

Privacy by Design (PbD) is a framework that advocates for privacy to be a key consideration throughout the entire engineering process. It involves proactive rather than reactive measures, and it views privacy as an essential component of the core functionality being delivered, not an add-on feature (Cavoukian, 2009).

Key Principles of Privacy by Design

1. **Proactive not Reactive; Preventative not Remedial**: The PbD principle asserts that the goal is to anticipate and prevent privacy-invasive events before they happen, rather than waiting for privacy risks to materialize (Cavoukian, 2009).

2. **Privacy as the Default Setting**: This principle ensures that personal data is automatically protected in any IT system or business practice. No action is required on the part of the individual to protect their privacy — it is built into the system, by default (Cavoukian, 2012).

3. **Privacy Embedded into Design**: Privacy is integrated into the design and architecture of IT systems and business practices. It is not a bolt-on, but an essential component of the core functionality (Hoepman, 2014).

4. **Full Functionality – Positive-Sum, not Zero-Sum**: PbD seeks to accommodate all legitimate interests and objectives in a win-win manner, not through trade-offs. It avoids the false dichotomies, such as privacy vs. security, demonstrating that it is possible to have both (Cavoukian & Jonas, 2012).

5. **End-to-End Security – Full Lifecycle Protection**: This principle emphasizes the need for secure data management from start to finish. It involves robust methods of data collection, retention, use, and deletion, ensuring secure and responsible lifecycle management of information (Cavoukian, 2009).

1. **Visibility and Transparency – Keep it Open**: PbD encourages openness and transparency in the practices and technologies used. Stakeholders should be informed about the business practices and technologies that affect their data, along with the measures in place to protect their privacy (Cavoukian, 2011).

2. **Respect for User Privacy – Keep it User-Centric**: This principle involves empowering individuals with privacy options and controls. User-centric approaches ensure that individuals have a voice in how their personal information is used (Cavoukian, 2010).

Challenges in Implementing Privacy by Design

Despite its comprehensive approach, implementing Privacy by Design in AI and Big Data faces several challenges:

1. **Complexity in AI Algorithms**: The complexity and often opaque nature of AI algorithms can make it difficult to incorporate privacy considerations from the outset.
2. **Evolving Nature of Technology and Data Use**: Rapid technological advancements and evolving ways of using data can make it challenging to anticipate future privacy risks and incorporate protective measures from the design phase.
3. **Balancing Innovation and Privacy**: Finding a balance between innovation in AI and Big Data and the stringent application of privacy principles can be challenging, as overly restrictive privacy measures may hinder technological advancement.

Incorporating Privacy by Design in AI and Big Data, as explored in "Data Titans," represents a proactive approach to privacy, ensuring that ethical considerations and data privacy are ingrained in technological innovations from the ground up. While challenges exist, Privacy by Design remains a pivotal methodology for harmonizing the rapid pace of technological advancement with the imperative to safeguard individual privacy rights and ethical standards.

Continuous Monitoring and Review:

Ethical and privacy considerations are not one-time efforts but require ongoing monitoring and review. As AI and Big Data technologies evolve, so too should the frameworks and policies governing their use, ensuring they remain relevant and effective (Mittelstadt, 2016).

IV. Regulatory Compliance and Governance

Ensuring compliance with international and national data protection laws, such as GDPR in Europe and various privacy laws in other regions, is essential for ethical AI and Big Data use. This involves understanding and adhering to legal requirements, which can vary significantly across jurisdictions (Kuner et al., 2017).

In the scholarly examination, significant attention is directed towards the crucial aspects of regulatory compliance and governance in the realm of ethical considerations and data privacy. This analytical discourse underscores the importance of adhering to regulatory standards and establishing effective governance mechanisms in managing AI and Big Data, highlighting the evolving landscape of legal and ethical norms in technology.

The Role of Regulatory Compliance in AI and Big Data

Regulatory compliance involves adhering to laws and regulations established by governing bodies. In the context of AI and Big Data, these regulations are designed to protect data privacy, ensure security, and promote ethical AI practices.

1. **Data Protection Regulations**: The General Data Protection Regulation (GDPR) in the European Union is a prime example of a regulatory framework that sets stringent rules for data protection and privacy. GDPR imposes obligations on data handling, consent mechanisms, and data subject rights, significantly impacting how AI and Big Data are utilized (Voigt & Von dem Bussche, 2017).

2. **AI-Specific Regulations**: As AI technology advances, several jurisdictions are contemplating or have implemented regulations specific to AI. These regulations aim to address issues like algorithmic transparency, bias, and accountability (Taddeo & Floridi, 2018).

Challenges in Regulatory Compliance and Governance

Compliance with regulations in the rapidly evolving field of AI and Big Data presents several challenges:

1. **Keeping Pace with Technological Advancements**: The fast-paced nature of technological innovation often outstrips the development of regulatory frameworks, leading to a lag in appropriate legal governance (Koops, 2016).

2. **Global Divergence in Regulations**: There is a lack of uniformity in AI and data privacy regulations across different countries, posing challenges for multinational operations and compliance strategies (Russell, Dewey, & Tegmark, 2015).

3. **Interpreting Ambiguous Legal Norms**: Many regulations, particularly those pertaining to AI, may be open to interpretation, requiring organizations to navigate ambiguities and make judgment calls on compliance matters (Bathaee, 2018).

Strategies for Effective Compliance and Governance

To navigate these challenges, the following strategies are recommended:

1. **Implementing Robust Data Governance Frameworks**: Establishing comprehensive data governance frameworks that include policies, procedures, and standards for data management is essential. These frameworks should align with regulatory requirements and ethical considerations (Weber, 2017).

2. **Regular Compliance Audits and Risk Assessments**: Conducting regular audits and assessments can help organizations stay compliant with existing regulations and adapt to new ones. This involves evaluating AI systems and data practices against regulatory standards and identifying areas of risk (Bostrom & Yudkowsky, 2014).

1. **Cross-Functional Compliance Teams**: Creating cross-functional teams involving legal, data privacy, cybersecurity, and AI ethics experts can facilitate a holistic approach to compliance. These teams can work collaboratively to ensure that all aspects of AI and data usage adhere to regulatory and ethical standards (Martin, 2019).

2. **Continuous Training and Awareness**: Investing in continuous training and awareness programs for employees about data privacy and AI ethics is vital. This helps create a culture of compliance and ethical consciousness within the organization (Cath et al., 2018).

3. **Engagement with Regulatory Bodies and Policy Makers**: Proactively engaging with regulatory bodies and contributing to policy discussions can help organizations stay ahead of regulatory changes and influence the development of pragmatic and effective AI governance models (Floridi et al., 2018).

Regulatory compliance and governance in the context of AI and Big Data, as analyzed in "Data Titans," are foundational to the ethical and responsible use of these technologies. Effective compliance strategies, underpinned by robust governance frameworks, are essential for navigating the complex legal landscape, safeguarding data privacy, and ensuring that AI systems operate within the bounds of ethical and legal norms.

Conclusion

In the narrative of "Data Titans," the exploration of ethical considerations and data privacy in the realm of AI and Big Data underscores their critical importance. It emphasizes that for AI and Big Data to reach their full potential, they must be harnessed in a manner that respects individual rights, promotes fairness and transparency, and safeguards privacy. This ethical and responsible approach is not just a legal imperative but a foundational pillar for building trust and acceptance in AI and Big Data technologies.

Navigating the Ethical Landscape of AI in Big Data:

Navigating the ethical landscape of artificial intelligence (AI) in the realm of big data necessitates a multifaceted approach, intertwining legal, ethical, and technological considerations. The burgeoning proliferation of AI systems utilizing extensive datasets has engendered pressing concerns regarding data privacy and ethical use of information. Paramount among these concerns is the imperative to uphold individual privacy rights while leveraging the potential of big data to foster technological advancement.

The confluence of AI and big data presents a paradoxical scenario. On one hand, the aggregation and analysis of large datasets can lead to unprecedented insights and innovations, significantly benefiting society (Mittelstadt, 2016). On the other hand, this same process raises profound privacy concerns, often involving sensitive personal information, thus necessitating stringent data protection measures (Taylor, Floridi, & van der Sloot, 2017).

A primary ethical consideration is the concept of informed consent. In traditional data collection paradigms, informed consent is a cornerstone of ethical practice, ensuring that individuals are aware of how their data is being used (Martin, 2019). However, in the context of AI and big data, obtaining explicit consent becomes challenging, as data is often repurposed for uses unforeseen at the time of collection (Zarsky, 2016).

Another critical aspect is the avoidance of algorithmic bias. AI systems, despite their computational prowess, are susceptible to biases present in their training data, which can lead to discriminatory outcomes (Barocas, Hardt, & Narayanan, 2019). Ensuring fairness and avoiding unintended harm are ethical imperatives in the deployment of AI systems.

Furthermore, the concept of data minimization, which advocates for collecting only the data that is strictly necessary, becomes crucial in this context (Koops, 2014). This principle not only helps in mitigating privacy risks but also aligns with ethical standards of responsible data management.

In conclusion, the intersection of AI and big data requires a harmonious balance between the pursuit of technological advancement and the upholding of ethical and privacy standards. As these technologies continue to evolve, so too must our approaches to ethical considerations and data privacy, ensuring that the benefits of AI and big data are harnessed responsibly and equitably.

Data Privacy Laws and AI Compliance:

The integration of Artificial Intelligence (AI) into big data analytics has necessitated a reevaluation of data privacy laws and their applicability in ensuring AI compliance. This complex interplay between evolving technologies and legal frameworks presents a critical juncture for both policymakers and technologists. The advent of AI in big data underscores the urgency for comprehensive laws that both facilitate technological innovation and protect individual privacy rights.

Contemporary discourse in data privacy laws emphasizes the imperative to address the unique challenges posed by AI. For instance, the General Data Protection Regulation (GDPR) in the European Union represents a paradigm shift in data privacy, introducing principles such as data protection by design and by default, and the right to explanation, specifically in the context of automated decision-making (European Parliament and Council, 2016). These principles are instrumental in establishing a legal framework that addresses the complexities introduced by AI technologies.

Moreover, compliance with data privacy laws in the AI context demands a meticulous approach to data handling practices. AI systems often require extensive datasets for training and operation, which may include sensitive personal information. Therefore, adherence to principles such as data minimization and purpose limitation, as stipulated in the GDPR, becomes crucial (Kamarinou, Millard, & Singh, 2016). These principles ensure that data collection and processing are conducted in a manner that respects individual privacy and aligns with legal standards.

Furthermore, AI's inherent capabilities, such as pattern recognition and predictive analytics, pose unique challenges to privacy. The ability of AI systems to infer personal information from seemingly unrelated data points raises concerns regarding consent and the scope of data usage (Barocas & Selbst, 2016). This necessitates a dynamic interpretation of consent, where individuals are adequately informed about the potential uses of their data in an AI-driven context.

In addition, there is an increasing recognition of the need for transparency and accountability in AI systems. The opacity of certain AI algorithms, particularly in deep learning, presents challenges in demonstrating compliance with data privacy laws (Burrell, 2016). As such, developing mechanisms for explainability and interpretability in AI systems is a focal point in aligning AI with privacy regulations.

In conclusion, the intersection of AI and data privacy laws is a dynamic and evolving domain, requiring ongoing dialogue and adaptation between technological advancements and legal frameworks. Ensuring AI compliance with data privacy laws involves a multi-faceted approach, encompassing legal compliance, ethical data handling practices, and transparency in AI operations. As AI continues to permeate various sectors, the imperative for robust and responsive privacy laws becomes increasingly paramount.

Building Trust and Transparency:

In the contemporary landscape of Artificial Intelligence (AI) and big data, building trust and transparency is paramount, not only as a regulatory compliance measure but also as an ethical obligation. This necessity stems from the increasing societal reliance on AI systems, whose decisions and processes significantly impact various aspects of daily life. Ethical considerations and data privacy are intertwined in this quest for trust and transparency, necessitating a comprehensive approach that balances technological innovation with societal norms and values.

Transparency in AI and data privacy is fundamentally about ensuring that stakeholders, including users, regulators, and the public, understand how AI systems operate, make decisions, and use personal data. This understanding is critical for building trust, as it allows individuals to ascertain the fairness, accuracy, and privacy implications of AI systems (Turilli & Floridi, 2009). Transparency, however, is not without its challenges. AI algorithms, particularly those based on deep learning, can be inherently opaque, making it difficult to discern how they process data and arrive at conclusions (Burrell, 2016).

To address these challenges, there has been a growing emphasis on the development of explainable AI (XAI). XAI aims to make the workings of AI systems more understandable to humans, thereby promoting accountability and trustworthiness (Gunning, 2017). This involves creating AI systems that can provide understandable explanations of their processes and decisions, aligning with both ethical standards and regulatory requirements, such as the right to explanation under the GDPR (Goodman & Flaxman, 2017).

Privacy, as a cornerstone of ethical AI, is intrinsically linked to trust. Ensuring data privacy means protecting personal data from unauthorized access and misuse, a vital aspect in the age of AI and big data. Privacy-by-design, a concept that involves integrating privacy protections into the development process of AI systems, is critical in this regard (Cavoukian, 2009). By prioritizing privacy from the outset, organizations can build systems that inherently respect user privacy and engender public trust.

Moreover, stakeholder engagement is a key element in building trust and transparency. Involving a diverse range of stakeholders, including ethicists, legal experts, and end-users, in the development and governance of AI systems, ensures a more holistic understanding of the ethical implications and helps in identifying potential privacy concerns (Mittelstadt et al., 2016). This collaborative approach not only enhances the ethical integrity of AI systems but also fosters a culture of trust among all involved parties.

In conclusion, building trust and transparency in the context of AI and data privacy is a multifaceted endeavor. It requires a concerted effort to develop transparent and explainable AI systems, integrate privacy considerations from the ground up, and engage with stakeholders comprehensively. As AI technologies continue to evolve, sustaining this balance between innovation and ethical responsibility will be crucial in maintaining public trust and upholding data privacy standards.

Chapter 5: The Future of AI in Big Data

In the realm of data-driven decision-making, the convergence of Artificial Intelligence (AI) and Big Data has brought forth a transformative synergy that continues to reshape industries and domains. As we peer into the future, it becomes increasingly evident that AI's role within the expansive realm of Big Data is poised for remarkable growth and sophistication, with profound implications for research, industry, and society at large.

Advanced Data Analytics and Machine Learning Integration:

The future of AI in Big Data revolves around the seamless integration of advanced data analytics and machine learning techniques. With the exponential growth of data volumes, traditional analytical tools and approaches are becoming obsolete. Machine learning algorithms, powered by AI, offer the capacity to uncover hidden patterns, detect anomalies, and predict trends with unparalleled accuracy (Kelleher, Mac Namee, & D'Arcy, 2015). This integration will enable organizations to extract deeper insights from their data, thereby enhancing decision-making processes.

The future of Artificial Intelligence (AI) in Big Data is indelibly linked to the advancement of data analytics and the integration of sophisticated machine learning techniques. This nexus is poised to usher in a new era of analytical capabilities, where the extraction of meaningful insights from vast and complex datasets becomes increasingly automated and precise. The trajectory of AI in the realm of

Big Data analytics is characterized by a relentless push towards more advanced, efficient, and context-aware systems.

Advanced data analytics, powered by AI, are set to revolutionize the way data is interpreted and utilized. The incorporation of AI into data analytics transcends traditional statistical methods, enabling the handling of unstructured data, such as text, images, and videos, with unprecedented proficiency (Hashem et al., 2015). This capability is crucial in an era where the majority of data generated is unstructured. AI-driven analytics are expected to evolve to a point where they can not only process this data but also derive context and semantic understanding, thereby offering deeper insights (Chen & Zhang, 2014).

Machine learning, particularly deep learning, is at the forefront of this transformative shift in data analytics. The integration of deep learning into Big Data analytics facilitates the discovery of intricate patterns and relationships within the data, which were previously imperceptible with conventional analytical methods (LeCun, Bengio, & Hinton, 2015). The future of machine learning in Big Data is likely to witness the development of more advanced neural network architectures that can handle increasingly complex datasets with greater accuracy and efficiency.

The convergence of AI and Big Data analytics also heralds significant advancements in predictive analytics. Leveraging machine learning algorithms, future AI systems will be capable of making highly accurate predictions based on Big Data, empowering decision-making in fields such as finance, healthcare, and urban planning (Jordan & Mitchell, 2015). These predictive models will continuously evolve, becoming more sophisticated over time as they are fed more data and further refined.

Another critical development in the future of AI in Big Data is the enhancement of real-time analytics. The integration of AI with Big Data technologies like Apache Hadoop and Spark enables the processing and analysis of vast datasets in real-time, providing instant insights and enabling swift decision-making (Zaharia et al., 2016). This is particularly important in applications where time is critical, such as fraud detection and emergency response.

Furthermore, the integration of AI with Big Data will continue to be shaped by advancements in computational hardware and algorithms. Developments in areas such as quantum computing and edge computing are expected to significantly expand the capabilities of AI in processing and analyzing Big Data, offering new possibilities for complex problem-solving (Castelvecchi, 2017).

In conclusion, the future of AI in Big Data, marked by advanced data analytics and machine learning integration, is set to transform how we understand and interact with large datasets. This evolution promises not only enhanced analytical capabilities but also the potential for unprecedented applications across various sectors.

Real-time Data Processing and IoT Synergy:

The proliferation of the Internet of Things (IoT) devices generates an incessant stream of real-time data. AI, in conjunction with Big Data technologies, will play a pivotal role in processing and analyzing this continuous influx of information (Deng, Liu, & Deng, 2016). This synergy holds the potential to revolutionize various sectors, including healthcare, transportation, and smart cities, by enabling proactive decision-making based on real-time insights.

The future of Artificial Intelligence (AI) in Big Data is inextricably tied to advancements in real-time data processing and the synergistic integration with the Internet of Things (IoT). This interplay is pivotal in an era where instantaneous data analysis and decision-making are increasingly critical across diverse domains. The burgeoning volume of data generated by IoT devices presents both a challenge and an opportunity for AI in Big Data, driving innovations focused on efficiency, speed, and contextual relevance.

Real-time data processing, facilitated by AI, is transforming the landscape of Big Data analytics. This transformation involves the ability to process and analyze data as it is generated, without significant delay. The integration of AI with stream processing technologies enables the handling of continuous data flows, allowing for immediate insights and responses. This immediacy is essential in applications where time-sensitive decisions are crucial, such as in autonomous vehicles, healthcare monitoring systems, and financial trading algorithms (Zaharia et al., 2013).

The synergy between AI and IoT is another cornerstone of this future landscape. IoT devices, ranging from sensors to smart appliances, generate a continuous stream of data. AI, with its advanced analytical capabilities, plays a crucial role in interpreting this data, enabling intelligent and automated decision-making. This integration is expected to lead to more sophisticated and autonomous IoT systems, capable of context-aware operations and adaptive responses (Gubbi et al., 2013).

Furthermore, the future of AI in Big Data will likely witness advancements in edge computing. Edge computing involves processing data closer to the source of data generation, i.e., near or at the IoT devices themselves. This approach reduces latency, alleviates bandwidth constraints, and enhances privacy by localizing data processing. The integration of AI at the edge is poised to enhance the efficiency and effectiveness of real-time data processing in IoT environments (Shi et al., 2016).

In addition to these technological advancements, the future of AI in Big Data will also be shaped by developments in AI algorithms optimized for real-time processing. These algorithms will need to balance the trade-off between speed and accuracy, ensuring rapid processing without significant loss in analytical precision. The evolution of machine learning techniques, such as online learning and incremental learning, will be key to this development (Losing et al., 2018).

Moreover, the increasing convergence of AI, Big Data, and IoT will necessitate robust frameworks for data governance and privacy. As real-time data processing becomes more prevalent, ensuring the security and privacy of data, especially in IoT networks, will be paramount. This will involve not only technological solutions but also regulatory and ethical considerations (Weber, 2010).

In conclusion, the future of AI in Big Data, with a focus on real-time data processing and IoT synergy, promises a transformative impact across various sectors. This future is characterized by the integration of advanced AI with cutting-edge technologies in data processing and IoT, leading to smarter, faster, and more contextually aware systems.

Enhanced Personalization and Customer Experience:

The future of AI in Big Data also promises a paradigm shift in personalization. Organizations will leverage AI-driven recommendation systems and predictive analytics to offer highly tailored experiences to individuals (Bishop, 2006). This level of personalization extends across domains such as e-commerce, entertainment, and healthcare, enhancing customer satisfaction and engagement.

The future of Artificial Intelligence (AI) in Big Data is poised to revolutionize the realm of personalized customer experience significantly. The symbiosis of AI and Big Data is catalyzing a paradigm shift towards more nuanced and individualized user interactions in various sectors. This shift is underpinned by the sophisticated analysis of large datasets, enabling the tailoring of services and products to meet the unique preferences and needs of individual customers.

Enhanced personalization, facilitated by AI and Big Data, is predicated on the capability to dissect and interpret vast quantities of data to glean insights about consumer behaviors, preferences, and trends. The utilization of machine learning algorithms, particularly those based on predictive analytics, plays a pivotal role in this process. These algorithms analyze historical and real-time data to forecast future customer behavior, thereby enabling businesses to offer highly targeted and relevant products and services (Huang & Rust, 2018).

In the retail sector, for instance, AI-driven personalization is transforming the shopping experience. Retailers are leveraging AI to provide personalized product recommendations, tailor marketing messages, and optimize the shopping experience based on individual consumer data (Choi, Hwang, & McMillan, 2020). This level of personalization not only enhances customer satisfaction but also increases business efficiency by aligning supply with consumer demand more accurately.

In the realm of online services, AI and Big Data are enabling the creation of highly individualized user experiences. Streaming services, for example, utilize AI algorithms to analyze viewing habits and preferences, thereby offering personalized content recommendations (Gomez-Uribe & Hunt, 2016). Similarly, AI in social media platforms analyzes user interactions and content preferences to customize news feeds and advertisements, creating a more engaging user experience.

The future of AI in Big Data also heralds advancements in customer service and support. AI-powered chatbots and virtual assistants, trained on large datasets, are becoming increasingly adept at providing real-time, personalized customer support. These AI systems can handle a wide range of queries, offer tailored solutions, and learn from each interaction, thereby continuously improving the quality of customer service (Davenport, Guha, Grewal, & Bressgott, 2020).

Furthermore, the integration of AI and Big Data in customer experience is expected to expand into more immersive and interactive technologies, such as augmented reality (AR) and virtual reality (VR). These technologies, powered by AI, can offer highly personalized and engaging experiences, further enhancing customer engagement and satisfaction (Javornik, 2016).

However, the enhanced personalization offered by AI and Big Data raises critical considerations regarding consumer privacy and data security. As businesses collect and analyze more personal data, ensuring the privacy and security of this data becomes paramount. This necessitates robust data governance policies and practices to protect consumer information and maintain trust (Martin, 2019).

In conclusion, the future of AI in Big Data in terms of enhanced personalization and customer experience is marked by the potential for profoundly individualized and engaging user interactions. This future, while promising significant benefits for both businesses and consumers, also calls for careful consideration of ethical and privacy concerns.

Ethical Considerations and Responsible AI:

As AI in Big Data becomes more pervasive, ethical considerations will continue to take center stage. Ensuring responsible AI practices, which respect privacy, mitigate bias, and adhere to regulatory frameworks, will be paramount (Floridi et al., 2018). Organizations and researchers must proactively address these ethical concerns to build trust and maintain societal acceptance.

The future of Artificial Intelligence (AI) in Big Data is inextricably linked with ethical considerations and the imperative for responsible AI. This connection underscores the necessity to address the profound moral and ethical implications as AI systems become more prevalent and influential in analyzing and interpreting vast quantities of data. The evolution of AI in the context of Big Data is not merely a technological or scientific progression, but also a social and ethical journey, necessitating a nuanced and responsible approach to AI development and deployment.

Ethical considerations in the future of AI and Big Data primarily revolve around issues such as privacy, bias, transparency, and accountability. The privacy concerns are particularly acute, as AI systems in Big Data environments often handle sensitive and personal information. Ensuring that these systems respect and protect individual privacy is paramount, and this involves not only robust data protection measures but also ethical design and deployment practices (Mittelstadt, Allo, Taddeo, Wachter, & Floridi, 2016).

Bias in AI is another critical ethical issue. AI systems, particularly those reliant on machine learning, can inadvertently perpetuate and amplify existing biases present in the training data, leading to unfair and discriminatory outcomes (Barocas, Hardt, & Narayanan, 2019). Future advancements in AI must focus on developing methods to detect, mitigate, and eliminate bias, ensuring that AI systems are fair and equitable.

Transparency and explainability in AI systems are essential to ensure trust and accountability, especially when these systems make decisions impacting human lives. The 'black box' nature of certain AI algorithms, especially in deep learning, poses a significant challenge to transparency. Future developments in AI should emphasize the creation of interpretable and explainable models, enabling stakeholders to understand and trust AI decision-making processes (Ribeiro, Singh, & Guestrin, 2016).

Responsible AI also involves ensuring that AI systems are secure and robust against manipulation and attacks, protecting both the integrity of the system and the data it handles. As AI systems become more complex and integrated into critical infrastructure, their vulnerability to cyber-attacks and other forms of manipulation becomes a significant concern (Taddeo & Floridi, 2018).

In addition to these technical and ethical considerations, the future of AI in Big Data also demands a regulatory and policy response. Developing and implementing appropriate regulations and guidelines that ensure ethical AI deployment while fostering innovation is a critical challenge for policymakers (Cath et al., 2018).

Furthermore, the ethical development of AI in Big Data requires a multidisciplinary approach, involving collaboration between technologists, ethicists, legal experts, and policymakers. This collaborative approach ensures a holistic understanding of the ethical implications and facilitates the development of AI systems that are not only technologically advanced but also socially responsible and ethically sound.

In conclusion, the future of AI in Big Data, with respect to ethical considerations and responsible AI, is a complex and multifaceted domain. It demands a concerted effort to address privacy, bias, transparency, and accountability issues, alongside a robust regulatory framework. Ensuring the ethical development and deployment of AI is crucial for harnessing its full potential while safeguarding societal values and individual rights.

Interdisciplinary Collaboration:

The future of AI in Big Data will be marked by interdisciplinary collaboration. Experts from diverse fields, including computer science, data ethics, and domain-specific domains, will collaborate to harness the full potential of AI-driven insights (Crawford, 2013). This collaborative approach will lead to innovative solutions to complex problems.

The future trajectory of Artificial Intelligence (AI) in Big Data is increasingly converging towards an interdisciplinary paradigm, where collaboration across diverse academic and professional disciplines becomes indispensable. This interdisciplinary collaboration is not merely beneficial but essential, given the multifaceted challenges and opportunities presented by the integration of AI in Big Data. The synthesis of insights from various fields such as computer science, ethics, law, social sciences, and domain-specific knowledge is crucial in navigating the complexities of AI in Big Data and harnessing its full potential responsibly.

Interdisciplinary collaboration in the context of AI and Big Data is anchored in the recognition that AI is not a standalone technology but rather an enabler of broader socio-technical systems. The development and deployment of AI in Big Data environments entail considerations beyond the technical aspects, encompassing ethical, legal, societal, and policy dimensions. For instance, addressing the ethical implications of AI, such as bias, fairness, and privacy, requires insights from ethicists, sociologists, and legal experts alongside AI researchers and practitioners (Mittelstadt et al., 2016).

Furthermore, the effective translation of AI and Big Data technologies into practical applications necessitates domain-specific expertise. For example, the application of AI in healthcare requires not only advanced AI algorithms but also a deep understanding of medical science, patient care, and healthcare systems (Topol, 2019). Similarly, leveraging AI for environmental sustainability calls for collaboration with environmental scientists, ecologists, and policy makers (Dignum, 2019).

The integration of AI with Big Data also presents significant technical challenges that demand interdisciplinary solutions. Issues such as data integration, scalability, real-time processing, and the handling of unstructured data require a combination of expertise in computer science, statistics, mathematics, and engineering (Hashem et al., 2015). Additionally, the design of user interfaces and user experience in AI systems benefits from the involvement of experts in human-computer interaction and design (Dunne, 2015).

Interdisciplinary collaboration extends to the development of regulatory frameworks and governance models for AI in Big Data. The rapid advancement of AI technologies and their societal implications necessitate informed policy making that balances innovation with ethical considerations and public interests. This requires dialogue and collaboration between technologists, policy makers, legal experts, and ethicists (Cath et al., 2018).

In the educational sphere, the future of AI in Big Data underscores the need for interdisciplinary education and training. Developing curricula that blend technical skills with ethical, legal, and domain-specific knowledge is essential in preparing a workforce capable of addressing the challenges and opportunities of AI in Big Data (Hagendorff, 2020).

The future of AI in Big Data is fundamentally linked to interdisciplinary collaboration. Such collaboration fosters a holistic understanding of the multifaceted nature of AI and its implications, enabling the development of AI technologies that are not only technologically advanced but also ethically sound, legally compliant, socially beneficial, and responsive to domain-specific needs.

In conclusion, the future of AI in Big Data is a compelling narrative of advancement and opportunity. As AI technologies mature and data volumes continue to expand, the potential for transformative impacts across industries and society is immense. However, this journey must be undertaken with a strong ethical compass and a commitment to responsible AI practices to ensure that the benefits are equitably distributed and that privacy and fairness are upheld.

Emerging Trends and Future Technologies:

The future of Artificial Intelligence (AI) in Big Data is intricately tied to emerging trends and forthcoming technologies that promise to reshape the landscape of data analysis and decision-making processes. This future trajectory is marked by a confluence of technological advancements, each playing a pivotal role in enhancing the capabilities and reach of AI in various sectors. The exploration of these trends and technologies offers a glimpse into a future where AI and Big Data not only coexist but synergistically evolve to address complex challenges and unlock new possibilities.

One of the foremost trends in this realm is the advancement of AI algorithms towards greater sophistication and efficiency. The development of deep learning and neural network architectures, which have been instrumental in recent AI breakthroughs, is expected to continue at an accelerated pace (LeCun, Bengio, & Hinton, 2015). Future advancements may include the evolution of self-learning and self-evolving AI systems, capable of adapting to new data and environments without explicit programming. This adaptability will be crucial in managing the dynamic and ever-growing datasets characteristic of Big Data environments.

Another significant trend is the integration of AI with quantum computing. Quantum computing offers the potential to process and analyze data at speeds far beyond the capabilities of classical computers (Castelvecchi, 2017). The intersection of quantum computing and AI could revolutionize Big Data analytics by enabling the handling of complex, multi-dimensional datasets with unprecedented efficiency, thereby opening new frontiers in fields such as genomics, climate modeling, and financial modeling.

The Internet of Things (IoT) is also a critical trend shaping the future of AI in Big Data. The proliferation of IoT devices is generating vast amounts of data, offering a rich source of information for AI systems (Atzori, Iera, & Morabito, 2017). The integration of AI with IoT has the potential to enhance the intelligence of these devices, leading to more autonomous and context-aware systems. This synergy could have profound implications in areas such as smart cities, healthcare monitoring, and industrial automation.

Augmented Reality (AR) and Virtual Reality (VR) are emerging as transformative technologies in the context of AI and Big Data. AR and VR can provide immersive and interactive platforms for data visualization and analysis, offering new ways to interpret and interact with complex datasets (Javornik, 2016). The integration of AI with AR and VR could lead to more intuitive and effective tools for data analysis, aiding in decision-making processes across various fields.

Edge computing is another trend that is poised to influence the future of AI in Big Data significantly. Edge computing involves processing data closer to where it is generated, reducing latency and bandwidth usage. The combination of AI and edge computing can lead to more efficient real-time data processing, particularly in IoT applications (Shi et al., 2016).

In conclusion, the future of AI in Big Data is intertwined with emerging trends and technologies that are set to expand the capabilities and impact of AI. These developments, from advanced AI algorithms and quantum computing to IoT, AR/VR, and edge computing, represent a trajectory towards more powerful, efficient, and versatile AI systems. As these technologies evolve, they will undoubtedly present new challenges but also offer extraordinary opportunities to harness the full potential of AI in Big Data.

AI, Big Data, and the Internet of Things (IoT):

The confluence of Artificial Intelligence (AI), Big Data, and the Internet of Things (IoT) is poised to engender a transformative impact in the forthcoming era, marking a significant paradigm shift in how data is collected, analyzed, and utilized for decision-making. This triadic integration is emblematic of an advanced technological epoch wherein AI's analytical prowess, IoT's expansive data generation capabilities, and Big Data's voluminous storage and processing facilities coalesce to foster unprecedented innovations across various sectors.

AI's role in this triad primarily revolves around its ability to imbue IoT devices with advanced data processing and decision-making capabilities. Leveraging machine learning algorithms, AI can analyze the vast streams of data generated by IoT devices, extracting actionable insights and facilitating real-time responses (Atzori, Iera, & Morabito, 2017). This integration is pivotal in realizing the potential of IoT, transforming it from a mere data collection framework to an intelligent system capable of autonomous operation and context-aware actions.

Big Data serves as the foundational bedrock for this integration, providing the necessary infrastructure for storing and managing the enormous volumes of data generated by IoT devices. The challenge of Big Data in the context of AI and IoT is not just its sheer volume but also the velocity, variety, and veracity of the data. Advanced Big Data analytics tools are essential to process and make sense of this data, enabling AI algorithms to perform efficiently and effectively (Hashem et al., 2015).

The synergy between AI, Big Data, and IoT is expected to revolutionize various industries. In smart cities, for instance, this integration can lead to more efficient urban management systems, where real-time data from IoT sensors is analyzed by AI to optimize traffic flow, energy usage, and emergency response services (Zanella et al., 2014). In healthcare, wearable IoT devices can continuously monitor patient health data, with AI algorithms providing personalized medical insights and early warnings of potential health issues (Islam et al., 2015).

The future of AI in Big Data in the context of IoT also brings to the fore the significance of edge computing. Edge computing involves processing data at the edge of the network, closer to where it is generated. This paradigm is crucial in reducing latency and bandwidth usage for IoT devices, thereby enhancing the efficiency and speed of AI-driven data analysis (Shi et al., 2016).

However, this integration raises critical concerns related to privacy, security, and ethics. The vast amounts of data collected by IoT devices, coupled with AI's ability to analyze this data in depth, pose significant privacy risks. Ensuring the security of this data against cyber threats and maintaining the privacy and trust of individuals become paramount (Weber, 2010). Moreover, ethical considerations regarding the autonomous decision-making of AI in IoT systems necessitate robust guidelines and regulatory frameworks.

In conclusion, the future of AI in Big Data, in the context of its integration with IoT, represents a frontier of technological advancement with the potential to radically alter the landscape of data-driven decision-making. This integration promises enhanced efficiency, personalization, and automation across various sectors but also requires careful navigation of the associated privacy, security, and ethical challenges.

Predictions for the Next Decade:

The next decade is poised to witness pivotal transformations in the realm of Artificial Intelligence (AI) and Big Data, with advancements that promise to redefine the boundaries of technology, society, and ethics. The confluence of these domains is expected to lead to groundbreaking innovations, along with challenges that necessitate careful navigation.

One of the foremost predictions for the next decade is the advancement in AI algorithms, particularly in deep learning and neural networks. These advancements will lead to AI systems that are more efficient, accurate, and capable of handling complex tasks that are currently beyond reach. The evolution of AI will likely see the development of algorithms that are better at generalizing from limited data, thus reducing the dependency on large datasets and mitigating issues related to data privacy (LeCun, Bengio, & Hinton, 2015).

In parallel, the role of Big Data is expected to become more nuanced. With the growing awareness of privacy concerns and the implementation of regulations like the GDPR, there will be a greater emphasis on privacy-preserving data analytics. Techniques such as federated learning, where AI models are trained across multiple decentralized devices or servers holding local data samples, are likely to gain prominence. This approach not only helps in safeguarding privacy but also reduces the costs and latency involved in data transmission (Konečný et al., 2016).

The integration of AI with quantum computing is another anticipated development. Quantum computing promises to significantly enhance the processing power available for data analysis, potentially enabling AI to solve complex problems much faster than current computers

(Castelvecchi, 2017). This could lead to major breakthroughs in fields such as drug discovery, climate modeling, and financial modeling.

The Internet of Things (IoT) is expected to continue its exponential growth, with AI playing a key role in analyzing the vast amounts of data generated by IoT devices. This synergy will be pivotal in realizing the potential of smart cities, autonomous vehicles, and personalized healthcare, where real-time data processing and decision-making are crucial (Atzori, Iera, & Morabito, 2017).

In terms of societal impact, the next decade will likely see AI becoming more embedded in everyday life, leading to significant changes in job markets, education, and social dynamics. While AI and automation may displace certain types of jobs, they are also expected to create new jobs and demand for skills in AI management and ethics (Manyika et al., 2017).

Ethical considerations will become even more central as AI systems become more autonomous and prevalent in decision-making. The development of ethical AI, focusing on fairness, transparency, and accountability, will be a key area of focus. This will require a multidisciplinary approach, involving collaboration between technologists, ethicists, policymakers, and other stakeholders (Mittelstadt et al., 2016).

In conclusion, the next decade in AI and Big Data is set to be a period of significant advancements and transformations. While these developments hold immense promise, they also present challenges that require thoughtful consideration and collaborative efforts across various domains to ensure that the benefits of AI and Big Data are realized responsibly and equitably.

Chapter 6:
Industry-Specific Applications

Artificial Intelligence (AI) has emerged as a game-changing force with the potential to revolutionize a myriad of industries. Its transformative impact stems from its adaptability and capacity to cater to industry-specific needs. This section explores the intricate web of industry-specific applications of AI, emphasizing the depth of innovation and potential disruption across sectors.

Healthcare and Medical Diagnosis:

In the domain of healthcare, AI is poised to redefine diagnosis, treatment, and patient care. Advanced machine learning algorithms have exhibited exceptional capabilities in analyzing medical imaging data (Litjens et al., 2017). AI-driven systems can assist radiologists in detecting diseases from X-rays, MRIs, and CT scans, thereby enhancing accuracy and early disease identification. Moreover, predictive models based on patient data can optimize treatment plans and improve healthcare outcomes (Obermeyer & Emanuel, 2016). The integration of AI into healthcare not only augments diagnostic precision but also reduces healthcare costs.

The healthcare industry stands at the forefront of reaping the benefits of Artificial Intelligence (AI) and Big Data analytics, embarking on a transformative journey towards precision medicine and enhanced patient care. This section delves into the intricate landscape of industry-specific applications in healthcare and medical diagnosis, emphasizing the profound impact of AI in revolutionizing healthcare delivery.

1. **Medical Imaging and Radiology**

   AI has made substantial inroads into the realm of medical imaging, notably in radiology. AI-driven algorithms are capable of analyzing complex medical images such as X-rays, Magnetic Resonance Imaging (MRI), and Computed Tomography (CT) scans with remarkable precision and speed (Litjens et al., 2017). These algorithms can detect anomalies, identify early signs of diseases, and assist radiologists in making more accurate diagnoses. For example, deep learning-based models have demonstrated exceptional performance in detecting breast cancer, lung nodules, and diabetic retinopathy (Esteva et al., 2017). This has the potential to significantly reduce diagnostic errors and improve patient outcomes.

2. **Disease Risk Prediction and Personalized Treatment**

   AI excels in harnessing vast datasets to predict disease risk and tailor treatment plans. Machine learning models can analyze electronic health records (EHRs), genomic data, and patient histories to identify individuals at high risk of developing specific diseases (Obermeyer & Emanuel, 2016). Additionally, AI-driven decision support systems can suggest personalized treatment options based on genetic profiles, enabling more effective and targeted therapies. The advent of precision medicine promises to revolutionize disease prevention and management.

3. **Drug Discovery and Development**

   The pharmaceutical industry is leveraging AI to expedite drug discovery and development processes. AI-driven algorithms can sift through vast chemical databases, predict molecular interactions, and identify potential drug candidates with higher success rates (Angermueller et al., 2016). This not only reduces the time and cost associated with drug development but also enables the discovery of novel therapies for previously untreatable conditions. AI is facilitating the emergence of targeted therapies and personalized medicine.

4. **Telemedicine and Remote Monitoring**

Telemedicine has gained prominence, particularly in the wake of the COVID-19 pandemic, and AI plays a pivotal role in enabling remote healthcare delivery. AI-powered chatbots and virtual assistants facilitate remote consultations and provide medical guidance. Wearable devices equipped with AI sensors monitor patients' vital signs and health parameters, enabling early intervention and reducing hospital readmissions (Wani et al., 2020). This trend towards remote healthcare is expected to enhance accessibility and reduce healthcare disparities.

5. **Healthcare Management and Resource Optimization**

AI-driven healthcare management systems optimize resource allocation and streamline administrative processes. Predictive analytics can forecast patient admissions, helping hospitals allocate staff and resources efficiently (Obermeyer & Emanuel, 2016). Additionally, AI enhances revenue cycle management, fraud detection, and billing accuracy, leading to cost savings and improved financial viability for healthcare institutions.

In conclusion, the integration of AI into healthcare and medical diagnosis is ushering in an era of precision medicine, data-driven decision-making, and improved patient care. These industry-specific applications not only enhance the accuracy and efficiency of diagnosis and treatment but also have the potential to significantly reduce healthcare costs and improve healthcare outcomes. As AI continues to evolve, its role in healthcare promises to be instrumental in shaping the future of medicine.

Finance and Algorithmic Trading:

The financial industry has been an early adopter of AI, particularly in algorithmic trading. AI-powered trading systems can process vast datasets and execute trades at lightning speed, capitalizing on market trends and anomalies (Cartea et al., 2015). These systems mitigate risks and enhance portfolio management, ushering in a new era of quantitative finance. Moreover, AI is instrumental in fraud detection and credit risk assessment, ensuring the security and stability of financial markets.

The financial industry has been a pioneering domain in harnessing the potential of Artificial Intelligence (AI) and data analytics. Specifically, the realm of finance and algorithmic trading has witnessed an unprecedented transformation with the infusion of advanced AI algorithms. This section explores the intricate landscape of industry-specific applications in finance, highlighting the profound impact of AI on quantitative finance and algorithmic trading.

1. **Algorithmic Trading and High-Frequency Trading (HFT)**

   Algorithmic trading, underpinned by AI, has revolutionized the way financial markets operate. These algorithms can process vast amounts of market data in real-time, execute trades with minimal latency, and identify arbitrage opportunities (Cartea et al., 2015). High-frequency trading (HFT) strategies, driven by AI algorithms, aim to capitalize on microsecond price discrepancies, thereby enhancing liquidity and market efficiency. AI-powered trading systems have become an integral component of modern financial markets.

2. **Risk Management and Portfolio Optimization**

   AI plays a pivotal role in risk management and portfolio optimization. Machine learning models can assess the risk associated with financial instruments and portfolios, enabling investors to make informed decisions (Lipton et al., 2018). These models consider multiple factors, including historical market data, macroeconomic indicators, and geopolitical events, to assess risk and optimize portfolios. AI-driven risk models help in minimizing losses and achieving better risk-adjusted returns.

3. **Sentiment Analysis and News Trading**

   The analysis of news and sentiment data using AI has gained traction in financial markets. Natural language processing (NLP) algorithms can analyze news articles, social media sentiment, and market commentary to gauge market sentiment and anticipate price movements (Bollen et al., 2011). Traders employ sentiment analysis to make informed trading decisions and capitalize on sentiment-driven market movements.

4. **Fraud Detection and Compliance**

   AI is instrumental in detecting fraudulent activities in the financial industry. Machine learning models can identify unusual patterns and anomalies in transaction data, flagging potential instances of fraud (Deng et al., 2013). Moreover, AI algorithms aid in ensuring regulatory compliance by automating compliance checks and reporting, thereby reducing compliance costs and risks.

5. **Robo-Advisors and Personalized Financial Services**

AI-driven robo-advisors are transforming the landscape of personal finance. These automated advisory platforms use machine learning to tailor investment recommendations to individual clients based on their financial goals, risk tolerance, and financial profiles (Botsman & Miles, 2016). Robo-advisors democratize access to professional financial advice and offer cost-effective investment solutions.

In conclusion, the infusion of AI into finance and algorithmic trading has ushered in a new era of quantitative finance, characterized by enhanced market efficiency, risk management, and personalized financial services. These industry-specific applications have not only reshaped the financial landscape but also highlighted the potential for AI to redefine traditional business models and strategies in the financial sector.

Manufacturing and Industry 4.0:

Manufacturing is undergoing a profound transformation with the advent of Industry 4.0. AI-driven automation and robotics are optimizing production processes and quality control (Mourtzis et al., 2016). Predictive maintenance powered by AI can significantly reduce downtime and maintenance costs. Furthermore, AI-based supply chain management enhances efficiency, demand forecasting, and inventory control. The integration of AI into manufacturing yields increased productivity and competitiveness.

The manufacturing sector is undergoing a profound transformation with the advent of Industry 4.0, characterized by the integration of advanced digital technologies and automation. Industry-specific applications in manufacturing are driving the evolution of smart manufacturing, revolutionizing processes, improving efficiency, and enhancing competitiveness. This section explores the intricate landscape of Industry 4.0 applications in manufacturing, emphasizing the profound impact of artificial intelligence (AI) and data analytics.

1. **Predictive Maintenance and Asset Management**

   AI-driven predictive maintenance is at the forefront of Industry 4.0 applications in manufacturing. Machine learning models analyze sensor data from machinery and equipment to predict when maintenance is required (Jardine et al., 2006). This proactive approach reduces downtime, minimizes unplanned repairs, and optimizes the lifespan of assets. Manufacturers can transition from reactive maintenance to a predictive and preventive maintenance model, leading to significant cost savings.

2. **Smart Manufacturing and IoT Integration**

   Industry 4.0 embraces the Internet of Things (IoT) to connect machines, devices, and sensors across the manufacturing floor. AI algorithms analyze data from these connected devices in real-time, enabling autonomous decision-making and process optimization (Monostori et al., 2016). This integration enhances visibility into manufacturing operations, streamlines supply chain management, and facilitates real-time adjustments to production processes.

3. **Quality Control and Defect Detection**

   AI-powered computer vision systems are transforming quality control in manufacturing. These systems can inspect products with high precision, identifying defects and deviations from standards (Litjens et al., 2017). Manufacturers can achieve higher quality standards, reduce waste, and ensure product consistency. Defect detection is particularly critical in industries such as automotive and electronics.

4. **Supply Chain Optimization**

   AI and data analytics optimize supply chain operations by predicting demand, managing inventory, and identifying potential disruptions (Korpela et al., 2017). Manufacturers can ensure the timely availability of materials and components, reduce excess inventory, and enhance supplier collaboration. This results in streamlined supply chains, cost savings, and improved customer satisfaction.

5. **Human-Machine Collaboration and Worker Safety**

Collaborative robots (cobots) equipped with AI algorithms are working alongside human operators in manufacturing environments (Siciliano et al., 2016). These cobots enhance productivity, perform repetitive or dangerous tasks, and improve worker safety. AI systems can monitor worker safety in real-time, detecting potential hazards and alerting workers to take preventive actions.

In conclusion, Industry 4.0 applications in manufacturing represent a transformative shift towards smart manufacturing, marked by data-driven decision-making, automation, and enhanced operational efficiency. These industry-specific applications leverage AI and data analytics to optimize processes, improve quality, and drive innovation. As the manufacturing sector continues to evolve, embracing Industry

4.0 technologies is essential for maintaining competitiveness in a rapidly changing global landscape.

Agriculture and Precision Farming:

Agriculture is experiencing a technological revolution through AI-enabled precision farming. AI-driven systems analyze environmental data, including soil conditions, weather, and crop health, to optimize planting, irrigation, and harvesting (Liu et al., 2017). This results in increased crop yields, reduced resource wastage, and sustainable agricultural practices. AI also aids in pest and disease detection, enabling timely interventions to protect crops.

Agriculture has entered a new era with the integration of advanced technologies, particularly in the form of precision farming and Industry 4.0 applications. These industry-specific applications are transforming the agricultural landscape by harnessing data-driven decision-making, automation, and artificial intelligence (AI). This section explores the intricate web of applications in agriculture, emphasizing the profound impact of precision farming.

1. **Precision Agriculture and Data-Driven Farming**

   Precision agriculture represents a paradigm shift in farming practices, driven by data analytics and IoT devices (Lowenberg-DeBoer et al., 2017). Soil sensors, drones, and satellite imagery collect data on soil quality, weather conditions, and crop health. AI algorithms process this data to provide farmers with real-time insights into crop conditions, allowing for precise resource management, including targeted irrigation, fertilization, and pest control. This data-driven approach optimizes crop yields, minimizes resource wastage, and reduces environmental impact.

2. **Automated Farm Machinery and Robotics**

   AI-powered farm machinery and robotics are enhancing productivity and efficiency in agriculture (Bargiel et al., 2018). Autonomous tractors, drones, and robotic harvesters perform tasks such as planting, harvesting, and weeding with precision and consistency. These technologies reduce labor costs, improve accuracy, and enable 24/7 farming operations. AI algorithms enable these machines to adapt to changing field conditions and avoid obstacles, making them invaluable tools for modern agriculture.

3. **Crop Monitoring and Disease Detection**

AI and computer vision systems are used for crop monitoring and disease detection (Xia et al., 2017). These systems analyze images and videos captured by drones or cameras mounted on tractors to identify early signs of crop diseases, nutrient deficiencies, or pest infestations. Early detection allows for timely interventions, minimizing crop losses and reducing the need for chemical treatments. AI also aids in crop identification and yield estimation, providing valuable information for harvest planning and marketing.

4. **Supply Chain Optimization and Traceability**

Industry 4.0 technologies facilitate supply chain optimization in agriculture (Zhong et al., 2016). Blockchain technology, combined with AI, enables end-to-end traceability of agricultural products from farm to consumer. Smart contracts and IoT sensors track the movement and conditions of agricultural products throughout the supply chain, enhancing transparency and reducing food fraud. AI-driven demand forecasting optimizes inventory management and reduces food waste.

5. **Sustainable Agriculture and Resource Conservation**

Precision farming promotes sustainable agriculture by optimizing resource use (Hobbs & Godwin, 2015). AI-based models consider various factors, including weather forecasts and historical data, to recommend optimal planting times and crop varieties. This leads to resource-efficient farming practices, reduced water usage, and minimized environmental impact. Precision farming aligns with the goals of sustainable agriculture by ensuring the long-term viability of farming operations.

In conclusion, industry-specific applications in agriculture and precision farming are ushering in a new era of agricultural productivity, sustainability, and efficiency. These applications leverage AI, IoT, and data analytics to empower farmers with real-time insights and automation capabilities. As the global population continues to grow, precision farming is poised to play a pivotal role in ensuring food security and sustainable agricultural practices.

Entertainment and Personalization:

In the realm of entertainment, AI is enhancing user experiences through content recommendation and personalization algorithms (Hsu, 2019). Streaming platforms leverage AI to suggest tailored content, increasing user engagement and satisfaction. Virtual reality (VR) and augmented reality (AR) technologies, driven by AI, create immersive experiences in gaming and entertainment.

The entertainment industry is undergoing a profound transformation through the integration of advanced technologies, particularly in the form of data analytics and artificial intelligence (AI). These industry-specific applications are revolutionizing user experiences, enhancing content delivery, and personalizing entertainment offerings. This section explores the intricate landscape of applications in entertainment, emphasizing the profound impact of personalization.

1. **Content Recommendation and Personalized Viewing**

   AI-driven recommendation systems have become an integral part of the entertainment landscape (Ricci et al., 2015). Streaming platforms such as Netflix and Amazon Prime employ advanced algorithms to analyze user preferences, viewing history, and behavioral data. Based on this analysis, personalized content recommendations are made to users, enhancing their viewing experiences. These recommendations not only increase user engagement but also drive content discovery.

2. **Targeted Advertising and Monetization**

   Personalization extends to advertising in the entertainment industry. AI algorithms analyze user data to deliver targeted advertisements (O'Keefe & Brown, 2019). Advertisers can tailor their messages to specific demographics, interests, and preferences, increasing the effectiveness of ad campaigns. This targeted advertising model benefits both advertisers and content providers by maximizing revenue while minimizing viewer intrusion.

3. **Immersive Experiences with Virtual and Augmented Reality**

   Virtual Reality (VR) and Augmented Reality (AR), powered by AI, are transforming the entertainment landscape (Schuemie et al., 2020). VR immerses users in interactive virtual worlds, enhancing gaming experiences and providing unique storytelling opportunities. AR overlays digital content onto the real world, creating interactive experiences through mobile apps and wearable devices. These technologies offer new avenues for immersive entertainment and personalization.

4. **Music Streaming and Personalized Playlists**

   The music industry leverages personalization to curate playlists and recommendations for users (Vall et al., 2017). AI algorithms analyze listening habits, musical preferences, and user behavior to generate personalized playlists. Music streaming services like Spotify use AI to understand users' moods and recommend songs accordingly. Personalized playlists enhance user engagement and satisfaction.

5. **Gaming and AI-Enhanced Gameplay**

In the gaming industry, AI is used to personalize gameplay experiences (Yannakakis et al., 2018). AI algorithms adapt game difficulty, levels, and challenges based on the player's skill level and preferences. Additionally, AI-driven NPCs (non-playable characters) exhibit dynamic behavior and adapt to player actions, providing a more immersive and personalized gaming experience.

Industry-specific applications in entertainment and personalization are redefining the way content is delivered and consumed. These applications leverage AI and data analytics to enhance user experiences, increase engagement, and drive revenue. As technology continues to evolve, personalization will remain a pivotal aspect of the entertainment industry, catering to the diverse preferences and expectations of audiences.

In conclusion, the applications of AI are manifold and industry-specific, heralding a transformative paradigm shift across various sectors. These examples illustrate the adaptability and versatility of AI in addressing unique challenges and driving innovation. As AI continues to evolve, its integration into industry-specific domains promises to reshape industries, redefine business models, and elevate the quality of products and services.

AI and Big Data in Healthcare:

The healthcare industry is witnessing a profound transformation driven by the integration of Artificial Intelligence (AI) and Big Data analytics. These industry-specific applications are revolutionizing healthcare by enhancing diagnosis, treatment, and patient care. This section explores the intricate landscape of AI and Big Data applications in healthcare, emphasizing their profound impact on the industry.

1. **Medical Imaging and Radiology**

   AI and Big Data have revolutionized medical imaging and radiology (Litjens et al., 2017). Advanced machine learning algorithms analyze vast amounts of medical images, including X-rays, Magnetic Resonance Imaging (MRI), and Computed Tomography (CT) scans, with exceptional accuracy. AI-driven systems assist radiologists in detecting diseases and anomalies, improving diagnostic precision. Big Data analytics enable the storage and retrieval of large image datasets, facilitating longitudinal studies and research.

2. **Predictive Analytics and Disease Prevention**

The integration of AI and Big Data enables predictive analytics for disease prevention (Obermeyer & Emanuel, 2016). Machine learning models analyze electronic health records (EHRs), genomic data, and patient histories to predict disease risk. These models identify individuals at high risk for specific diseases, allowing for early interventions and tailored preventive measures. Big Data analytics handle the vast amount of patient data required for predictive modeling.

3. **Drug Discovery and Personalized Medicine**

AI and Big Data play a pivotal role in drug discovery and personalized medicine (Angermueller et al., 2016). AI algorithms expedite the drug discovery process by analyzing vast chemical databases, predicting molecular interactions, and identifying potential drug candidates. Big Data analytics assist in managing and analyzing genomics data for personalized treatment plans. This results in targeted therapies, reduced side effects, and improved patient outcomes.

4. **Telemedicine and Remote Monitoring**

Telemedicine and remote monitoring are thriving with AI and Big Data integration (Wani et al., 2020). AI-powered chatbots and virtual assistants enable remote consultations, expanding access to healthcare. Wearable devices equipped with AI sensors monitor patients' vital signs and health parameters, transmitting data for real-time analysis. AI algorithms detect abnormalities, enabling timely interventions and reducing hospital readmissions.

5. **Healthcare Management and Cost Optimization**

AI and Big Data enhance healthcare management and cost optimization (Obermeyer & Emanuel, 2016). Predictive analytics forecast patient admissions, allowing hospitals to allocate resources efficiently. AI-driven revenue cycle management streamlines administrative processes, detects fraud, and ensures billing accuracy, leading to cost savings. Big Data analytics help healthcare institutions manage the vast amount of administrative and patient data generated daily.

In conclusion, industry-specific applications of AI and Big Data in healthcare represent a transformative paradigm shift, redefining patient care, diagnosis, and treatment. These applications leverage the power of AI to process vast datasets, provide predictive insights, and enhance the quality of care. As the healthcare industry continues to evolve, AI and Big Data will play an increasingly pivotal role in delivering personalized and efficient healthcare services.

Revolutionizing Retail with AI and Big Data:

The retail industry is undergoing a radical transformation through the integration of Artificial Intelligence (AI) and Big Data analytics. These industry-specific applications are reshaping the retail landscape by improving customer experiences, optimizing operations, and boosting profitability. This section delves into the intricate landscape of AI and Big Data applications in retail, emphasizing their profound impact on the industry.

1. **Personalized Customer Experiences**

   AI and Big Data enable retailers to provide personalized customer experiences (Verhoef et al., 2017). AI algorithms analyze customer behavior, purchase history, and online interactions to create tailored recommendations and marketing campaigns. Personalization enhances customer engagement, increases sales, and fosters brand loyalty. Big Data analytics handle the massive volume of customer data required for effective personalization.

2. **Inventory Management and Demand Forecasting**

   AI-driven inventory management and demand forecasting are transforming retail operations (Davenport, 2014). Machine learning models analyze historical sales data, seasonality, and market trends to optimize inventory levels. AI systems predict demand patterns, reducing stockouts and overstock situations. Big Data analytics support the processing of vast amounts of sales and inventory data for accurate forecasting.

3. **Visual Search and Augmented Reality**

Visual search and augmented reality applications powered by AI are enhancing the shopping experience (Kaplan et al., 2019). Visual search allows customers to find products by simply uploading images. Augmented reality apps enable virtual try-ons and product visualization. AI algorithms identify products from images and provide relevant information, creating immersive shopping experiences. Big Data supports the storage and retrieval of product images and metadata.

4. **Supply Chain Optimization**

AI and Big Data optimize supply chains, reducing costs and enhancing efficiency (Najjar & Kanso, 2019). AI-driven algorithms analyze data from suppliers, distribution centers, and transportation networks to optimize logistics and reduce lead times. Big Data analytics aggregate and process data from various supply chain components, enabling real-time decision-making and streamlined operations.

5. **Fraud Detection and Security**

Retailers leverage AI and Big Data to enhance fraud detection and security measures (Sahin et al., 2018). AI algorithms analyze transaction data to detect suspicious activities and anomalies. Big Data analytics store and process large volumes of transaction and customer data for retrospective analysis and forensic investigations. This combination improves payment security and minimizes financial losses.

In conclusion, industry-specific applications of AI and Big Data are revolutionizing the retail sector, enhancing customer experiences, optimizing operations, and increasing profitability. These applications harness the power of AI to analyze vast datasets, predict consumer behavior, and improve decision-making. As the retail industry continues to evolve, AI and Big Data will remain pivotal in reshaping the future of retail.

AI-Driven Strategies in Finance and Banking:

The finance and banking sector is at the forefront of harnessing the transformative power of Artificial Intelligence (AI). These industry-specific applications are reshaping the landscape of financial services by enhancing efficiency, risk management, and customer experience. This section explores the intricate web of AI-driven strategies in finance and banking, emphasizing their profound impact on the industry.

1. Algorithmic Trading and Market Analysis

AI-driven algorithms have revolutionized trading strategies and market analysis (Cartea et al., 2015). Machine learning models analyze vast amounts of market data, news sentiment, and historical trends to identify trading opportunities and execute orders with minimal latency. AI-driven trading systems can adapt to changing market conditions and optimize trading strategies in real time.

The finance and banking industry has been revolutionized by the integration of Artificial Intelligence (AI) into its operations. One of the most significant applications of AI in this sector is in algorithmic trading and market analysis. This section explores the intricate landscape of AI-driven strategies in finance and banking, emphasizing their profound impact on trading and market dynamics.

Algorithmic Trading:

Algorithmic trading, also known as algo-trading or automated trading, leverages AI algorithms to execute trading strategies at speeds and frequencies impossible for human traders (Cartea et al., 2015). These AI-driven systems analyze vast amounts of market data, including price movements, trading volumes, news sentiment, and historical trends, to identify potential trading opportunities. Key aspects of AI-powered algorithmic trading include:

1. **High-Frequency Trading (HFT):** AI algorithms enable high-frequency traders to make split-second decisions and execute trades. These algorithms can analyze and process data at microsecond intervals, capitalizing on the smallest market inefficiencies.

2. **Market Microstructure Analysis:** AI models delve deep into the market microstructure, examining order book dynamics, trade execution patterns, and liquidity conditions. This analysis helps traders optimize their strategies for specific market conditions.

3. **Statistical Arbitrage:** AI-driven trading strategies employ statistical methods to identify pricing anomalies and arbitrage opportunities. These strategies are capable of identifying and exploiting market inefficiencies across various asset classes.

4. **Risk Management:** Advanced risk management techniques are integral to algorithmic trading systems. AI models continuously monitor and adjust trading positions to mitigate risk, prevent large losses, and optimize returns.

Market Analysis:

AI-driven market analysis goes beyond traditional methods by utilizing machine learning and deep learning algorithms to extract valuable insights from vast datasets (Lo, 2017). Key components of AI-powered market analysis include:

1. **Sentiment Analysis:** Natural language processing (NLP) algorithms analyze news articles, social media feeds, and other textual data sources to gauge market sentiment. Sentiment analysis helps traders understand market sentiment shifts and their potential impact on asset prices.

2. **Predictive Analytics:** Machine learning models are employed to make predictions about future market movements. These models consider a wide range of factors, including historical price data, economic indicators, and geopolitical events, to forecast market trends.

3. **Pattern Recognition:** AI algorithms excel at recognizing complex patterns in market data. They can identify technical chart patterns, trend reversals, and anomalies that may not be apparent to human analysts.

4. **Portfolio Optimization:** AI-driven portfolio optimization models help investors construct well-balanced portfolios that maximize returns while managing risk. These models consider factors such as correlation, volatility, and diversification.

Benefits and Challenges:

AI-driven strategies in finance and banking offer several benefits, including increased efficiency, reduced trading costs, enhanced risk management, and improved decision-making. However, they also pose challenges related to data quality, model transparency, regulatory compliance, and the potential for systemic risks.

In conclusion, AI-driven strategies in finance and banking, particularly in algorithmic trading and market analysis, have ushered in a new era of sophisticated trading and investment practices. These applications harness the power of AI to process massive datasets, identify trading opportunities, and make data-driven investment decisions, ultimately reshaping the landscape of financial markets.

II. Risk Assessment and Fraud Detection

AI plays a pivotal role in risk assessment and fraud detection (Deng et al., 2013). Machine learning models analyze transaction data, customer behavior, and historical patterns to identify potential fraud or anomalies. AI algorithms assess credit risk, monitor portfolio health, and calculate risk exposure, aiding in more informed lending decisions and risk management.

The finance and banking industry has experienced a paradigm shift in risk assessment and fraud detection through the integration of Artificial Intelligence (AI). AI-driven strategies have emerged as powerful tools in identifying and managing risks while also detecting fraudulent activities. This section explores the intricate landscape of AI-driven risk assessment and fraud detection in finance and banking, highlighting their profound impact on security and financial stability.

Risk Assessment:

AI plays a pivotal role in risk assessment within the financial sector (Deng et al., 2013). Machine learning models analyze vast datasets encompassing market data, customer profiles, transaction history, and macroeconomic indicators to evaluate credit risk, market risk, and operational risk. Key aspects of AI-driven risk assessment include:

1. **Credit Risk Analysis:** AI models assess the creditworthiness of individuals and businesses by analyzing credit histories, financial statements, and alternative data sources. These models provide more accurate credit scores, enabling lenders to make informed lending decisions and tailor loan terms.

2. **Market Risk Management:** AI algorithms analyze market data to assess exposure to market volatility and potential losses. Real-time monitoring of market conditions enables institutions to react swiftly to adverse developments, reducing the impact of market risks.

3. **Operational Risk Mitigation:** AI-driven strategies monitor internal processes, transaction data, and employee behavior to identify and mitigate operational risks. Proactive risk management prevents system failures, errors, and fraud, preserving the institution's reputation and financial stability.

4. **Portfolio Risk Optimization:** AI models optimize investment portfolios by considering factors such as asset correlation, volatility, and diversification. These models help investors construct portfolios that maximize returns while managing risk.

Fraud Detection:

AI is a formidable weapon against fraudulent activities in finance and banking (Sahin et al., 2018). Machine learning models analyze transaction data, customer behavior, and historical patterns to detect anomalies and potential fraud. Key aspects of AI-driven fraud detection include:

1. **Anomaly Detection:** AI algorithms continuously monitor transaction data to identify unusual patterns or outliers. Deviations from established behavioral norms trigger alerts, enabling rapid intervention to prevent fraud.
2. **Pattern Recognition:** AI models excel at recognizing complex patterns in transaction data. They can detect suspicious trends, irregular spending behavior, and coordinated attacks that may elude human analysts.
3. **Predictive Analytics:** AI-driven fraud detection uses predictive models to assess the likelihood of fraudulent activities. These models consider a wide range of factors, including historical fraud patterns and emerging threats.
4. **Real-time Monitoring:** AI systems provide real-time monitoring of transactions, allowing institutions to detect and block fraudulent activities as they occur. This immediate response reduces financial losses and protects customers.

Benefits and Challenges:

AI-driven strategies in risk assessment and fraud detection offer numerous benefits, including enhanced accuracy, faster detection, reduced false positives, and improved customer trust. However, they also pose challenges related to data privacy, model interpretability, regulatory compliance, and adversarial attacks.

In conclusion, AI-driven strategies in finance and banking have redefined risk assessment and fraud detection. These applications leverage the power of AI to process massive datasets, evaluate risks, and detect fraudulent activities, ultimately bolstering security and maintaining financial stability in the industry.

III. Customer Relationship Management (CRM)

AI-driven CRM systems enhance customer experience and relationship management (Verhoef et al., 2017). These systems analyze customer data, transaction history, and communication patterns to provide personalized recommendations and tailored financial services. Chatbots and virtual assistants powered by AI provide 24/7 customer support, answering queries and assisting with routine transactions.

In the finance and banking industry, Customer Relationship Management (CRM) has undergone a profound transformation with the integration of Artificial Intelligence (AI). AI-driven CRM strategies have become pivotal in understanding, engaging, and retaining customers in this highly competitive sector. This section explores the intricate landscape of AI-driven CRM in finance and banking, emphasizing its profound impact on customer engagement and satisfaction.

The Role of AI in CRM:

AI is reshaping CRM strategies by enabling financial institutions to collect, analyze, and utilize vast amounts of customer data more effectively (Verhoef et al., 2017). AI-driven CRM encompasses various aspects, including:

1. **Data Collection and Integration:** AI systems collect and integrate customer data from multiple sources, such as transaction history, online interactions, social media, and communication channels. This consolidated data forms a comprehensive view of each customer.

2. **Personalization:** AI algorithms analyze customer data to provide personalized product recommendations, marketing messages, and offers. Personalization enhances customer engagement and drives cross-selling and upselling opportunities.

3. **Chatbots and Virtual Assistants:** AI-powered chatbots and virtual assistants provide 24/7 customer support, answering

queries, assisting with routine transactions, and even guiding customers through complex financial processes.

4. **Predictive Analytics:** AI models employ predictive analytics to forecast customer behavior, such as the likelihood of churning or the potential for high-value purchases. This enables proactive customer retention efforts.

5. **Sentiment Analysis:** Natural language processing (NLP) algorithms analyze customer feedback, social media mentions, and online reviews to gauge sentiment. Financial institutions can respond to customer concerns and feedback promptly, improving overall satisfaction.

Benefits of AI-Driven CRM:

AI-driven CRM in finance and banking offers several significant advantages:

1. **Enhanced Customer Engagement:** Personalized interactions and recommendations based on AI analysis lead to higher customer engagement and satisfaction.

2. **Efficient Operations:** AI-powered chatbots and virtual assistants reduce the workload on customer service teams, allowing for more efficient operations and cost savings.

3. **Cross-Selling and Upselling:** Personalized product recommendations drive cross-selling and upselling opportunities, increasing revenue.

4. **Churn Reduction:** Predictive analytics help identify customers at risk of churning, allowing for targeted retention efforts.

5. **Data-Driven Decision-Making:** AI-driven insights inform strategic decision-making by providing a deep understanding of customer preferences and behaviors.

Challenges and Considerations:

Despite the many advantages of AI-driven CRM, there are also challenges and considerations:

1. **Data Privacy and Security:** Handling sensitive customer data requires stringent data privacy and security measures to protect against breaches and regulatory non-compliance.
2. **Model Transparency:** Ensuring AI models are transparent and interpretable is essential for building trust with customers and regulators.
3. **Regulatory Compliance:** Financial institutions must navigate complex regulatory frameworks when implementing AI in CRM to ensure compliance with data protection and consumer protection laws.

In conclusion, AI-driven CRM is revolutionizing customer interactions in the finance and banking sector. These applications harness the power of AI to collect and analyze vast datasets, enabling personalized customer experiences, enhanced engagement, and more efficient operations. As the industry continues to evolve, AI-driven CRM will remain central to maintaining and strengthening customer relationships.

IV. Regulatory Compliance and Reporting

AI facilitates regulatory compliance and reporting in the finance sector (Brear et al., 2018). AI algorithms automatically detect and report suspicious activities, ensuring adherence to anti-money laundering (AML) and know-your-customer (KYC) regulations. Big Data analytics handle the storage and retrieval of vast amounts of transaction and compliance data, facilitating audits and reporting.

The increasing complexity of regulatory frameworks has compelled institutions to explore innovative solutions for compliance and reporting. Artificial Intelligence (AI)-driven strategies have emerged as powerful tools for navigating this regulatory landscape, offering efficient ways to ensure adherence to standards while optimizing reporting processes. This section explores the intricate landscape of AI-driven strategies in regulatory compliance and reporting within finance and banking, emphasizing their profound impact on risk management and operational efficiency.

The Role of AI in Regulatory Compliance and Reporting:

AI is playing a pivotal role in helping financial institutions manage the intricate web of regulatory requirements. These AI-driven strategies encompass various aspects, including:

1. **Data Management and Integration:** AI systems enable financial institutions to collect, aggregate, and integrate data from disparate sources, including transaction records, customer information, and regulatory filings. This consolidation ensures that all relevant data is readily accessible for compliance purposes.

2. **Real-Time Monitoring:** AI algorithms provide real-time monitoring of transactions, customer activities, and market conditions. These systems can detect irregularities, suspicious transactions, or potential compliance violations as they occur, allowing for immediate intervention.

3. **Predictive Analytics:** AI models employ predictive analytics to forecast potential compliance issues or emerging risks. By analyzing historical data and identifying patterns, financial institutions can anticipate compliance challenges and proactively address them.

4. **Automation of Reporting:** AI-driven solutions automate the process of preparing and generating regulatory reports. These systems can extract relevant data, generate required reports, and ensure accuracy while reducing the time and resources required for manual reporting.

5. **Anti-Money Laundering (AML) and Know Your Customer (KYC):** AI-powered solutions can enhance AML and KYC processes by analyzing customer data, transaction patterns, and

screening against watchlists. Suspicious activities or customers can be flagged for further investigation.

Benefits of AI-Driven Compliance and Reporting:

AI-driven strategies in regulatory compliance and reporting offer several significant advantages:

1. **Efficiency:** Automation and real-time monitoring streamline compliance processes, reducing the time and effort required for reporting.
2. **Accuracy:** AI systems minimize errors in reporting by automating data collection and validation.
3. **Risk Mitigation:** Predictive analytics and real-time monitoring enable financial institutions to identify and mitigate compliance risks promptly.
4. **Cost Reduction:** Automation reduces operational costs associated with manual reporting and compliance activities.
5. **Adaptability:** AI systems can adapt to changing regulatory requirements, ensuring that financial institutions remain compliant as regulations evolve.

Challenges and Considerations:

Despite the benefits, AI-driven compliance and reporting also present challenges and considerations:

1. **Data Privacy and Security:** Handling sensitive customer and financial data requires robust data privacy and security measures to prevent breaches and regulatory violations.
2. **Model Interpretability:** Ensuring AI models used for compliance and reporting are transparent and interpretable is crucial for compliance officers, regulators, and auditors.

3. **Regulatory Compliance:** Financial institutions must ensure that AI solutions used for compliance adhere to regulatory standards and guidelines.

In conclusion, AI-driven strategies in regulatory compliance and reporting are transforming the finance and banking sector by providing efficient and effective tools to manage complex regulatory requirements. These applications leverage the power of AI to automate reporting processes, enhance monitoring, and mitigate compliance risks, ultimately improving operational efficiency and risk management in the industry.

V. Credit Scoring and Loan Approval

AI-driven credit scoring models enhance the loan approval process (Biblioteca et al., 2018). Machine learning models analyze credit history, income, and alternative data sources to assess creditworthiness. These models provide more accurate credit scores, enabling financial institutions to make informed lending decisions and offer customized loan terms.

The finance and banking sector has witnessed a transformative shift in credit scoring and loan approval processes through the integration of Artificial Intelligence (AI). AI-driven strategies are revolutionizing how financial institutions assess creditworthiness, make lending decisions, and tailor loan terms. This section explores the intricate landscape of AI-driven credit scoring and loan approval in finance and banking, emphasizing their profound impact on risk management and customer satisfaction.

The Role of AI in Credit Scoring and Loan Approval:

AI is playing a pivotal role in reshaping credit scoring and loan approval processes. These AI-driven strategies encompass various aspects, including:

1. **Data Integration:** AI systems aggregate and integrate diverse data sources, such as credit histories, financial statements, income

records, and alternative data (e.g., social media activity and utility payments). This comprehensive data collection ensures a holistic view of an applicant's financial profile.

2. **Predictive Modeling:** Machine learning models analyze historical data to predict credit risk more accurately. These models consider various factors, such as payment history, outstanding debt, credit utilization, and behavior trends, to assess an applicant's creditworthiness.

3. **Alternative Data:** AI-driven credit scoring incorporates alternative data sources to assess individuals with limited credit histories or no traditional credit profiles. This inclusivity benefits underserved populations and enhances financial inclusion.

4. **Real-time Analysis:** AI algorithms provide real-time analysis of applicant data, enabling faster and more informed lending decisions. Financial institutions can respond swiftly to loan applications, reducing the time-to-approval.

5. **Customization:** AI systems allow financial institutions to tailor loan terms and interest rates based on the applicant's risk profile. Personalized offers improve customer satisfaction and enhance the likelihood of loan acceptance.

Benefits of AI-Driven Credit Scoring and Loan Approval:

AI-driven strategies in credit scoring and loan approval offer several significant advantages:

1. **Accuracy:** AI models provide more accurate credit scores and risk assessments, reducing the likelihood of defaults and loan losses.

2. **Efficiency:** Automation streamlines loan approval processes, reducing the time and effort required for manual credit assessments.

3. **Inclusivity:** Incorporating alternative data sources widens access to credit, benefiting individuals with limited credit histories or those underserved by traditional credit scoring methods.
4. **Personalization:** AI enables personalized loan offers, improving customer experience and satisfaction.
5. **Risk Mitigation:** Advanced risk assessment helps financial institutions make informed lending decisions, reducing the potential for non-performing loans.

Challenges and Considerations:

Despite the benefits, AI-driven credit scoring and loan approval also present challenges and considerations:

1. **Data Privacy:** Handling sensitive financial and personal data necessitates robust data privacy and security measures to protect against breaches and regulatory violations.
2. **Model Transparency:** Ensuring AI models used for credit scoring are transparent and interpretable is crucial for both regulators and applicants.
3. **Fairness and Bias:** AI models must be carefully designed to avoid bias and discrimination, ensuring fair lending practices.

AI-driven strategies in credit scoring and loan approval are transforming the finance and banking sector by providing more accurate, efficient, and inclusive ways to assess creditworthiness and make lending decisions. These applications leverage the power of AI to automate processes, enhance risk assessment, and offer tailored financial solutions, ultimately reshaping the landscape of credit and lending in the industry.

In conclusion, industry-specific applications of AI-driven strategies are redefining the finance and banking sector, offering unparalleled opportunities for improved decision-making, risk management, and customer engagement. These applications leverage the power of AI to analyze massive datasets, optimize financial processes, and enhance regulatory compliance. As the financial industry continues to evolve, AI-driven strategies will remain pivotal in shaping the future of finance and banking.

Chapter 7: Overcoming Challenges and Limitations

The rapid advancement of Artificial Intelligence (AI) and Big Data technologies has ushered in transformative possibilities across various industries. However, this progress has not been without its challenges and limitations. This section explores the multifaceted landscape of addressing these obstacles while striving for the full realization of AI and Big Data's potential.

Challenges in AI and Big Data:

Data Privacy and Security:

As the volume of data collected and analyzed increases, ensuring the privacy and security of sensitive information becomes paramount (Davenport & Harris, 2007). Data breaches, cyberattacks, and unauthorized access pose significant risks. Addressing these challenges requires robust encryption, access controls, and compliance with data protection regulations.

The growth of data in the digital age, coupled with the pervasive use of Artificial Intelligence (AI) and Big Data analytics, has brought unprecedented opportunities and challenges, none more significant than those related to data privacy and security. This section delves into the multifaceted landscape of overcoming challenges and limitations associated with data privacy and security in AI and Big Data, emphasizing the critical role of safeguarding sensitive information in an interconnected world.

Challenges in Data Privacy and Security:

1. **Data Breaches and Unauthorized Access:** The rising number of data breaches and incidents of unauthorized access pose significant threats (Cavoukian & Castro, 2016). Malicious actors seek to exploit vulnerabilities in systems to gain unauthorized access to sensitive data.

2. **Data Ownership and Consent:** The ownership and consent regarding personal data are often unclear, leading to ethical and legal dilemmas (Mittelstadt et al., 2016). Users may not fully understand how their data is used or may not have control over its dissemination.

3. **Regulatory Compliance:** Evolving data protection regulations, such as the General Data Protection Regulation (GDPR) and the California Consumer Privacy Act (CCPA), pose compliance challenges (Greenleaf & Cottier, 2019). Organizations must navigate complex legal requirements.

4. **Data Anonymization and De-identification:** Traditional methods of data anonymization may not be foolproof (Ohm, 2010). Re-identification attacks can compromise the privacy of individuals, even in supposedly anonymized datasets.

Strategies for Overcoming Challenges:

1. **Privacy by Design:** Adopting a "Privacy by Design" approach ensures that privacy considerations are integrated into every stage of AI and Big Data projects (Cavoukian, 2009). This includes anonymizing data, implementing access controls, and minimizing data collection.

2. **Encryption and Secure Data Storage:** Encrypting data both in transit and at rest provides a fundamental layer of security

(Schneier, 1996). Strong encryption algorithms and secure storage solutions protect data from unauthorized access.

3. **User Education and Consent:** Ensuring that users are well-informed about data usage and obtaining explicit consent is vital (Kosta et al., 2017). Transparency regarding data collection practices builds trust and complies with regulations.

4. **Continuous Monitoring and Threat Detection:** Implementing robust monitoring and threat detection mechanisms helps identify and respond to security incidents promptly (Kumar & Spafford, 2004). AI-based anomaly detection systems can detect suspicious activities.

5. **Data Minimization:** Collecting only the data necessary for a specific purpose reduces the risk associated with data breaches (Greenleaf, 2017). Organizations should adhere to the principle of collecting "just enough" data.

Ethical Considerations:

1. **Algorithmic Fairness:** Ensuring fairness in AI algorithms is essential (Diakopoulos et al., 2016). Bias in algorithms can perpetuate discriminatory outcomes, particularly when using historical data.

2. **Algorithmic Transparency:** Transparency and explainability in AI models are crucial (Gunning, 2017). Understanding how AI systems make decisions is essential for accountability and trust.

As AI and Big Data continue to reshape industries and societies, addressing the challenges and limitations related to data privacy and security becomes paramount. Privacy by design, encryption, user education, and continuous monitoring are essential strategies. Ethical considerations, such as algorithmic fairness and transparency, further enhance responsible data handling. In an interconnected world, safeguarding sensitive information is not merely a legal requirement but a moral obligation.

Bias and Fairness:

AI algorithms can inherit biases present in training data, leading to discriminatory outcomes (Barocas et al., 2019). Ensuring fairness in AI models is a critical challenge. Mitigating bias requires transparent algorithms, diverse training datasets, and continuous monitoring.

In the era of Artificial Intelligence (AI) and Big Data analytics, addressing bias and ensuring fairness has emerged as a central concern. These technologies, while offering transformative potential, can inadvertently perpetuate and exacerbate societal biases. This section explores the multifaceted landscape of overcoming challenges and limitations related to bias and fairness in AI and Big Data, emphasizing the critical importance of mitigating discrimination and promoting ethical AI practices.

Challenges in Bias and Fairness:

1. **Data Bias:** Biased training data can result in AI systems that reflect historical inequalities (Barocas et al., 2019). When data contains pre-existing biases, AI models may perpetuate these biases in their predictions.

2. **Algorithmic Bias:** The algorithms themselves can introduce bias based on their design and optimization objectives (Diakopoulos et al., 2016). This bias may manifest as discriminatory outcomes in decision-making.

3. **Lack of Diversity:** The lack of diversity in AI development teams can lead to cultural and demographic blind spots (Crawford & Calo, 2016). This can result in biased assumptions and narrow perspectives during algorithm development.

4. **Transparency and Explainability:** Ensuring transparency and explainability in AI systems is challenging (Gunning, 2017). Many AI models are complex "black boxes," making it difficult to understand their decision-making processes.

Strategies for Overcoming Bias and Ensuring Fairness:

1. **Diverse Data:** Ensuring diverse and representative training data is essential (Hajian et al., 2016). This includes actively seeking data from underrepresented groups to reduce bias in algorithms.
2. **Bias Mitigation Techniques:** Employing bias mitigation techniques, such as re-weighting training data or modifying algorithms, can help reduce bias (Hardt et al., 2016).
3. **Algorithmic Auditing:** Conducting audits of AI systems to assess their fairness and impact is crucial (Barocas et al., 2019). These audits can identify bias and discriminatory patterns.
4. **Fairness Metrics:** Developing fairness metrics and evaluation criteria can help quantify and measure bias in AI systems (Dwork et al., 2012). These metrics provide a basis for assessing and improving fairness.
5. **Ethical AI Principles:** Adhering to ethical AI principles and guidelines, such as those outlined by organizations like the Partnership on AI, promotes responsible AI development (Partnership on AI, 2017).

Ethical Considerations:

1. **Algorithmic Transparency:** Ensuring transparency and explainability in AI models is vital (Gunning, 2017). Understanding how AI systems make decisions is essential for accountability and trust.
2. **Accountability:** Establishing clear lines of accountability for AI decisions and outcomes is essential (Jobin et al., 2019). This includes identifying who is responsible for AI system behavior.

Bias and fairness in AI and Big Data are pivotal ethical considerations that must be addressed to ensure responsible and equitable deployment of these technologies. By addressing data and algorithmic biases, promoting diverse development teams, and adhering to ethical AI principles, organizations can mitigate discrimination and work toward the development of AI systems that benefit all members of society.

Interoperability and Integration:

Integrating AI and Big Data solutions into existing systems can be complex (Provost & Fawcett, 2013). Ensuring seamless interoperability with legacy systems and data sources is a challenge that organizations must address for successful implementation.

The proliferation of Artificial Intelligence (AI) and Big Data technologies has brought about a wealth of possibilities for organizations across diverse sectors. However, along with the potential benefits, there are significant challenges and limitations, particularly concerning the interoperability and integration of these technologies. This section explores the multifaceted landscape of overcoming challenges related to interoperability and integration in AI and Big Data, emphasizing their critical role in achieving seamless data-driven solutions.

Challenges in Interoperability and Integration:

1. **Diverse Data Sources:** Organizations often deal with heterogeneous data sources that vary in format, structure, and quality (Bertino et al., 2011). These disparities make it challenging to integrate data effectively.

2. **Legacy Systems:** Many organizations rely on legacy systems that may not be easily compatible with modern AI and Big Data solutions (Vasudevan & Zadeh, 2018). Integrating these systems into a unified data ecosystem can be complex.

3. **Silos and Fragmentation:** Data silos, where data is isolated within departments or systems, hinder cross-functional collaboration (Archer et al., 2008). Silos can lead to redundancy and inefficiency.

4. **Data Governance:** Ensuring data quality, consistency, and governance across integrated systems is a persistent challenge (Dhar, 2013). Data governance frameworks must be established.

Strategies for Overcoming Interoperability and Integration Challenges:

1. **Data Standardization:** Standardizing data formats, naming conventions, and metadata across systems facilitates interoperability (Vasudevan & Zadeh, 2018). This ensures that data can be easily exchanged and integrated.

2. **APIs and Middleware:** Implementing Application Programming Interfaces (APIs) and middleware solutions can bridge the gap between disparate systems (Cugola & Margara, 2012). These technologies enable data flow between applications.

3. **Cloud-Based Solutions:** Leveraging cloud platforms for data storage and processing offers scalability and flexibility (Gubbi et al., 2013). Cloud services often provide built-in tools for data integration.

4. **Master Data Management (MDM):** Implementing MDM solutions helps organizations maintain consistent and accurate master data across systems (Redman, 2008). MDM improves data quality and integration.

5. **Data Integration Platforms:** Utilizing data integration platforms and tools can simplify the process of connecting and harmonizing data from diverse sources (Inmon et al., 2016).

Ethical Considerations:

1. **Data Privacy and Security:** Integrating data from various sources requires robust data privacy and security measures to protect sensitive information (Schneier, 1996). Ensuring compliance with data protection regulations is essential.

2. **Ethical Data Usage:** Organizations must establish ethical guidelines for data usage when integrating sensitive or personal data (Floridi et al., 2018). Data should be used in ways that respect individual privacy and consent.

Interoperability and integration are pivotal challenges in the successful deployment of AI and Big Data solutions. By standardizing data, leveraging APIs and middleware, and embracing cloud-based technologies, organizations can unlock the full potential of their data assets. Ethical considerations, such as data privacy and responsible data usage, must remain at the forefront of these efforts to ensure that integration efforts align with ethical and legal standards.

Data Quality:

The accuracy and reliability of data used for AI and Big Data analytics are fundamental to their effectiveness (Batini et al., 2009). Data cleansing, validation, and quality assurance processes are essential to overcome this limitation.

In the realm of Artificial Intelligence (AI) and Big Data, the quality of data plays a paramount role in the success of analytics and decision-making processes. However, ensuring data quality in this era of massive data volumes and diversity poses a significant challenge. This section explores the multifaceted landscape of overcoming challenges related to data quality in AI and Big Data, highlighting the importance of high-quality data for accurate insights and meaningful outcomes.

Challenges in Data Quality:

1. **Volume and Velocity:** The sheer volume and velocity of data generated today can overwhelm traditional data quality measures (Laney, 2001). Rapid data accumulation may lead to inaccuracies and inconsistencies.
2. **Data Variety:** Big Data encompasses diverse data types, including structured, semi-structured, and unstructured data (Manyika et al., 2011). Managing data variety is challenging, as different formats require tailored quality checks.
3. **Data Cleansing:** Identifying and rectifying errors and inconsistencies in Big Data can be complex and resource-intensive (Batini et al., 2009). Manual data cleansing efforts may not scale effectively.

4. **Data Integration:** Integrating data from disparate sources may introduce quality issues, such as schema conflicts and data mapping challenges (Dhar, 2013). Maintaining consistency is a persistent challenge.

Strategies for Overcoming Data Quality Challenges:

1. **Data Quality Assessment:** Implementing data quality assessment processes is essential (Batini et al., 2009). This involves profiling data, detecting anomalies, and measuring data quality using relevant metrics.
2. **Data Governance:** Establishing data governance frameworks ensures data quality and consistency (Dhar, 2013). This includes data lineage, metadata management, and data stewardship practices.
3. **Data Validation and Cleansing Tools:** Leveraging data validation and cleansing tools automates the identification and correction of data errors (Wang et al., 2011). These tools enhance efficiency.
4. **Master Data Management (MDM):** Implementing MDM solutions helps organizations maintain consistent and accurate master data across systems (Redman, 2008). MDM improves data quality and integration.
5. **Data Quality Monitoring:** Continuous monitoring of data quality is crucial (Lee et al., 2002). Automated monitoring tools can alert organizations to deviations from established data quality standards.

Ethical Considerations:

1. **Data Privacy and Security:** Data quality efforts must align with data privacy and security regulations (Floridi et al., 2018). Protecting sensitive information is paramount.

2. **Ethical Data Usage:** Organizations must ensure that data quality measures align with ethical data usage principles (Floridi et al., 2018). Data should be used responsibly and ethically.

Conclusion:

Data quality remains a fundamental challenge in the realm of AI and Big Data analytics. Accurate insights and meaningful outcomes are contingent on the reliability and consistency of data. By implementing data quality assessment processes, governance frameworks, automation tools, and continuous monitoring, organizations can overcome data quality challenges and harness the full potential of AI and Big Data for informed decision-making.

Strategies for Overcoming Challenges:

Ethical Guidelines and Regulation:

Establishing ethical guidelines and regulatory frameworks for AI and Big Data usage is essential (Floridi et al., 2018). Regulations such as the General Data Protection Regulation (GDPR) and ethical AI principles provide a foundation for responsible deployment.

In the rapidly evolving landscape of Artificial Intelligence (AI) and Big Data, addressing ethical concerns and ensuring responsible use of these technologies are of paramount importance. Ethical challenges such as bias, data privacy, and transparency necessitate the establishment of clear ethical guidelines and regulatory frameworks. This section explores the multifaceted landscape of strategies for overcoming challenges through ethical guidelines and regulation in AI and Big Data, emphasizing their critical role in promoting ethical AI practices.

The Role of Ethical Challenges:

1. **Bias and Fairness:** AI systems can inadvertently perpetuate biases present in training data (Barocas et al., 2019). Ethical guidelines and regulations aim to mitigate bias and ensure fair decision-making.

2. **Data Privacy and Security:** Protecting individuals' data privacy and ensuring the security of sensitive information are ethical imperatives (Floridi et al., 2018). Regulations provide a framework for data protection.

3. **Transparency and Accountability:** Ensuring transparency in AI decision-making processes and holding organizations accountable for their actions are ethical considerations (Gunning, 2017). Ethical guidelines promote transparency and accountability.

Strategies for Ethical Guidelines and Regulation:

1. **Development of Ethical Frameworks:** Establishing ethical frameworks and guidelines for AI development and deployment is crucial (Floridi et al., 2018). These frameworks should encompass principles such as fairness, transparency, and accountability.

2. **Regulatory Compliance:** Governments and regulatory bodies can enact laws and regulations that govern the use of AI and Big Data (Partnoy & Rasmussen, 2019). For example, the General Data Protection Regulation (GDPR) addresses data privacy.

3. **Industry Self-Regulation:** Industry associations and organizations can develop self-regulatory codes of conduct to ensure ethical practices among their members (Jobin et al., 2019). These codes align with broader ethical principles.

4. **Ethical Impact Assessments:** Conducting ethical impact assessments before deploying AI systems helps identify and mitigate potential ethical risks (Floridi et al., 2018). These assessments ensure responsible AI development.

5. **Transparency and Explainability Standards:** Establishing standards for AI system transparency and explainability promotes accountability (Gunning, 2017). AI systems should be designed to provide understandable explanations for their decisions.

Ethical Considerations:

1. **Collaborative Responsibility:** Ethical guidelines emphasize shared responsibility among stakeholders, including developers, organizations, regulators, and users (Jobin et al., 2019). Collaborative efforts are essential.

2. **Balancing Innovation and Ethics:** Striking a balance between technological innovation and ethical considerations is challenging (Floridi et al., 2018). Ethical guidelines seek to ensure responsible innovation.

Ethical guidelines and regulatory frameworks are essential strategies for addressing challenges and ensuring the responsible use of AI and Big Data technologies. By developing ethical frameworks, enacting regulations, and promoting industry self-regulation, organizations can navigate the ethical landscape while continuing to harness the transformative power of AI and Big Data for societal benefit.

Transparency and Explainability:

Ensuring the transparency and explainability of AI algorithms is crucial (Diakopoulos et al., 2016). Organizations can employ interpretable models, documentation, and audit trails to increase transparency.

In the age of Artificial Intelligence (AI) and Big Data, the opacity of AI systems has raised concerns about their decision-making processes. To address these concerns and build trust, strategies for transparency and explainability are crucial. This section explores the multifaceted landscape of strategies for overcoming challenges through transparency and explainability in AI and Big Data, emphasizing their role in promoting responsible and accountable AI practices.

The Role of Transparency and Explainability:

1. **Opaque AI Decisions:** Many AI models, particularly deep learning models, are often viewed as "black boxes" due to their complexity (Gunning, 2017). Understanding their decision-making processes is challenging.

2. **Accountability and Trust:** Transparency and explainability are essential for holding AI systems accountable for their actions (Jobin et al., 2019). Users and stakeholders must trust AI decisions.

3. **Bias and Fairness:** Transparency can help identify and rectify biases in AI systems, ensuring fairness (Barocas et al., 2019). Explainability aids in understanding how bias may occur.

Strategies for Transparency and Explainability:

1. **Interpretable Models:** Developing AI models that are inherently interpretable, such as decision trees or linear regression, can enhance transparency (Lipton, 2016). These models offer clearer insights into decision logic.

2. **Model Visualization:** Visualizing model outputs, feature importance, and decision paths can make AI decisions more understandable (Chen et al., 2018). Visualization tools aid transparency.

3. **Explainable AI (XAI) Techniques:** Employing XAI techniques, such as LIME (Local Interpretable Model-Agnostic Explanations) or SHAP (SHapley Additive exPlanations), can provide post-hoc explanations of AI model predictions (Ribeiro et al., 2016; Lundberg & Lee, 2017).

4. **Transparency Reports:** Organizations can produce transparency reports that outline their AI systems' data sources, training processes, and decision-making logic (Diakopoulos et al., 2016). These reports enhance accountability.

5. **Algorithmic Auditing:** Conducting algorithmic audits to assess the fairness and transparency of AI systems can identify issues and drive improvements (Barocas et al., 2019).

Ethical Considerations:

1. **Balancing Transparency and Complexity:** Striking a balance between transparency and the complexity of AI models is challenging (Gunning, 2017). Some models may require trade-offs between interpretability and performance.
2. **Data Privacy:** Ensuring that transparency efforts do not compromise data privacy is crucial (Floridi et al., 2018). Sensitive information should not be disclosed.

Transparency and explainability are integral strategies for overcoming challenges in AI and Big Data. By developing interpretable models, visualization tools, and XAI techniques, organizations can demystify AI decision-making processes, foster trust, and mitigate bias. Ethical considerations, such as data privacy and the complexity of AI models, must be carefully navigated to ensure responsible and accountable AI practices.

Diverse Data Sources:

Addressing bias requires diversifying training datasets and using representative data (O'Neil, 2016). Organizations should actively seek data from underrepresented groups and continuously monitor model outcomes for fairness.

In the era of Big Data and Artificial Intelligence (AI), organizations face the challenge of harnessing valuable insights from a myriad of diverse data sources. These sources encompass structured, semi-structured, and unstructured data, each with its unique characteristics and complexities. This section delves into strategies for overcoming challenges posed by diverse data sources in AI and Big Data, emphasizing the importance of data integration and harmonization.

The Complexity of Diverse Data Sources:

1. **Heterogeneity:** Diverse data sources come in various formats, structures, and languages (Manyika et al., 2011). This heterogeneity makes integration and analysis complex.

2. **Data Volume:** The sheer volume of data generated from diverse sources can be overwhelming (Chen et al., 2014). Managing and processing such vast amounts of data require robust strategies.

3. **Data Velocity:** Data from different sources may arrive at varying speeds, from real-time streaming to batch updates (Gubbi et al., 2013). Handling this velocity is crucial.

Strategies for Overcoming Challenges:

1. **Data Standardization:** Standardizing data formats, naming conventions, and metadata across diverse sources is fundamental (Manyika et al., 2011). This facilitates seamless integration and ensures data consistency.

2. **Data Integration Platforms:** Utilizing data integration platforms and tools streamlines the process of connecting and harmonizing data from disparate sources (Inmon et al., 2016). These platforms enable data flow and transformation.

3. **Data Transformation:** Employing data transformation techniques to convert data into a common format or structure aids integration (Rahm & Do, 2000). ETL (Extract, Transform, Load) processes are valuable in this regard.

4. **Master Data Management (MDM):** Implementing MDM solutions helps organizations maintain consistent and accurate master data across systems (Redman, 2008). MDM improves data quality and integration.

5. **Data Catalogs:** Creating data catalogs that document the metadata and lineage of diverse data sources enhances discoverability and usability (Mandler et al., 2016).

Ethical Considerations:

1. **Data Privacy:** Integrating diverse data sources should not compromise data privacy (Floridi et al., 2018). Sensitive information must be protected and anonymized when necessary.
2. **Ethical Data Usage:** Ethical guidelines must govern the use of data from diverse sources (Floridi et al., 2018). Data should be employed in ways that respect individual privacy and consent.

Diverse data sources offer immense potential for gaining valuable insights and making data-driven decisions in AI and Big Data applications. However, the complexity of these sources necessitates effective strategies for integration and harmonization. By standardizing data, utilizing integration platforms, implementing transformation processes, and adhering to ethical considerations, organizations can unlock the full potential of diverse data sources while maintaining data quality and privacy.

Cybersecurity Measures:

Implementing robust cybersecurity measures, including encryption, intrusion detection, and access controls, is vital to protect data (Scarfone et al., 2008). Regular security audits and penetration testing can identify vulnerabilities.

In the area of Artificial Intelligence (AI) and Big Data, the significance of cybersecurity measures cannot be overstated. The increasing volume and complexity of data, coupled with the rapid growth of AI applications, present significant cybersecurity challenges. This section explores the multifaceted landscape of strategies for overcoming challenges through cybersecurity measures in AI and Big Data, emphasizing the importance of safeguarding data and systems.

The Evolving Cybersecurity Landscape:

1. **Data Vulnerabilities:** The vast amounts of sensitive data in AI and Big Data environments make them attractive targets for cyberattacks (Scarfone et al., 2019). Data breaches can lead to severe consequences.

2. **AI-Driven Attacks:** AI can be weaponized for cyberattacks, including the generation of highly convincing phishing emails and automated attacks (Gavai et al., 2019). Defending against AI-driven threats is essential.

3. **IoT and Edge Devices:** The proliferation of Internet of Things (IoT) and edge devices introduces additional attack surfaces and vulnerabilities (Zheng et al., 2015). Securing these devices is challenging.

Strategies for Cybersecurity Measures:

1. **Data Encryption:** Encrypting data both at rest and in transit helps protect sensitive information from unauthorized access (Scarfone et al., 2019). Strong encryption algorithms are essential.

2. **Access Control:** Implementing robust access control mechanisms ensures that only authorized users can access data and systems (Bertino et al., 2018). Role-based access control is commonly employed.

3. **Anomaly Detection:** Employing machine learning-based anomaly detection systems can identify unusual patterns indicative of cyberattacks (Gavai et al., 2019). These systems enable early threat detection.

4. **Secure Development Practices:** Following secure coding practices during the development of AI and Big Data applications helps prevent vulnerabilities (Zheng et al., 2015). Regular code audits and testing are crucial.

5. **Incident Response Plans:** Developing comprehensive incident response plans and conducting drills ensures a rapid and effective response to cyber incidents (Scarfone et al., 2019). This minimizes damage.

Ethical Considerations:

1. **Data Privacy:** Cybersecurity measures must align with data privacy regulations (Floridi et al., 2018). Protecting personal and sensitive data is paramount.
2. **Ethical Use of AI:** Organizations must ensure that AI is used ethically in cybersecurity, avoiding harmful or malicious applications (Floridi et al., 2018).

Cybersecurity measures are indispensable in the AI and Big Data landscape to safeguard sensitive data, mitigate cyber threats, and protect the integrity of systems. By implementing robust encryption, access control, anomaly detection, secure development practices, and incident response plans, organizations can fortify their defenses against evolving cyber threats. Ethical considerations, including data privacy and responsible AI use, must be central to these efforts.

Data Governance:

Establishing data governance frameworks ensures data quality and consistency (Dhar, 2013). This includes data lineage, metadata management, and data stewardship practices.

In the era of Big Data and Artificial Intelligence (AI), the effective management and governance of data have become pivotal for organizations seeking to harness its transformative potential. Data governance encompasses a set of practices, policies, and standards aimed at ensuring data quality, integrity, and compliance. This section explores the multifaceted landscape of strategies for overcoming challenges through data governance in AI and Big Data, emphasizing the importance of establishing a robust data governance framework.

The Significance of Data Governance:

1. **Data Proliferation:** The exponential growth of data sources and volumes can lead to data chaos without proper governance (Manyika et al., 2011). Managing this proliferation is essential.

2. **Data Quality:** Ensuring data quality is a fundamental challenge (Batini et al., 2009). Inaccurate or inconsistent data can lead to erroneous AI and Big Data insights.

3. **Compliance and Regulation:** Adhering to data privacy and security regulations, such as GDPR, requires meticulous data governance (Floridi et al., 2018). Non-compliance can result in severe penalties.

Strategies for Data Governance:

1. **Data Governance Framework:** Establishing a formal data governance framework with defined roles, responsibilities, and policies is fundamental (Redman, 2008). This framework provides a structure for governance efforts.

2. **Data Quality Assurance:** Implementing data quality assessment processes, including data profiling and cleansing, ensures data accuracy (Batini et al., 2009). Data quality should be monitored continuously.

3. **Metadata Management:** Managing metadata, which provides information about data assets, facilitates data discovery and lineage tracking (Mandler et al., 2016). Metadata catalogs are valuable tools.

4. **Data Stewardship:** Appointing data stewards responsible for data assets and their quality promotes accountability (Dhar, 2013). Stewards ensure data conforms to governance policies.

5. **Data Classification and Tagging:** Classifying data based on sensitivity and tagging it accordingly supports data protection and compliance efforts (Floridi et al., 2018). This helps in data access control.

Ethical Considerations:

1. **Data Privacy and Security:** Data governance practices must align with data privacy and security regulations (Floridi et al., 2018). Protecting sensitive information is paramount.
2. **Ethical Data Usage:** Organizations must ensure that data governance efforts promote ethical data usage principles (Floridi et al., 2018). Data should be handled responsibly and ethically.

Data governance is a cornerstone of success in AI and Big Data endeavors. By establishing a robust data governance framework, implementing data quality assurance processes, managing metadata, appointing data stewards, and ensuring data classification and tagging, organizations can overcome data governance challenges. Ethical considerations, including data privacy and responsible data usage, must be embedded in these governance efforts to ensure compliance and ethical data practices.

Leveraging AI for Solutions:

AI for Security:

AI-driven cybersecurity solutions can proactively detect and respond to threats (Mahmood et al., 2018). Machine learning algorithms can analyze network traffic patterns to identify anomalies indicative of cyberattacks.

Artificial Intelligence (AI) has emerged as a powerful tool in addressing the evolving challenges of security in a digitally connected world. The complex and dynamic nature of contemporary security threats necessitates innovative solutions, and AI offers a promising avenue. This section explores the multifaceted landscape of leveraging AI for security solutions, emphasizing its role in enhancing threat detection, prevention, and response.

The Shifting Security Landscape:

1. **Sophisticated Threats:** Security threats have become increasingly sophisticated, with attackers employing advanced

techniques and evasive tactics (Scarfone et al., 2019). Traditional security measures are often inadequate.

2. **Big Data and Complexity:** The volume and complexity of security data, including logs and network traffic, overwhelm human analysts (Gubbi et al., 2013). Effectively sifting through this data is challenging.

3. **Real-time Threats:** Many security threats unfold in real-time, necessitating rapid detection and response (Gavai et al., 2019). Manual monitoring is often insufficient.

Leveraging AI for Security Solutions:

1. **Anomaly Detection:** AI-based anomaly detection systems can identify unusual patterns and behaviors indicative of security threats (Gavai et al., 2019). Machine learning models excel at recognizing deviations from normalcy.

2. **Behavioral Analysis:** AI-driven behavioral analysis can establish baselines for normal user and system behavior and flag deviations (Scarfone et al., 2019). This aids in identifying insider threats and advanced persistent threats (APTs).

3. **Natural Language Processing (NLP):** NLP algorithms can analyze textual data, such as security incident reports and threat intelligence feeds, to extract actionable insights (Zhou et al., 2018).

4. **Predictive Analysis:** AI enables predictive analysis to anticipate potential security breaches by assessing historical data and identifying vulnerabilities (Gubbi et al., 2013).

5. **Security Automation:** AI-powered security automation can rapidly respond to threats, mitigate risks, and apply patches or updates (Gavai et al., 2019). This reduces response times.

Ethical Considerations:

1. **Data Privacy and Compliance:** Leveraging AI for security must align with data privacy and compliance regulations (Floridi et al., 2018). Personal and sensitive data must be protected.
2. **Algorithmic Fairness:** AI models used in security must be fair and unbiased, avoiding discrimination against individuals or groups (Barocas et al., 2019). Ethical considerations are essential.

AI offers a transformative approach to addressing the ever-evolving security challenges in the digital landscape. By employing AI for anomaly detection, behavioral analysis, NLP, predictive analysis, and security automation, organizations can bolster their security posture. Ethical considerations, such as data privacy and algorithmic fairness, must underpin these efforts to ensure responsible and effective AI-driven security solutions.

AI for Bias Mitigation:

AI itself can be used to identify and mitigate bias in algorithms (Hardt et al., 2016). Counter-bias techniques, such as re-weighting training data, can help address bias issues.

Artificial Intelligence (AI) systems have the potential to revolutionize numerous domains, but they also carry the risk of perpetuating biases present in the data they are trained on. Addressing bias in AI algorithms has become a critical concern, particularly in applications where fairness and equity are paramount. This section explores the multifaceted landscape of leveraging AI for bias mitigation, emphasizing its role in promoting fairness and mitigating harmful biases.

The Challenge of Bias in AI:

1. **Data Bias:** AI models learn from historical data, which may contain biases reflecting societal prejudices (Barocas et al., 2019). Biased training data can lead to discriminatory outcomes.
2. **Algorithmic Bias:** The algorithms themselves can introduce bias during data processing, feature selection, or model

optimization (Diakopoulos et al., 2016). Understanding these biases is complex.

3. **Ethical Concerns:** Biased AI systems can perpetuate unfair practices and discrimination, raising ethical and legal concerns (Floridi et al., 2018). Fairness and equity are essential considerations.

Leveraging AI for Bias Mitigation:

1. **Fairness-aware Algorithms:** Developing fairness-aware AI algorithms that consider protected attributes (e.g., gender, race) during model training and decision-making (Zafar et al., 2017). These algorithms aim to mitigate disparate impacts.

2. **De-biasing Techniques:** Employing de-biasing techniques that preprocess data to remove biases or reweight samples to achieve fairness (Kamiran et al., 2012). Adversarial training and re-sampling are common approaches.

3. **Explainable AI (XAI):** XAI techniques can provide insights into why AI systems make certain decisions, helping identify and rectify bias (Ribeiro et al., 2016). This transparency aids in accountability.

4. **Auditing and Monitoring:** Implementing auditing and monitoring tools to continuously assess AI systems for bias during deployment (Hardt et al., 2016). Regular audits help in bias detection.

5. **Diverse and Representative Data:** Ensuring that training data is diverse and representative of the population to minimize biases in the first place (Barocas et al., 2019). Data collection efforts must be thorough.

Ethical Considerations:

1. **Transparency:** Maintaining transparency in AI bias mitigation efforts is essential (Floridi et al., 2018). Stakeholders should understand how bias is addressed.
2. **Algorithmic Fairness:** Striking a balance between fairness and other performance metrics is challenging (Barocas et al., 2019). Trade-offs may be necessary.

Leveraging AI for bias mitigation is a critical step toward ensuring fairness and equity in AI systems. By adopting fairness-aware algorithms, de-biasing techniques, XAI methods, auditing, and diverse data practices, organizations can work toward minimizing bias in AI decision-making processes. Ethical considerations, including transparency and algorithmic fairness, should guide these efforts to create AI systems that promote fairness and mitigate harmful biases.

AI for Data Quality:

Machine learning models can assist in data quality improvement by identifying inconsistencies and anomalies (Zhu et al., 2017). These models can be integrated into data validation processes.

The quality of data is paramount in the success of Artificial Intelligence (AI) applications. Poor data quality can lead to erroneous predictions and flawed decision-making. This section explores the multifaceted landscape of leveraging AI for enhancing data quality, emphasizing its role in overcoming challenges and limitations associated with data reliability, accuracy, and completeness.

The Importance of Data Quality in AI:

1. **Impact on AI Performance:** The accuracy and reliability of AI models are directly influenced by the quality of input data (Dhar, 2013). Low-quality data can lead to biased, unreliable results.
2. **Garbage In, Garbage Out (GIGO):** In the AI context, GIGO holds true, as inaccurate or incomplete data can render even the most sophisticated algorithms ineffective (Domingos, 2012). Data quality is the foundation of AI.

3. **Data Volume and Complexity:** The sheer volume and complexity of data generated in modern applications make manual data quality management impractical (Chen et al., 2014). AI can automate these processes.

Leveraging AI for Data Quality Enhancement:

1. **Data Cleansing and Standardization:** AI-driven data cleansing techniques automatically detect and rectify inaccuracies, inconsistencies, and missing values in datasets (Chen et al., 2014). Standardization ensures uniformity.
2. **Machine Learning for Data Validation:** Machine learning models can validate data by identifying outliers, anomalies, and patterns indicative of data quality issues (Liu et al., 2016). This aids in data validation.
3. **Natural Language Processing (NLP):** NLP algorithms can analyze textual data for quality issues, such as grammatical errors or inconsistencies (Pakhira et al., 2018). They can also suggest improvements.
4. **Predictive Quality Modeling:** AI can predict data quality issues based on historical data patterns and deviations (Zhou et al., 2018). This enables proactive data quality management.
5. **Automated Data Governance:** AI can automate data governance tasks, including metadata management, lineage tracking, and quality monitoring (Wang et al., 2016). This ensures ongoing data quality.

Ethical Considerations:

1. **Bias Mitigation:** AI solutions for data quality enhancement must be designed to avoid introducing bias or perpetuating existing biases (Floridi et al., 2018). Bias-aware AI algorithms are crucial.

2. **Data Privacy:** AI must be employed for data quality enhancement in compliance with data privacy regulations (Floridi et al., 2018). Sensitive information must be protected.

Leveraging AI for data quality enhancement is a critical step in ensuring reliable and accurate AI-driven insights and decision-making. By applying AI to data cleansing, validation, NLP analysis, predictive modeling, and automated governance, organizations can overcome data quality challenges. Ethical considerations, such as bias mitigation and data privacy, should guide these efforts to maintain data integrity and compliance.

Conclusion:

AI and Big Data hold immense potential for innovation and progress across various domains. However, realizing this potential requires addressing the challenges and limitations associated with these technologies. Through ethical guidelines, transparency, diverse data sources, robust cybersecurity measures, and the responsible use of AI, organizations can overcome obstacles and harness the full power of AI and Big Data for the betterment of society.

Addressing Data Quality and Quantity Issues:

In the age of Big Data and Artificial Intelligence (AI), the availability of vast amounts of data is both a blessing and a challenge. While the sheer quantity of data promises new insights and opportunities, the quality and quantity of data can pose significant obstacles. This section explores the multifaceted landscape of addressing data quality and quantity issues in the context of AI and Big Data, emphasizing strategies to overcome challenges associated with data reliability, accuracy, completeness, and volume.

Data Quality Challenges:

1. **Inaccuracies and Inconsistencies:** Data may contain inaccuracies, inconsistencies, and errors introduced during data collection or integration (Wang & Strong, 1996). These issues can lead to unreliable results.
2. **Missing Data:** Gaps or missing data points in datasets can hinder analysis and modeling, potentially biasing AI outcomes (Little & Rubin, 2002). Imputation methods may be necessary.
3. **Data Bias:** Biased data, reflecting systemic prejudices or under-representation, can lead to biased AI models and decisions (Barocas et al., 2019). Bias detection and mitigation are critical.

Data Quantity Challenges:

1. **Data Volume:** The exponential growth of data can overwhelm storage and processing capabilities, making it challenging to manage and analyze large datasets (Manyika et al., 2011).
2. **Data Scalability:** Scalability issues arise when AI algorithms struggle to process and learn from massive datasets efficiently (Chen et al., 2014). This can lead to extended processing times.

Strategies for Addressing Data Quality Issues:

1. **Data Profiling and Cleaning:** Data profiling tools can identify inconsistencies and errors, enabling data cleaning and validation (Batini et al., 2009). Automated data cleaning processes can rectify issues.
2. **Data Imputation:** Imputation methods, such as mean imputation or machine learning-based imputation, can fill in missing data points (Little & Rubin, 2002). Imputation techniques should align with data characteristics.
3. **Data Validation:** Implementing data validation checks at various stages of data collection and integration helps prevent data

quality issues (Wang & Strong, 1996). Validation rules should be defined.

4. **Bias Detection and Mitigation:** Employing bias detection algorithms and fairness-aware AI techniques to identify and mitigate biases in datasets and AI models (Barocas et al., 2019).

Strategies for Addressing Data Quantity Issues:

1. **Data Sampling:** Sampling methods can reduce data volume while preserving statistical properties, making it more manageable for AI algorithms (Manyika et al., 2011). Proper sampling techniques are essential.
2. **Distributed Computing:** Leveraging distributed computing frameworks, such as Hadoop and Spark, allows parallel processing of large datasets (Chen et al., 2014). This enhances scalability.
3. **Feature Selection:** Identifying and selecting relevant features from high-dimensional data can reduce the data dimensionality (Guyon & Elisseeff, 2003). Feature selection algorithms help identify critical variables.

Ethical Considerations:

1. **Bias Mitigation:** Ethical considerations include addressing biases in data, which can perpetuate discrimination (Floridi et al., 2018). Transparency and fairness are vital.
2. **Privacy Preservation:** Data quality improvements must not compromise data privacy or violate regulations (Floridi et al., 2018). Data anonymization and encryption may be necessary.

Addressing data quality and quantity issues is fundamental to the success of AI and Big Data applications. By implementing data profiling, cleaning, imputation, validation, and bias detection techniques, organizations can enhance data quality. Strategies such as data sampling, distributed computing, and feature selection aid in managing data quantity. Ethical considerations, including bias mitigation and privacy preservation, must guide these efforts to ensure responsible and effective data handling.

AI Model Explainability and Bias:

As Artificial Intelligence (AI) becomes increasingly integrated into decision-making processes across various domains, the need for transparency, fairness, and accountability in AI models has never been greater. This section explores the intricate landscape of addressing challenges and limitations associated with AI model explainability and bias mitigation, emphasizing strategies to ensure interpretable and unbiased AI systems.

The Challenge of AI Model Complexity:

1. **Black-Box Nature:** Many AI models, especially deep learning neural networks, are often considered "black boxes" due to their complex architectures (Ribeiro et al., 2016). Understanding their decision-making processes can be challenging.
2. **Lack of Interpretability:** Interpreting how AI models arrive at specific predictions or classifications is essential for gaining trust and insight (Caruana et al., 2015). Lack of interpretability can hinder adoption.

The Challenge of Bias in AI Models:

1. **Data Bias Propagation:** AI models can perpetuate biases present in training data, leading to biased decisions (Barocas et al., 2019). This can result in discrimination against certain groups.
2. **Unintentional Bias:** Bias in AI models may be unintentional and emerge from complex interactions within the model (Zafar et al., 2017). Identifying and mitigating such bias is challenging.

Strategies for AI Model Explainability:

1. **Interpretable Models:** Using inherently interpretable models, such as decision trees or linear regression, when possible (Ribeiro et al., 2016). These models provide direct insights into decision factors.
2. **Feature Importance Analysis:** Employing feature importance techniques to understand which variables influence AI model predictions (Lundberg & Lee, 2017). This aids in understanding model behavior.
3. **Local Explanations:** Generating local explanations for specific predictions, such as LIME (Local Interpretable Model-agnostic Explanations) (Ribeiro et al., 2016). These provide insights into individual cases.

Strategies for Bias Mitigation:

1. **Fairness-aware Algorithms:** Utilizing fairness-aware AI algorithms that aim to minimize disparate impacts on different demographic groups (Zafar et al., 2017). These models explicitly consider fairness during training.
2. **Bias Auditing:** Conducting bias audits to detect and quantify bias in AI models and data (Hardt et al., 2016). Regular audits help maintain fairness.
3. **Ethical Guidelines:** Adhering to ethical guidelines and principles that promote fairness and transparency in AI model development and deployment (Floridi et al., 2018).

Ethical Considerations:

1. **Algorithmic Fairness:** Striking a balance between model accuracy and fairness is challenging (Barocas et al., 2019). Trade-offs may be necessary, and ethical considerations are paramount.

2. **Transparency:** Ensuring that AI model explainability does not compromise proprietary information while maintaining transparency for stakeholders (Floridi et al., 2018).

Addressing the challenges and limitations in AI model explainability and bias mitigation is essential for responsible AI deployment. By employing interpretable models, analyzing feature importance, providing local explanations, using fairness-aware algorithms, conducting bias audits, and adhering to ethical guidelines, organizations can enhance model transparency and mitigate bias. Ethical considerations, including algorithmic fairness and transparency, should guide these efforts to ensure the development of trustworthy and equitable AI systems.

Scalability and Maintenance of AI Systems in Big Data:

As the volume and complexity of data continue to grow exponentially, the scalability and maintenance of AI systems in the context of Big Data pose significant challenges. This section explores the multifaceted landscape of addressing challenges and limitations associated with the scalability and maintenance of AI systems, emphasizing strategies to ensure reliable, efficient, and sustainable solutions.

The Challenge of Scalability:

1. **Data Volume:** The ever-increasing volume of data requires AI systems to scale horizontally and vertically to handle massive datasets (Chen et al., 2014). Traditional systems may struggle to keep up.
2. **Computational Resources:** Scaling AI systems necessitates substantial computational resources, including processing power and memory (Chen et al., 2014). Resource allocation becomes crucial.

The Challenge of Maintenance:

1. **Model Drift:** Over time, AI models can experience "model drift" as data distributions change, affecting model performance (Gama et al., 2014). Regular model retraining is necessary.
2. **Algorithm Updates:** AI algorithms evolve, and staying up-to-date with the latest advancements is essential to maintain optimal performance (Chen et al., 2014). Algorithmic maintenance is ongoing.

Strategies for Scalability:

1. **Distributed Computing:** Leveraging distributed computing frameworks such as Apache Hadoop and Spark to parallelize data processing and model training (Chen et al., 2014). This enhances scalability.
2. **Containerization:** Containerization technologies like Docker enable easy deployment and scaling of AI applications across different environments (Boettiger, 2015). Containers simplify resource management.

Strategies for Maintenance:

1. **Continuous Monitoring:** Implementing continuous monitoring of AI models to detect model drift and performance degradation (Gama et al., 2014). Regular monitoring helps in timely updates.
2. **Automated Pipelines:** Setting up automated data pipelines for data collection, preprocessing, model training, and deployment (Chen et al., 2014). Automation reduces maintenance efforts.

Ethical Considerations:

1. **Data Privacy:** Ethical considerations include ensuring data privacy and compliance with data protection regulations during AI system maintenance (Floridi et al., 2018). Data anonymization and encryption may be necessary.
2. **Bias Mitigation:** Ongoing maintenance should include bias detection and mitigation efforts to prevent unintended discrimination (Barocas et al., 2019). Regular audits are essential.

Conclusion:

Overcoming challenges and limitations in the scalability and maintenance of AI systems in Big Data is essential to harness the potential of AI-driven insights and decision-making. By leveraging distributed computing, containerization, continuous monitoring, and automated pipelines, organizations can enhance scalability and reduce maintenance efforts. Ethical considerations, including data privacy and bias mitigation, must guide these efforts to ensure responsible and sustainable AI system development and deployment.

Chapter 8: Building a Career in AI and Big Data

The fields of Artificial Intelligence (AI) and Big Data have witnessed unprecedented growth in recent years, creating a wealth of opportunities for individuals looking to build a career in these domains. This section explores the multifaceted landscape of career development in AI and Big Data, emphasizing key skills, educational pathways, and ethical considerations.

The Growth of AI and Big Data:

Explosive Industry Growth:

The AI and Big Data industries are experiencing exponential growth, with increasing demand for skilled professionals (Manyika et al., 2011). Job opportunities abound.

The fields of Artificial Intelligence (AI) and Big Data have experienced unprecedented growth in recent years, establishing themselves as dominant forces in the technological landscape. This section delves into the remarkable expansion of AI and Big Data, elucidating the profound implications it holds for those seeking to build a career in these dynamic domains.

The Ubiquity of AI and Big Data:

1. **Exponential Data Generation:** The digital age has ushered in an era of data abundance, with the world generating vast

amounts of data daily (Manyika et al., 2011). This data deluge is a core driver of AI and Big Data.

2. **Technological Advancements:** Breakthroughs in computing power, machine learning algorithms, and data storage have accelerated the adoption of AI and Big Data technologies (Chen et al., 2014). These advancements have made previously unfeasible tasks achievable.

Explosive Industry Growth:

1. **Diverse Industry Applications:** AI and Big Data have transcended boundaries and found applications in a wide array of sectors, including healthcare, finance, e-commerce, and autonomous vehicles (Chen et al., 2014). The versatility of these technologies has fueled their growth.

2. **Economic Impact:** The economic impact of AI and Big Data is profound, with significant contributions to GDP growth and productivity improvements (Manyika et al., 2011). This has led to substantial investments and job opportunities.

3. **Proliferation of Startups:** The startup ecosystem in AI and Big Data is flourishing, with entrepreneurial ventures driving innovation and shaping the industry landscape (Chen et al., 2014). This entrepreneurial dynamism offers diverse career paths.

The Role of Data in the Digital Age:

1. **Data as a Strategic Asset:** Data is now recognized as a strategic asset, and organizations are increasingly data-driven (Manyika et al., 2011). This shift underscores the importance of professionals skilled in data analytics and AI.

2. **Personalization and Automation:** AI and Big Data enable personalization of services and automation of processes, enhancing user experiences and operational efficiency (Chen et al., 2014).

This creates demand for professionals who can harness these capabilities.

The explosive growth of AI and Big Data has positioned these fields at the forefront of technological innovation and economic development. For those aspiring to build a career in AI and Big Data, the dynamic nature of these domains offers abundant opportunities for growth, innovation, and societal impact. As AI and Big Data continue to evolve, individuals with the skills and expertise to navigate and harness their potential are poised to shape the future of technology and industry.

Cross-Industry Relevance:

AI and Big Data are not limited to a single industry; they have applications in healthcare, finance, manufacturing, and more (Chen et al., 2014). Versatile career paths exist.

The rapid expansion of Artificial Intelligence (AI) and Big Data technologies has not been confined to a single industry but has permeated virtually every sector of the global economy. This section explores the extensive cross-industry relevance of AI and Big Data, shedding light on the diverse career opportunities that arise as a result of this pervasive influence.

AI and Big Data's Reach Across Industries:

1. **Healthcare:** In healthcare, AI and Big Data facilitate disease diagnosis, drug discovery, patient care optimization, and predictive analytics (Chen et al., 2014). Professionals in this field analyze medical data, develop predictive models, and ensure data privacy compliance.

2. **Finance:** The finance industry relies on AI for algorithmic trading, risk assessment, fraud detection, and personalized financial recommendations (Manyika et al., 2011). Careers span from quantitative analysis to AI-driven trading strategy development.

3. **Manufacturing:** AI-driven predictive maintenance, quality control, and supply chain optimization are transforming the manufacturing sector (Chen et al., 2014). Career opportunities range from data engineering to AI implementation in production processes.

4. **Retail:** In the retail sector, AI-powered recommendation systems, demand forecasting, and inventory management enhance customer experiences (Manyika et al., 2011). Professionals work on data-driven marketing, customer analytics, and supply chain optimization.

5. **Automotive:** The automotive industry utilizes AI for autonomous vehicles, driver assistance systems, and predictive maintenance (Chen et al., 2014). Career paths involve AI research and development, data analysis, and software engineering.

6. **Energy:** Energy companies employ AI and Big Data for predictive maintenance of infrastructure, energy consumption optimization, and grid management (Manyika et al., 2011). Professionals focus on data analytics and AI applications in the energy sector.

Diverse Career Paths:

1. **Data Scientists and Analysts:** Individuals with expertise in data analysis, statistics, and machine learning are in high demand across industries (Chen et al., 2014). They extract valuable insights from data.

2. **Machine Learning Engineers:** Engineers skilled in developing machine learning models and AI algorithms play a crucial role in AI-driven applications (Manyika et al., 2011).

3. **Data Engineers:** Data engineers are responsible for data collection, storage, and processing pipelines, ensuring the availability of quality data for analysis (Chen et al., 2014).

4. **AI Ethicists and Compliance Officers:** With the growing emphasis on ethics and data privacy, careers focused on AI

ethics, compliance, and data protection are emerging (Floridi et al., 2018).

Adaptability and Versatility:

1. **Interdisciplinary Knowledge:** Professionals with interdisciplinary knowledge bridging AI, Big Data, and specific industry domains are highly sought after (Chen et al., 2014).
2. **Lifelong Learning:** Given the rapid advancements in technology, a commitment to lifelong learning and staying updated with industry trends is essential for career growth (Chen et al., 2014).

The cross-industry relevance of AI and Big Data underscores the vast and varied career opportunities available to those aspiring to build a career in these domains. As AI and Big Data continue to evolve and permeate industries, professionals with diverse skill sets and adaptability will find themselves at the forefront of innovation and problem-solving in a multitude of sectors.

Key Skills for Success:

Data Analysis and Interpretation:

Proficiency in data analysis tools, statistical methods, and data visualization is crucial (Chen et al., 2014). The ability to draw insights from data is highly valued.

Machine Learning and AI Algorithms: Understanding machine learning algorithms, neural networks, and AI frameworks is essential (Goodfellow et al., 2016). Practical experience in model development is valuable.

In the rapidly evolving landscape of AI and Big Data, proficiency in data analysis and interpretation stands as one of the foundational and indispensable skills for individuals seeking to forge successful careers. This section elucidates the critical role of data analysis and interpretation and explores the skill sets required for excellence in this domain.

The Significance of Data Analysis:

1. **Data as the Raw Material:** Data is the lifeblood of AI and Big Data, serving as the raw material from which insights and knowledge are extracted (Chen et al., 2014). Effective data analysis is the linchpin of the entire process.
2. **Driving Informed Decisions:** In today's data-driven world, organizations rely on data analysis to make informed decisions, optimize operations, and gain a competitive edge (Manyika et al., 2011).

Key Skills for Success:

1. **Statistical Proficiency:** A strong foundation in statistics is fundamental for data analysis. Knowledge of probability, hypothesis testing, and regression analysis is invaluable (Chen et al., 2014).
2. **Data Visualization:** The ability to present data effectively through charts, graphs, and visualizations aids in conveying insights to stakeholders (Tufte, 2001).
3. **Programming Skills:** Proficiency in programming languages such as Python and R is essential for data manipulation, analysis, and scripting (Chollet, 2018).
4. **Machine Learning:** Familiarity with machine learning techniques enables data analysts to build predictive models and uncover hidden patterns in data (Goodfellow et al., 2016).
5. **Domain Knowledge:** Understanding the specific domain in which data analysis is applied, whether it's finance, healthcare, or marketing, enhances the ability to generate meaningful insights (Dhar, 2013).

Ethical Considerations:

1. **Data Privacy:** Data analysts must be well-versed in data privacy regulations and best practices to ensure the responsible handling of sensitive information (Floridi et al., 2018).

2. **Bias Awareness:** Ethical data analysis involves recognizing and addressing biases in data and algorithms to prevent discriminatory outcomes (Barocas et al., 2019).

Continuous Learning and Adaptation:

1. **Rapid Technological Advancements:** The field of data analysis is continually evolving with new tools, techniques, and methodologies. Professionals must commit to lifelong learning to stay current (Chen et al., 2014).
2. **Interdisciplinary Collaboration:** Collaborating with professionals from diverse fields, including data engineers, data scientists, and domain experts, enriches data analysis and interpretation (Chen et al., 2014).

Data analysis and interpretation form the bedrock of AI and Big Data, enabling organizations to transform raw data into actionable insights. As the demand for data-driven decision-making intensifies, individuals equipped with the essential skills and a commitment to ethical data analysis will find themselves at the forefront of innovation and problem-solving in a multitude of industries.

Programming Languages:

Proficiency in programming languages such as Python and R is fundamental for data manipulation and modeling (Chollet, 2018).

In the fast-paced world of AI and Big Data, proficiency in programming languages is an essential skill for individuals seeking to excel in these domains. This section elucidates the pivotal role of programming languages and explores the specific languages that hold significant relevance.

Programming Languages as the Backbone:

1. **Data Manipulation:** Programming languages serve as the primary tools for data manipulation, transformation, and analysis

(Chen et al., 2014). They facilitate the extraction of insights from large and complex datasets.

2. **Algorithm Implementation:** AI and Big Data solutions heavily rely on algorithms. Programming languages enable the implementation of machine learning algorithms and data processing pipelines (Chen et al., 2014).

Key Programming Languages for AI and Big Data:

1. **Python:** Python stands out as the predominant programming language in AI and Big Data. Its simplicity, readability, and extensive libraries, such as NumPy, pandas, and scikit-learn, make it an ideal choice for data manipulation and machine learning (Chollet, 2018).
2. **R:** R is another language specially tailored for data analysis and statistical computing. It offers a wide range of statistical packages and data visualization libraries (Chen et al., 2014).
3. **Java:** Java is widely used in Big Data processing frameworks like Hadoop and Spark. It excels in handling large-scale data processing tasks in distributed computing environments (Zaharia et al., 2010).
4. **Scala:** Scala is gaining popularity for its compatibility with Apache Spark. It combines functional and object-oriented programming paradigms and is well-suited for Big Data analytics (Odersky et al., 2004).
5. **SQL:** Structured Query Language (SQL) is indispensable for database management and querying. Proficiency in SQL is essential for working with structured data in AI and Big Data applications (Chen et al., 2014).

The Role of Specialized Libraries and Frameworks:

1. **TensorFlow and PyTorch:** These libraries are essential for deep learning and neural network development. Python integration makes them accessible to a wide range of developers (Chollet, 2018).
2. **Apache Hadoop and Spark:** These frameworks facilitate the distributed processing of large datasets. They rely on languages like Java and Scala for implementation (Zaharia et al., 2010).

Continuous Learning and Adaptation:

1. **Language Evolution:** Programming languages and libraries evolve over time. Professionals must stay updated with the latest versions and enhancements (Chen et al., 2014).
2. **Interdisciplinary Collaboration:** Collaborating with data scientists, engineers, and domain experts necessitates proficiency in languages commonly used in those domains (Chen et al., 2014).

Proficiency in programming languages is a cornerstone skill for anyone aspiring to excel in AI and Big Data. Python, R, Java, Scala, and SQL are among the key languages that empower professionals to manipulate data, implement algorithms, and develop AI and Big Data solutions. As the industry continues to evolve, individuals adept at programming languages will remain at the forefront of innovation and problem-solving.

Educational Pathways:

Bachelor's Degree:

A bachelor's degree in computer science, data science, or a related field is often the first step (Chen et al., 2014). It provides foundational knowledge.

A solid educational foundation is paramount for individuals aspiring to establish successful careers in the dynamic fields of Artificial Intelligence (AI) and Big Data. Pursuing a bachelor's degree in relevant disciplines lays the groundwork for understanding the fundamental principles, theories, and applications within these domains.

The Importance of a Bachelor's Degree:

1. **Foundational Knowledge:** A bachelor's degree program provides students with essential foundational knowledge in computer science, data science, statistics, mathematics, and related fields (Chen et al., 2014). These subjects form the basis of AI and Big Data expertise.
2. **Structured Learning:** Bachelor's degree programs offer a structured curriculum designed to cover core concepts, theories, and practical skills. Students gain a well-rounded education in data analysis, programming, and problem-solving (Dhar, 2013).

Relevant Bachelor's Degree Programs:

1. **Computer Science:** A bachelor's degree in computer science is a common pathway into AI and Big Data careers. It equips students with programming skills, algorithms, and data structures (Chen et al., 2014).
2. **Data Science:** Some universities offer specialized bachelor's programs in data science. These programs focus on data analysis, statistical methods, and machine learning (Chen et al., 2014).
3. **Statistics and Mathematics:** Degrees in statistics or mathematics provide a strong quantitative foundation, which is crucial for data analysis and modeling (Chen et al., 2014).
4. **Engineering:** Engineering programs, particularly those with a focus on computer or electrical engineering, offer a solid technical background that aligns with AI and Big Data (Chen et al., 2014).

Skill Development:

1. **Programming Skills:** Bachelor's degree programs often include coursework in programming languages like Python, Java, or R. Proficiency in these languages is essential for data manipulation and analysis (Chen et al., 2014).
2. **Mathematical and Statistical Proficiency:** Courses in mathematics and statistics equip students with the mathematical rigor necessary for advanced data analysis and modeling (Dhar, 2013).

Practical Experience:

1. **Internships and Projects:** Many bachelor's degree programs encourage students to participate in internships or complete projects that apply AI and Big Data concepts in real-world scenarios (Dhar, 2013).

Ethical Considerations:

1. **Ethical Training:** Bachelor's programs often include ethics courses, which are essential for understanding the ethical implications of AI and Big Data (Floridi et al., 2018).

A bachelor's degree in a relevant field serves as a foundational stepping stone for those aiming to embark on a career in AI and Big Data. These programs impart essential knowledge, skills, and ethical perspectives, equipping graduates to tackle the complex challenges and opportunities within these rapidly evolving domains.

Master's Degree:

Pursuing a master's degree in AI, data science, or a specialized field offers in-depth expertise (Dhar, 2013). Many AI professionals hold advanced degrees.

For individuals aiming to excel in the burgeoning fields of Artificial Intelligence (AI) and Big Data, pursuing a master's degree offers an elevated educational pathway that equips them with advanced knowledge, specialized skills, and the depth of expertise necessary to address complex challenges and lead innovation in these domains.

The Significance of a Master's Degree:

1. **Specialization and Depth:** A master's degree program provides students with an opportunity to delve deeply into the intricacies of AI and Big Data. It enables them to acquire specialized skills and expertise (Chen et al., 2014).
2. **Advanced Research:** Master's programs often involve research projects or theses, allowing students to engage in cutting-edge research and contribute to the advancement of the field (Dhar, 2013).

Relevant Master's Degree Programs:

1. **Master of Science (MSc) in Artificial Intelligence:** These programs focus on advanced AI concepts, machine learning, natural language processing, and robotics. They prepare students for careers in AI research and development (Russell & Norvig, 2020).
2. **Master of Data Science (MDS):** MDS programs emphasize advanced data analysis, statistical modeling, and machine learning. Graduates are well-equipped to work as data scientists or analysts in various industries (Chen et al., 2014).
3. **Master of Business Analytics (MBA):** These programs combine data analytics with business acumen, preparing graduates for leadership roles in data-driven decision-making within organizations (Davenport & Harris, 2007).
4. **Master of Computer Science (MCS):** MCS programs offer specialized tracks in AI and Big Data, providing in-depth knowledge and practical experience in these domains (Russell & Norvig, 2020).

Advanced Skill Development:

1. **Advanced Algorithms:** Master's programs delve into advanced algorithms, including deep learning, reinforcement learning, and optimization techniques (Goodfellow et al., 2016).
2. **Big Data Technologies:** Students learn to work with Big Data technologies such as Hadoop, Spark, and NoSQL databases, gaining proficiency in distributed data processing (Zaharia et al., 2010).
3. **Ethics and Responsible AI:** Master's programs often include coursework on the ethical considerations and responsible development of AI and Big Data solutions (Floridi et al., 2018).

Research and Innovation:

1. **Thesis Projects:** Many master's programs require students to complete a thesis project, enabling them to conduct original research in AI and Big Data (Dhar, 2013).

Networking and Collaboration:

1. **Research Opportunities:** Master's students often have the opportunity to collaborate with faculty on research projects, expanding their professional network (Dhar, 2013).

A master's degree in AI and Big Data offers a transformative educational experience, providing students with specialized knowledge, advanced skills, and research opportunities. Graduates of these programs are well-prepared to contribute to the cutting-edge developments, ethical considerations, and real-world applications within these rapidly evolving fields.

Online Courses and Certifications:

Online courses and certifications, such as those from Coursera and edX, provide flexible learning options (Ng et al., 2017).

In the rapidly evolving landscape of Artificial Intelligence (AI) and Big Data, the pursuit of online courses and certifications has emerged as a flexible and accessible educational pathway for individuals seeking to establish or advance their careers. This section explores the significance of online education and the benefits it offers to aspiring professionals.

The Value of Online Courses and Certifications:

1. **Accessibility and Flexibility:** Online courses and certifications are accessible to learners worldwide, irrespective of geographical location. They provide the flexibility to study at one's own pace and convenience (Zheng et al., 2018).

2. **Cost-Effective Learning:** Many online courses are more affordable than traditional degree programs, making education accessible to a broader audience (Balakrishnan et al., 2017).

Relevance to AI and Big Data:

1. **Specialized Content:** Numerous online courses and certifications cater specifically to AI and Big Data. They offer specialized content designed to impart the latest knowledge and skills required in these fields (Balakrishnan et al., 2017).

2. **Cutting-Edge Curriculum:** Online courses are often updated regularly to align with the rapidly evolving technologies and methodologies in AI and Big Data (Zheng et al., 2018).

Online Courses and Certifications in AI and Big Data:

1. **Machine Learning:** Courses like "Machine Learning" on platforms like Coursera offer in-depth coverage of machine learning algorithms and applications (Ng, 2021).

2. **Data Science:** Certifications such as "Data Science Professional Certificate" on edX provide comprehensive training in data analysis, data visualization, and machine learning (edX, n.d.).
3. **Big Data Technologies:** "Big Data Specialization" on Coursera focuses on the practical aspects of working with Big Data tools like Hadoop and Spark (Coursera, n.d.).
4. **AI Ethics:** Courses such as "AI Ethics" explore the ethical considerations and responsible development of AI technologies (Floridi et al., 2018).

Benefits and Considerations:

1. **Self-Paced Learning:** Learners can tailor their online education to their needs, emphasizing specific topics or skills relevant to their career goals (Balakrishnan et al., 2017).
2. **Certification Validation:** Many online courses offer certificates upon completion, which can serve as proof of skills and knowledge to potential employers (Zheng et al., 2018).
3. **Networking Opportunities:** Online courses often provide access to global communities of learners and experts, facilitating networking and collaboration (Balakrishnan et al., 2017).

Ethical Considerations:

1. **Quality Assurance:** Choosing reputable platforms and institutions is crucial to ensure the quality and credibility of online courses and certifications (Zheng et al., 2018).

Online courses and certifications present a viable and accessible pathway for individuals aspiring to build a career in AI and Big Data. They offer specialized, up-to-date knowledge, and skills, empowering learners to stay competitive in these rapidly evolving fields. However, learners must exercise discretion in selecting high-quality courses and certifications to maximize their educational investment.

Ethical Considerations:

Data Privacy and Ethics:

Ethical considerations are crucial in AI and Big Data careers, including respect for data privacy and compliance with regulations (Floridi et al., 2018).

In the era of Artificial Intelligence (AI) and Big Data, professionals embarking on careers in these fields are confronted with profound ethical considerations, particularly concerning data privacy and ethics. This section elucidates the ethical imperatives that individuals must navigate as they harness the power of data in their careers.

Data Privacy: A Paramount Concern

1. **Personal Data Protection:** The collection and processing of personal data are central to AI and Big Data applications. Professionals must prioritize the privacy rights of individuals and ensure compliance with data protection laws (Mittelstadt, 2017).

2. **Informed Consent:** Ethical practices demand that individuals provide informed consent for the use of their data. Professionals should be diligent in obtaining clear and informed consent (Floridi et al., 2018).

3. **Data Minimization:** Adhering to the principle of data minimization, professionals must collect only the data necessary for specific purposes, reducing the risk of misuse (Mittelstadt, 2017).

Ethical Considerations in Data Handling

1. **Fairness and Bias Mitigation:** Professionals must be vigilant in identifying and rectifying biases in AI algorithms and Big Data analyses to ensure equitable outcomes (Barocas et al., 2019).

2. **Transparency and Explainability:** Ethical data practices entail making AI and Big Data processes transparent and providing

explanations for automated decisions, fostering trust and accountability (Floridi et al., 2018).

3. **Data Security:** Safeguarding data against breaches and unauthorized access is an ethical imperative. Professionals should implement robust security measures (Barocas et al., 2019).

Ethics in AI and Big Data Research and Development

1. **Ethical Frameworks:** Professionals should operate within established ethical frameworks, such as the principles of beneficence, non-maleficence, and autonomy, to guide their research and development (Floridi et al., 2018).

2. **Responsible Innovation:** Ethical considerations extend to the development and deployment of AI and Big Data technologies. Responsible innovation involves anticipating and mitigating potential risks (Floridi et al., 2018).

Educational and Professional Development

1. **Ethics Training:** Aspiring professionals should seek out courses and resources on data ethics and privacy to ensure they possess the necessary knowledge and ethical awareness (Floridi et al., 2018).

2. **Industry Standards:** Staying informed about evolving industry standards and best practices in data ethics is essential for career development (Mittelstadt, 2017).

Ethical Oversight and Accountability

1. **Ethics Committees:** Some organizations establish ethics committees or boards to review and oversee AI and Big Data projects, ensuring ethical compliance (Floridi et al., 2018).

2. **Accountability Mechanisms:** Professionals should advocate for accountability mechanisms within their organizations to address ethical lapses or breaches (Barocas et al., 2019).

Navigating Ethical Complexities

As AI and Big Data professionals forge their careers, they are entrusted with a profound responsibility to uphold the highest ethical standards. Data privacy, fairness, transparency, and ethical considerations in research and development are imperative for building trust, ensuring societal benefit, and avoiding unintended harm. Navigating these ethical complexities is an essential aspect of a successful and ethically sound career in AI and Big Data.

Bias Mitigation:

Addressing bias in AI models and data is an ethical imperative (Barocas et al., 2019). Ethical AI practitioners actively work to prevent bias.

As professionals embark on careers in Artificial Intelligence (AI) and Big Data, they encounter a critical ethical imperative: mitigating bias. Bias in AI and Big Data systems can perpetuate discrimination and inequity. This section explores the ethical dimensions of bias mitigation and its significance in these fields.

The Ethical Imperative of Bias Mitigation

1. **Recognizing Bias:** Professionals must acknowledge that bias can manifest in data, algorithms, and decision-making processes. This recognition is the first step toward ethical practice (Diakopoulos, 2016).
2. **Promoting Fairness:** Bias mitigation is integral to ensuring fairness and equity in AI and Big Data applications, particularly in areas like hiring, lending, and criminal justice (Barocas et al., 2019).

Sources of Bias in AI and Big Data

1. **Data Bias:** Biased training data can lead to skewed AI models. Professionals should scrutinize data sources to identify and rectify potential sources of bias (O'Neil, 2016).
2. **Algorithmic Bias:** Algorithms can perpetuate biases present in training data or inadvertently introduce new biases. Professionals must continuously monitor and evaluate algorithmic decisions (Diakopoulos, 2016).

Bias Mitigation Strategies

1. **Data Preprocessing:** Professionals should implement techniques like data preprocessing, oversampling, and undersampling to balance datasets and reduce bias (Chen & Song, 2018).
2. **Algorithmic Fairness:** Developing and utilizing fairness-aware algorithms that explicitly consider fairness criteria can mitigate bias (Hardt et al., 2016).
3. **Bias Audits:** Regular audits of AI systems can reveal bias and provide insights for bias mitigation efforts (Barocas et al., 2019).

Ethical Considerations in Bias Mitigation

1. **Ethical Guidelines:** Professionals should adhere to established ethical guidelines and principles for bias mitigation in AI and Big Data (Floridi et al., 2018).
2. **Transparency:** Transparency in AI and Big Data systems is essential. Professionals should ensure that the decision-making processes are explainable and interpretable (Diakopoulos, 2016).
3. **Accountability:** Organizations and professionals must take responsibility for the consequences of biased AI and Big Data systems (Barocas et al., 2019).

Ethical Training and Education

1. **Ethics Courses:** Aspiring professionals should seek education in ethics, especially as it pertains to AI and Big Data, to develop a strong ethical foundation (Floridi et al., 2018).
2. **Continuous Learning:** Staying current with evolving best practices in bias mitigation is essential for ethical AI and Big Data practice (Chen & Song, 2018).

Collaboration and Diverse Teams

1. **Interdisciplinary Collaboration:** Working with professionals from diverse backgrounds can help uncover and address hidden biases (Diakopoulos, 2016).
2. **Inclusive Teams:** Building diverse teams can foster more equitable and unbiased AI and Big Data solutions (Barocas et al., 2019).

Ethical Imperative of Bias Mitigation

In the pursuit of careers in AI and Big Data, professionals must recognize that bias mitigation is a fundamental ethical obligation. Mitigating bias promotes fairness, transparency, and accountability, aligning with the ethical principles that underpin the responsible development and deployment of AI and Big Data systems. Navigating the complexities of bias mitigation is a crucial aspect of building an ethical and impactful career in these fields.

Networking and Professional Development:

Participation in AI Communities:

Joining AI and data science communities, attending conferences, and engaging in online forums can expand professional networks (Chen et al., 2014).

Networking and active participation in AI communities play a pivotal role in the career development of professionals in the fields of Artificial Intelligence (AI) and Big Data. This section explores the significance of engaging with AI communities and the various benefits it offers to individuals seeking to excel in these domains.

The Significance of AI Communities

1. **Knowledge Exchange:** AI communities serve as platforms for knowledge sharing, enabling professionals to stay updated with the latest advancements, research findings, and best practices (Zheng et al., 2018).
2. **Networking Opportunities:** These communities provide a forum for connecting with like-minded individuals, experts, and potential collaborators, fostering valuable professional relationships (Guo et al., 2013).
3. **Continuous Learning:** Participation in AI communities promotes lifelong learning and skill development, as professionals gain insights from peers and mentors (Chen & Song, 2018).

Types of AI Communities

1. **Online Forums:** Platforms like Reddit's r/MachineLearning and Stack Overflow offer AI practitioners a space for discussing challenges, sharing insights, and seeking advice (Zheng et al., 2018).
2. **Professional Associations:** Organizations such as the Association for Computing Machinery (ACM) and the Institute of Electrical and Electronics Engineers (IEEE) have AI-specific special interest groups and conferences (Guo et al., 2013).
3. **AI Meetup Groups:** Local AI and Big Data meetup groups offer opportunities for face-to-face networking and knowledge exchange (Chen & Song, 2018).

Benefits of Active Participation

1. **Access to Resources:** AI communities provide access to resources like research papers, code repositories, and tutorials, aiding professionals in their work (Zheng et al., 2018).
2. **Mentorship:** Engaging with experienced members of AI communities can lead to mentorship opportunities, accelerating career growth (Guo et al., 2013).
3. **Professional Recognition:** Actively contributing to AI communities can enhance one's professional reputation and visibility within the field (Chen & Song, 2018).

Ethical Considerations

1. **Respectful Engagement:** Professionals should engage respectfully in AI communities, adhering to community guidelines and ethical norms (Zheng et al., 2018).
2. **Avoiding Plagiarism:** When sharing knowledge or code, it is imperative to give proper credit to original authors and respect intellectual property rights (Guo et al., 2013).

Educational Opportunities

1. **Online Courses and Workshops:** Many AI communities organize online courses and workshops, providing opportunities for skill enhancement (Chen & Song, 2018).
2. **Conferences and Symposia:** AI community events offer a platform for presenting research, gaining feedback, and expanding one's knowledge base (Zheng et al., 2018).

Building a Personal Brand

1. **Blogging and Publishing:** Some professionals maintain blogs or publish articles on AI-related topics, establishing themselves as thought leaders in the field (Guo et al., 2013).

2. **Open-Source Contributions:** Contributing to open-source AI projects can showcase expertise and commitment to the community (Chen & Song, 2018).

Leveraging AI Communities for Career Advancement

Active participation in AI communities is not only a valuable source of knowledge but also a pathway to professional growth and recognition. Networking with peers, engaging in discussions, and contributing to the collective learning of the community can accelerate career development and establish individuals as influential figures in the exciting and rapidly evolving domains of AI and Big Data.

Continual Learning:

AI and Big Data professionals must commit to lifelong learning to stay updated with evolving technologies and methodologies (Chen et al., 2014).

In the dynamic fields of Artificial Intelligence (AI) and Big Data, continual learning is not only advantageous but essential for professionals seeking to build a successful career. This section explores the significance of continuous learning and its role in professional development within these domains.

The Imperative of Continual Learning

1. **Rapid Technological Advancements:** AI and Big Data technologies evolve swiftly, necessitating professionals to stay current with the latest tools, methodologies, and research findings (Zheng et al., 2018).
2. **Adaptability:** Continuous learning enhances adaptability, enabling professionals to pivot, tackle new challenges, and capitalize on emerging opportunities (Guo et al., 2013).
3. **Competitive Advantage:** Professionals who invest in continual learning gain a competitive edge by acquiring in-demand skills and expertise (Chen & Song, 2018).

Continuous Learning Strategies

1. **Online Courses and Specializations:** Platforms like Coursera, edX, and Udacity offer a plethora of AI and Big Data courses, allowing professionals to choose topics aligned with their career goals (Zheng et al., 2018).
2. **Professional Certifications:** Acquiring certifications from reputable organizations in AI and Big Data, such as Google's TensorFlow Developer Certificate, can validate one's expertise (Guo et al., 2013).
3. **Academic Programs:** Pursuing advanced degrees or enrolling in part-time academic programs can provide a comprehensive and structured learning experience (Chen & Song, 2018).

Networking for Learning

1. **Peer Interaction:** Engaging with peers, colleagues, and mentors can lead to knowledge exchange, collaborative projects, and exposure to diverse perspectives (Guo et al., 2013).
2. **Conferences and Workshops:** Attending AI and Big Data conferences and workshops offers opportunities for intensive learning, networking, and exposure to cutting-edge research (Zheng et al., 2018).

Active Engagement with Research

1. **Reading Academic Papers:** Regularly reading research papers and publications in AI and Big Data journals keeps professionals informed about the latest advancements (Chen & Song, 2018).
2. **Contributions to Research:** Actively participating in research projects or publishing one's findings fosters a deeper understanding and application of AI and Big Data concepts (Guo et al., 2013).

Ethical Considerations in Continuous Learning

1. **Academic Integrity:** Professionals must maintain academic integrity by crediting original authors and respecting copyright laws when utilizing academic resources (Zheng et al., 2018).
2. **Responsible Research:** Ethical research practices, including informed consent and data privacy, should be adhered to during continual learning (Chen & Song, 2018).

Balancing Work and Learning

1. **Time Management:** Professionals must efficiently manage their time to balance work commitments and continuous learning (Guo et al., 2013).
2. **Setting Goals:** Establishing clear learning objectives and goals helps professionals prioritize their continual learning efforts (Zheng et al., 2018).

Continual Learning for Success

In the ever-evolving domains of AI and Big Data, continuous learning is not merely an option but a necessity for career advancement. Professionals who commit to lifelong learning are better positioned to excel, adapt to change, and contribute meaningfully to the rapidly expanding frontiers of AI and Big Data.

Conclusion:

Building a successful career in AI and Big Data is both rewarding and intellectually stimulating. By acquiring key skills, pursuing relevant education, and adhering to ethical principles, individuals can embark on a fulfilling journey in these rapidly growing fields. Networking, professional development, and a commitment to continual learning are essential for long-term success in the ever-evolving landscape of AI and Big Data.

Essential Skills and Educational Pathways:

A career in Artificial Intelligence (AI) and Big Data is characterized by its dynamism and the ever-evolving nature of technology. To excel in this field, professionals must possess a diverse set of essential skills and engage in specific educational pathways. This section explores the crucial skills and educational routes required to establish a successful career in AI and Big Data.

Essential Skills for Success

1. **Programming Proficiency:** Proficiency in programming languages such as Python, R, and Java is fundamental for AI and Big Data professionals (Kelleher et al., 2015). These languages are commonly used for data analysis, machine learning, and building AI models.

2. **Data Manipulation:** A solid grasp of data manipulation techniques, including data cleaning, transformation, and feature engineering, is essential (VanderPlas, 2016). These skills are critical for working with large datasets.

3. **Machine Learning and Deep Learning:** Understanding machine learning algorithms and deep learning frameworks like TensorFlow and PyTorch is indispensable for AI practitioners (Goodfellow et al., 2016). Proficiency in model development, training, and evaluation is crucial.

4. **Statistics and Probability:** A strong foundation in statistics and probability theory is necessary for data analysis and making data-driven decisions (Hastie et al., 2009). Statistical concepts underpin many AI and Big Data techniques.

5. **Data Visualization:** Effective communication of insights and findings is facilitated by data visualization skills (Wickham, 2016). Professionals should be adept at creating clear and informative visual representations of data.

6. **Domain Knowledge:** Domain-specific knowledge is valuable, as it allows professionals to apply AI and Big Data techniques

effectively in specific industries, such as healthcare, finance, or manufacturing (Provost & Fawcett, 2013).

7. **Ethical Awareness:** Ethical considerations in data handling, privacy, and bias mitigation are essential. Professionals must operate with a strong ethical foundation (Floridi et al., 2018).

Educational Pathways

1. **Bachelor's Degree:** Many professionals start their journey with a Bachelor's degree in fields such as computer science, data science, or engineering (Provost & Fawcett, 2013). These programs provide a strong foundational knowledge of AI and Big Data concepts.
2. **Master's Degree:** Pursuing a Master's degree in AI, data science, or related disciplines offers more specialized knowledge and research opportunities (Provost & Fawcett, 2013). It is often a preferred choice for career advancement.
3. **Online Courses and Certifications:** Numerous online platforms offer courses and certifications in AI and Big Data, allowing professionals to upskill while working (Coursera, edX, Udacity) (Zheng et al., 2018).
4. **Ph.D. Programs:** For those interested in research and academia, Ph.D. programs in AI or related fields provide in-depth knowledge and the opportunity to contribute to the field's advancement (Provost & Fawcett, 2013).

Continuous Learning

1. **Stay Informed:** AI and Big Data professionals should continuously update their knowledge by reading research papers, blogs, and industry news (Zheng et al., 2018).

2. **Professional Development:** Participating in workshops, conferences, and webinars keeps professionals updated with the latest trends and technologies (Guo et al., 2013).

Building a Resilient Career

A career in AI and Big Data demands a commitment to continual learning and skill development. Professionals with a strong foundation in essential skills and a relevant educational background are well-prepared to navigate the evolving landscape of technology, making valuable contributions to their organizations and the broader field of AI and Big Data.

Career Opportunities and Growth Prospects:

The career landscape in Artificial Intelligence (AI) and Big Data is characterized by unparalleled opportunities and remarkable growth prospects. As the demand for AI and data-driven solutions continues to surge across industries, professionals entering these fields are presented with a dynamic and promising career trajectory. This section explores the expansive career opportunities and the potential for growth in AI and Big Data.

The Booming AI and Big Data Job Market

1. **Unprecedented Demand:** The global demand for AI and Big Data professionals has reached unprecedented levels, driven by businesses seeking to harness data for informed decision-making and innovation (McAfee & Brynjolfsson, 2017).

2. **Diverse Industries:** AI and Big Data applications span across diverse industries, including healthcare, finance, manufacturing, e-commerce, and more, offering professionals the flexibility to choose domains aligned with their interests (Davenport & Harris, 2007).

Career Opportunities

1. **Data Scientist:** Data scientists analyze and interpret complex data sets, extracting valuable insights that inform business strategies (Provost & Fawcett, 2013).
2. **Machine Learning Engineer:** These professionals design and implement machine learning models and algorithms, contributing to AI-powered applications (Chollet, 2018).
3. **AI Researcher:** AI researchers explore cutting-edge AI technologies, developing new algorithms, and pushing the boundaries of AI capabilities (Russell & Norvig, 2021).
4. **Big Data Analyst:** Big Data analysts manage and analyze large volumes of data to derive actionable intelligence for organizations (Chen et al., 2012).
5. **AI Ethicist:** Ethical considerations in AI are gaining prominence, creating opportunities for professionals to ensure responsible AI development and deployment (Floridi et al., 2018).

Growth Prospects

1. **Rapid Advancements:** AI and Big Data are dynamic fields where new technologies, tools, and techniques continually emerge. Professionals can expect to witness and contribute to rapid advancements (Provost & Fawcett, 2013).
2. **Management Roles:** As professionals gain experience, they can transition into leadership roles such as Chief Data Officer (CDO) or Chief AI Officer (CAIO), overseeing AI and data strategies at the organizational level (Davenport & Harris, 2007).
3. **Consulting and Entrepreneurship:** Seasoned professionals often explore consulting or entrepreneurship opportunities, leveraging their expertise to provide AI and Big Data solutions to a broader market (McAfee & Brynjolfsson, 2017).

4. **Interdisciplinary Roles:** AI and Big Data professionals have the potential to work in interdisciplinary roles, collaborating with experts in fields like healthcare, climate science, and social sciences to tackle complex global challenges (Russell & Norvig, 2021).

Educational and Skill Requirements for Advancement

1. **Continuous Learning:** Professionals must commit to continuous learning to stay updated with the latest developments in AI and Big Data (Provost & Fawcett, 2013).
2. **Advanced Degrees:** Pursuing advanced degrees, such as Master's or Ph.D. programs, can open doors to specialized roles and research opportunities (Russell & Norvig, 2021).
3. **Networking:** Building a strong professional network within the AI and Big Data community can lead to collaborations, mentorship, and career opportunities (Guo et al., 2013).

Conclusion: A Thriving Career in AI and Big Data

For those entering or considering a career in AI and Big Data, the prospects are undeniably promising. The combination of soaring demand, diverse job opportunities, and growth potential makes these fields highly attractive for aspiring professionals. Embracing a commitment to continual learning and staying at the forefront of technological advancements will be key to capitalizing on the expansive career landscape offered by AI and Big Data.

Advice from Industry Experts:

Building a successful career in the dynamic and rapidly evolving fields of Artificial Intelligence (AI) and Big Data often benefits from insights and guidance from industry experts who have navigated these domains. Drawing from the wisdom of seasoned professionals and thought leaders, this section presents valuable advice for aspiring individuals seeking to embark on a fulfilling career journey in AI and Big Data.

Continuous Learning and Adaptation

1. **Stay Curious and Inquisitive:** Experts emphasize the importance of nurturing curiosity and a hunger for knowledge. Be eager to explore new technologies, research, and methodologies to keep pace with the ever-changing landscape of AI and Big Data (Hastie et al., 2009).

2. **Embrace Lifelong Learning:** The AI and Big Data fields demand continuous learning. Seek opportunities for professional development, whether through formal education, online courses, or self-study, to stay relevant and competitive (Provost & Fawcett, 2013).

Skills and Expertise

3. **Master Fundamental Skills:** Experts recommend focusing on mastering fundamental skills such as programming, data manipulation, and statistical analysis. A strong foundation in these areas is essential for success (Kelleher et al., 2015).

1. **Deep Specialization vs. Broad Knowledge:** Consider whether you want to specialize deeply in a particular niche or acquire a broad knowledge base. Both paths can lead to fulfilling careers, but it's crucial to align your choice with your interests and career goals (Russell & Norvig, 2021).

Networking and Collaboration

1. **Network Actively:** Building professional relationships within the AI and Big Data community is invaluable. Attend conferences, meetups, and online forums to connect with peers, mentors, and potential collaborators (Guo et al., 2013).

2. **Collaborate Across Disciplines:** AI and Big Data often intersect with other fields, such as healthcare, finance, and environmental science. Experts advise being open to interdisciplinary collaborations, as they can lead to innovative solutions and career opportunities (Provost & Fawcett, 2013).

Ethical Considerations

1. **Prioritize Ethics and Responsible AI:** With the growing impact of AI on society, experts stress the importance of ethical AI development. Make ethical considerations, such as fairness, transparency, and privacy, a core part of your practice (Floridi et al., 2018).

Mentorship and Career Advancement

1. **Seek Mentorship:** Consider finding a mentor who can provide guidance, share experiences, and offer insights into career advancement. Mentorship can significantly accelerate your professional growth (Zheng et al., 2018).
2. **Leadership Opportunities:** As you progress in your career, explore leadership roles that allow you to influence AI and Big Data strategies at an organizational level. Leadership positions often come with increased responsibility and impact (Davenport & Harris, 2007).

Adapting to Technological Advances

1. **Anticipate Technological Shifts:** AI and Big Data are continually evolving. Be prepared to adapt to technological shifts, embrace new tools and frameworks, and keep an eye on emerging trends (McAfee & Brynjolfsson, 2017).

Conclusion:

Insights for a Rewarding Career

The guidance provided by industry experts in the fields of AI and Big Data offers invaluable insights for those embarking on or advancing their careers. By maintaining a commitment to lifelong learning, cultivating essential skills, nurturing professional relationships, and embracing ethical considerations, individuals can set themselves on a path to a rewarding and impactful career journey in AI and Big Data.

APPENDICES

Appendix A: Glossary of Key Terms:

This glossary serves as a reference guide to clarify and define essential terminology related to Artificial Intelligence (AI) and Big Data, as discussed in the main text. Understanding these key terms is crucial for individuals pursuing a career or engaging with these fields.

A

- **Algorithm:** A step-by-step set of instructions or procedures followed to complete a specific task or solve a problem in AI and data analysis.

B

- **Big Data:** Extremely large and complex datasets that cannot be effectively managed or analyzed with traditional data processing methods.

D

- **Data Cleaning:** The process of identifying and correcting errors or inconsistencies in datasets to ensure data accuracy.
- **Data Mining:** The practice of extracting valuable patterns, information, or insights from large datasets.

- **Deep Learning:** A subfield of machine learning that focuses on training artificial neural networks with multiple layers to perform complex tasks.

E

- **Ethics in AI:** The ethical considerations and principles that guide the development and use of AI systems, including issues related to fairness, transparency, and accountability.

F

- **Machine Learning:** A subset of AI that involves training algorithms to improve their performance on a specific task through data analysis and learning from experience.

I

- **Interoperability:** The ability of different AI or data systems to work together and exchange information seamlessly.

M

- **Machine Vision:** The field of AI that focuses on enabling computers to interpret and understand visual information from the world, similar to human vision.

N

- **Natural Language Processing (NLP):** A branch of AI that deals with the interaction between computers and human language, enabling machines to understand, interpret, and generate human language.

P

- **Predictive Analytics:** The process of using data, statistical algorithms, and machine learning techniques to identify the likelihood of future outcomes based on historical data.

R

- **Reinforcement Learning:** A type of machine learning where an agent learns to make decisions by interacting with an environment and receiving rewards or penalties.

S

- **Supervised Learning:** A machine learning approach where a model is trained on a labeled dataset, with each input-output pair explicitly provided during training.
- **Unsupervised Learning:** A machine learning approach where a model learns patterns and structures from unlabeled data, identifying hidden relationships or clusters.

T

- **TensorFlow:** An open-source deep learning framework developed by Google for building and training machine learning and deep learning models.

U

- **Unstructured Data:** Data that lacks a predefined structure or schema, often including text, images, audio, and video.

V

- **Validation:** The process of assessing the performance of a machine learning model using a separate dataset not used during training to ensure its generalization ability.

This glossary aims to provide a foundation for understanding the terminology commonly encountered in the fields of AI and Big Data. It is important to consult relevant resources and references for in-depth explanations of these terms in specific contexts.

Appendix B: Further Reading and Resources:

This appendix serves as a curated list of recommended books, articles, websites, and other resources for individuals seeking to delve deeper into the fields of Artificial Intelligence (AI) and Big Data. These resources offer in-depth insights, practical knowledge, and valuable guidance for those interested in expanding their understanding and expertise.

Books

1. **"Artificial Intelligence: A Modern Approach" by Stuart Russell and Peter Norvig:** A comprehensive textbook that provides a thorough introduction to AI concepts, algorithms, and applications.
2. **"Python Machine Learning" by Sebastian Raschka and Vahid Mirjalili:** A hands-on guide to machine learning using Python, offering practical examples and code.
3. **"Big Data: A Revolution That Will Transform How We Live, Work, and Think" by Viktor Mayer-Schönberger and Kenneth Cukier:** Explains the impact of big data on society and businesses, highlighting its potential and challenges.

4. **"Deep Learning" by Ian Goodfellow and Yoshua Bengio and Aaron Courville:** An essential resource for those interested in deep learning, covering both theory and practical aspects.

Online Courses and MOOCs

1. **Coursera:** Offers various AI and machine learning courses from top universities and institutions, including Stanford University's "Machine Learning" and the University of Washington's "Machine Learning Specialization."
2. **edX:** Provides a range of courses related to AI, Big Data, and data science, including the "Data Science MicroMasters" program.

Websites and Online Resources

1. **Towards Data Science:** A popular Medium publication with articles, tutorials, and case studies on data science and machine learning topics.
2. **Kaggle:** A platform for data science competitions and datasets, with a vast community and resources for learning and practicing data science.
3. **AI Ethics Guidelines by IEEE:** A collection of resources and guidelines related to ethical considerations in AI development and deployment.

Research Journals and Papers

1. **"Nature Machine Intelligence" and "Journal of Artificial Intelligence Research (JAIR)":** Journals that publish research papers and articles on AI and machine learning advancements.
2. **"Big Data" Journal:** A journal dedicated to the latest developments in the field of big data analytics.

AI and Big Data Conferences

1. **NeurIPS (Conference on Neural Information Processing Systems):** An annual conference on machine learning and AI, featuring cutting-edge research and industry insights.
2. **Strata Data Conference:** A conference focused on big data, data science, and AI, offering tutorials, workshops, and networking opportunities.

Online Forums and Communities

1. **Stack Overflow:** A popular Q&A platform where you can find answers to technical questions related to AI, machine learning, and programming.
2. **Reddit Communities:** Subreddits like r/MachineLearning and r/datascience provide a platform for discussions, questions, and sharing resources.

These resources offer a starting point for individuals looking to explore and deepen their knowledge in the fields of AI and Big Data. The dynamic nature of these fields encourages continuous learning and staying up-to-date with the latest developments through both traditional and online resources.

REFERENCES

- Aggarwal, C. C. (2013). Outlier analysis. In Data mining (pp. 237-263). Springer, Boston, MA.
- Agrawal, A., Gans, J., & Goldfarb, A. (2018). Prediction machines: The simple economics of artificial intelligence. Harvard Business Press.
- Aigner, W., Miksch, S., Schumann, H., & Tominski, C. (2011). Visualization of Time-Oriented Data. Springer.
- Alpaydin, E. (2020). Introduction to machine learning (4th ed.). MIT Press.
- Ananny, M., & Crawford, K. (2018). Seeing without knowing: Limitations of the transparency ideal and its application to algorithmic accountability. New Media & Society, 20(3), 973-989.
- Angermueller, C., Pärnamaa, T., Parts, L., & Stegle, O. (2016). Deep Learning for Computational Biology. *Molecular Systems Biology*, 12(7), 878.
- Archer, N. P., Bharadwaj, A., & Srinivasan, V. (2008). An Integrated Framework for Information Quality Management. *International Journal of Information Management*, 28(6), 469-478.
- Atzori, L., Iera, A., & Morabito, G. (2010). The internet of things: A survey. Computer networks, 54(15), 2787-2805.
- Atzori, L., Iera, A., & Morabito, G. (2017). Understanding the Internet of Things: definition, potentials, and societal role of a fast-evolving paradigm. *Ad Hoc Networks, 56,* 122-140.

- Balakrishnan, V., Lim, Y. S., & Teo, T. W. (2017). Massive Open Online Courses (MOOCs): A Review of Usage, Challenges, and Future Directions. *International Journal of Information Management, 37*(6), 572-582.
- Bargiel, D., Kuboń, M., & Natkaniec, M. (2018). A Review of Autonomous Agricultural Machinery Classification. *Agricultural Engineering, 22*(2), 5-18.
- Barocas, S., & Selbst, A. D. (2016). Big data's disparate impact. *California Law Review, 104,* 671-732.
- Barocas, S., Hardt, M., & Narayanan, A. (2019). *Fairness and Abstraction in Sociotechnical Systems.* ACM FAT* 2019, 59-68. https://doi.org/10.1145/3351095.3372874
- Barocas, S., Hardt, M., & Narayanan, A. (2019). *Fairness and abstraction in sociotechnical systems.* ACM Conference on Fairness, Accountability, and Transparency, 59-68.
- Barocas, S., Hardt, M., & Narayanan, A. (2019). Fairness and Machine Learning. *Big Data, 7*(6), 291-306.
- Barocas, S., Hardt, M., & Narayanan, A. (2019). Fairness and Machine Learning. [Chapter in "Fairness and Machine Learning," Coursera]. Retrieved from https://fairmlbook.org/
- Bathaee, Y. (2018). The artificial intelligence black box and the failure of intent and causation. Harvard Journal of Law & Technology, 31, 889.
- Batini, C., Cappiello, C., Francalanci, C., & Maurino, A. (2009). Methodologies for Data Quality Assessment and Improvement. *ACM Computing Surveys (CSUR),* 41(3), 1-52.
- Bellman, R. (1961). Adaptive control processes: A guided tour. Princeton University Press.
- Bengio, Y., Courville, A., & Vincent, P. (2013). Representation Learning: A Review and New Perspectives. IEEE Transactions on Pattern Analysis and Machine Intelligence, 35(8), 1798-1828.

- Bergstra, J., & Bengio, Y. (2012). Random search for hyper-parameter optimization. Journal of Machine Learning Research, 13(Feb), 281-305.
- Bertino, E. (2009). Data privacy for pervasive computing. IEEE Pervasive Computing, 8(3), 2-4.
- Bertino, E., Castano, S., & Ferrari, E. (2011). Big Data Security and Privacy. *ACM Computing Surveys (CSUR)*, 46(4), 1-41.
- Bertino, E., Islam, S. M. R., Islam, M. S., & Mehedi, M. M. (2018). Role-Based Access Control: Issues and Challenges. In *International Conference on Cyber Security and Cloud Computing* (pp. 1-6).
- Bertsimas, D., & Kallus, N. (2020). From predictive to prescriptive analytics. Management Science, 66(3), 1025-1044.
- Bhattacharyya, S., Jha, S., Tharakunnel, K., & Westland, J. C. (2011). Data mining for credit card fraud: A comparative study. Decision Support Systems, 50(3), 602-613.
- Bholat, D., Hansen, S., Santos, P., & Schonhardt-Bailey, C. (2015). Text mining for central banks: Handbook – No 33. Centre for Central Banking Studies.
- Biblioteca, M., Marchiori, M., Vali, M., & Falcone, A. (2018). A Comparative Analysis of Supervised Learning Algorithms for Credit Scoring Purposes. *Expert Systems with Applications*, 114, 154-167.
- Bird, S., Klein, E., & Loper, E. (2009). Natural Language Processing with Python. O'Reilly Media, Inc.
- Bishop, C. M. (2006). *Pattern Recognition and Machine Learning.* springer.
- Bizer, C., Heath, T., & Berners-Lee, T. (2009). Linked data - The story so far. International Journal on Semantic Web and Information Systems (IJSWIS), 5(3), 1-22.
- Boettiger, C. (2015). An Introduction to Docker for Reproducible Research. *ACM SIGOPS Operating Systems Review*, 49(1), 71-79.

- Bollen, J., Mao, H., & Zeng, X. (2011). Twitter Mood Predicts the Stock Market. *Journal of Computational Science*, 2(1), 1-8.
- Borgman, C. L. (2012). The conundrum of sharing research data. Journal of the American Society for Information Science and Technology, 63(6), 1059-1078.
- Bostrom, N. (2014). Superintelligence: Paths, dangers, strategies. Oxford University Press.
- Bostrom, N., & Yudkowsky, E. (2014). The ethics of artificial intelligence. In The Cambridge Handbook of Artificial Intelligence, eds. W. Ramsey and K. Frankish. Cambridge University Press.
- Bostrom, N., & Yudkowsky, E. (2014). The ethics of artificial intelligence. The Cambridge Handbook of Artificial Intelligence, 316-334.
- Botsman, R., & Miles, A. (2016). The Evolution of Trust. *New Economic Perspectives*, 24(2), 22-26.
- Bottou, L., & Bousquet, O. (2008). The tradeoffs of large scale learning. In Advances in neural information processing systems (pp. 161-168).
- Brear, M., Berry, J., & Sinha, R. (2018). Regulatory Technology (RegTech) and Financial Crime: Evidence across Anti-Money Laundering (AML) and Know Your Customer (KYC) Compliance. *Journal of Money Laundering Control*, 21(3), 249-263.
- Brynjolfsson, E., & McAfee, A. (2014). The second machine age: Work, progress, and prosperity in a time of brilliant technologies. W.W. Norton & Company.
- Buolamwini, J., & Gebru, T. (2018). Gender Shades: Intersectional Accuracy Disparities in Commercial Gender Classification. Proceedings of Machine Learning Research, 81, 1-15. Retrieved from http://proceedings.mlr.press/v81/buolamwini18a.html
- Burrell, J. (2016). How the machine 'thinks': Understanding opacity in machine learning algorithms. Big Data & Society, 3(1).
- Cartea, Á., Jaimungal, S., & Penalva, J. (2015). Algorithmic trading with learning. *Mathematics and Financial Economics*, 9(1), 3-40.

- Caruana, R., Lou, Y., Gehrke, J., Koch, P., Sturm, M., Elhadad, N., & Wallace, B. (2015). Intelligible Models for Healthcare: Predicting Pneumonia Risk and Hospital 30-day Readmission. In *Proceedings of the 21th ACM SIGKDD International Conference on Knowledge Discovery and Data Mining* (KDD'15), 1721-1730.
- Castelvecchi, D. (2016). Can we open the black box of AI? Nature News, 538(7623), 20.
- Castelvecchi, D. (2017). Quantum computers ready to leap out of the lab in 2017. *Nature, 541*(7635), 9-10.
- Cath, C., Wachter, S., Mittelstadt, B., Taddeo, M., & Floridi, L. (2018). Artificial intelligence and the 'good society': The US, EU, and UK approach. Science and Engineering Ethics, 24(2), 505-528.
- Cavoukian, A. (2009). Privacy by Design: The 7 Foundational Principles. *Information and Privacy Commissioner of Ontario.*
- Cavoukian, A. (2010). Privacy by design: The definitive workshop. Identity in the Information Society, 3(2), 247-251.
- Cavoukian, A. (2011). Privacy by design in law, policy and practice: A white paper for decision-makers. Information and Privacy Commissioner of Ontario, Canada.
- Cavoukian, A. (2012). Privacy by default: The next generation of privacy protection. In The Law of Electronic Commerce. Edward Elgar Publishing.
- Cavoukian, A., & Castro, D. (2016). Big Data and Innovation, Setting the Record Straight: De-identification Does Work. *Privacy Analytics Inc.*
- Cavoukian, A., & Jonas, J. (2012). Privacy by design in the age of big data. Information and Privacy Commissioner of Ontario, Canada.
- Chaudhuri, S., Dayal, U., & Narasayya, V. (2011). An overview of business intelligence technology. Communications of the ACM, 54(8), 88-98.

- Chawla, N. V., Bowyer, K. W., Hall, L. O., & Kegelmeyer, W. P. (2002). SMOTE: synthetic minority over-sampling technique. Journal of artificial intelligence research, 16, 321-357.
- Chen, J., & Song, L. (2018). Improving fairness in machine learning systems: What do industry practitioners need? In *Proceedings of the 2018 CHI Conference on Human Factors in Computing Systems* (pp. 168).
- Chen, J., Pan, X., Monga, R., Bengio, Y., & Jozefowicz, R. (2014). Revisiting Distributed Synchronous SGD. arXiv preprint arXiv:1604.00981.
- Chen, J., Song, L., Wainwright, M. J., & Jordan, M. I. (2018). Learning to Explain: An Information-Theoretic Perspective on Model Interpretation. In *Proceedings of the 35th International Conference on Machine Learning* (ICML'18), 883-892.
- Chen, M., & Zhang, Y. (2014). Big data: Challenges, opportunities, and realities. *Effective Big Data Management and Opportunities for Implementation*, 1-25.
- Chen, M., Mao, S., & Liu, Y. (2014). Big Data: A Survey. *Mobile Networks and Applications*, 19(2), 171-209.
- Chen, M., Mao, S., Zhang, Y., & Leung, V. C. (2014). Big Data: Related Technologies, Challenges and Future Prospects. Springer.
- Chen, T., Li, M., Li, Y., Lin, M., Wang, N., Wang, M., ... & Zhang, Z. (2014). MXNet: A flexible and efficient machine learning library for heterogeneous distributed systems. arXiv preprint arXiv:1512.01274.
- Choi, Y., Hwang, J., & McMillan, S. (2020). Gearing up for the future: The role of big data analytics in retailing. *Journal of Business Research, 117*, 1-6.
- Chollet, F. (2018). *Deep Learning with Python*. Manning Publications.

- Coursera. (n.d.). *Big Data Specialization.* [Coursera Course]. Retrieved from https://www.coursera.org/specializations/big-data
- Crawford, K. (2013). The Hidden Biases in Big Data. *Harvard Business Review*, 1-6.
- Crawford, K., & Calo, R. (2016). There Is a Blind Spot in AI Research. *Nature*, 538(7625), 311-313.
- Cugola, G., & Margara, A. (2012). Processing Flows of Information: From Data Stream to Complex Event Processing. *ACM Computing Surveys (CSUR)*, 44(3), 1-62.
- Cunningham, J. P., & Ghahramani, Z. (2015). Linear dimensionality reduction: Survey, insights, and generalizations. Journal of Machine Learning Research, 16, 2859-2900.
- Davenport, T. H. (2013). Analytics in big data. International Institute for Analytics, 19.
- Davenport, T. H. (2014). Big Data in Big Companies. *Harvard Business Review*, 92(10), 60-68.
- Davenport, T. H., & Harris, J. (2007). Competing on Analytics: The New Science of Winning. *Harvard Business Press.*
- Davenport, T. H., & Patil, D. J. (2012). Data Scientist: The sexiest job of the 21st century. Harvard Business Review, 90(10), 70-76.
- Davenport, T. H., Guha, A., Grewal, D., & Bressgott, T. (2020). How artificial intelligence will change the future of marketing. *Journal of the Academy of Marketing Science, 48*(1), 24-42.
- De Fauw, J., Ledsam, J. R., Romera-Paredes, B., Nikolov, S., Tomasev, N., Blackwell, S., ... & Ronneberger, O. (2018). Clinically applicable deep learning for diagnosis and referral in retinal disease. Nature Medicine, 24(9), 1342-1350.
- Dean, J., & Ghemawat, S. (2008). MapReduce: Simplified data processing on large clusters. Communications of the ACM, 51(1), 107-113.
- Deng, J., Liu, X., & Deng, X. (2016). The Promise and Challenges of IoT in Industry. *IEEE Transactions on Industrial Informatics*, 12(6), 2716-2722.

- Deng, X., Liu, X., & Deng, X. (2013). Applied Data-Centric Social Sciences: Concepts, Data, Computation, and Theory. *Springer Science & Business Media.*
- Deng, X., Liu, X., & Deng, X. (2013). Applied Data-Centric Social Sciences: Concepts, Data, Computation, and Theory. *Springer Science & Business Media.*
- Dhar, V. (2013). Data Science and Prediction. *Communications of the ACM,* 56(12), 64-73.
- Diakopoulos, N. (2016). Accountability in algorithmic decision making. Communications of the ACM, 59(2), 56-62.
- Diakopoulos, N. (2016). Algorithmic Accountability: A Primer. *Data & Society Research Institute.* Retrieved from https://datasociety.net/pubs/ia/DataAndSociety_Algorithmic_Accountability_Primer_2016.pdf
- Diakopoulos, N., Friedler, S., Arenas, M., Barocas, S., Hardt, M., & Narayanan, A. (2016). Principles for Accountable Algorithms and a Social Impact Statement for Algorithms. *arXiv preprint arXiv:1606.08813.*
- Díaz, M., Hogan, A., & Lau, T. (2019). Interactive and interpretable machine learning models for human machine collaboration. ACM Transactions on Interactive Intelligent Systems (TiiS), 9(2-3), 1-23.
- Dignum, V. (2019). Responsible artificial intelligence: How to develop and use AI in a responsible way. *Springer.*
- Dixon, J. (2010). Pentaho, Hadoop, and Data Lakes. Pentaho Big Data Blog.
- Domingos, P. (2012). A Few Useful Things to Know About Machine Learning. *Communications of the ACM,* 55(10), 78-87.
- Donalek, C., Djorgovski, S. G., Cioc, A., Wang, A., Zhang, J., Lawler, E., ... & Longo, G. (2014). Immersive and Collaborative Data Visualization Using Virtual Reality Platforms. In 2014 IEEE International Conference on Big Data (Big Data) (pp. 609-614). IEEE.

- Doshi-Velez, F., & Kim, B. (2017). Towards a rigorous science of interpretable machine learning. arXiv preprint arXiv:1702.08608.
- Doshi-Velez, F., Kortz, M., Budish, R., Bavitz, C., Gershman, S., O'Brien, D., ... & Waldo, J. (2017). Accountability of AI under the law: The role of explanation. Berkman Klein Center Research Publication, 2017-2018.
- Dulac-Arnold, G., Evans, R., van Hasselt, H., Sunehag, P., Lillicrap, T., Hunt, J., ... & Coppin, B. (2015). Deep reinforcement learning in large discrete action spaces. arXiv preprint arXiv:1512.07679.
- Dunne, A. (2015). Hertzian Tales: Electronic Products, Aesthetic Experience, and Critical Design. *MIT Press.*
- Dwork, C. (2008). Differential privacy: A survey of results. In Theory and Applications of Models of Computation (pp. 1-19). Springer, Berlin, Heidelberg.
- Dwork, C., Hardt, M., Pitassi, T., Reingold, O., & Zemel, R. (2012). Fairness and Machine Learning. In *Proceedings of the 3rd Innovations in Theoretical Computer Science Conference* (pp. 117-129).
- edX. (n.d.). *Data Science Professional Certificate.* [edX Certification]. Retrieved from https://www.edx.org/professional-certificate/ibm-data-science
- Ekman, F., Koutsopoulos, H. N., & Jenelius, E. (2018). Real-time short-term traffic forecasting using machine learning and streaming data. Transportation Research Record, 2672(45), 45-55.
- Esteva, A., Kuprel, B., Novoa, R. A., Ko, J., Swetter, S. M., Blau, H. M., & Thrun, S. (2019). Dermatologist-level classification of skin cancer with deep neural networks. Nature, 542(7639), 115–118.
- Esteva, A., Kuprel, B., Novoa, R. A., Ko, J., Swetter, S. M., Blau, H. M., & Thrun, S. (2017). Dermatologist-level Classification of Skin Cancer with Deep Neural Networks. *Nature*, 542(7639), 115-118.

- European Parliament and Council. (2016). Regulation (EU) 2016/679 of the European Parliament and of the Council of 27 April 2016 on the protection of natural persons with regard to the processing of personal data and on the free movement of such data (General Data Protection Regulation).
- Fan, J., Han, F., & Liu, H. (2014). Challenges of big data analysis. National Science Review, 1(2), 293-314.
- Fan, J., Lau, R. Y., & Vojnovic, M. (2014). On the complexity of multi-dimensional data clustering and classification. Proceedings of the 2014 IEEE International Conference on Big Data (Big Data).
- Few, S. (2009). Now you see it: Simple visualization techniques for quantitative analysis. Analytics Press.
- Few, S. (2009). Now You See It: Simple Visualization Techniques for Quantitative Analysis. Analytics Press.
- Fjeld, J., Achten, N., Hilligoss, H., Nagy, A., & Srikumar, M. (2020). Principled Artificial Intelligence: Mapping Consensus in Ethical and Rights-Based Approaches to Principles for AI. Berkman Klein Center Research Publication, (2020-1).
- Floridi, L. (2016). The fourth revolution: How the infosphere is reshaping human reality. Oxford University Press.
- Floridi, L., & Cowls, J. (2019). A unified framework of five principles for AI in society. Harvard Data Science Review, 1(1).
- Floridi, L., Cowls, J., Beltrametti, M., Chatila, R., Chazerand, P., Dignum, V., ... & Engelmann, L. (2018). AI4People—An Ethical Framework for a Good AI Society: Opportunities, Risks, Principles, and Recommendations. *Minds and Machines*, 28(4), 689-707.
- Gama, J., Žliobaitė, I., Bifet, A., Pechenizkiy, M., & Bouchachia, A. (2014). A Survey on Concept Drift Adaptation. *ACM Computing Surveys (CSUR)*, 46(4), 1-37.
- Gandomi, A., & Haider, M. (2015). Beyond the hype: Big data concepts, methods, and analytics. International Journal of Information Management, 35(2), 137-144.

- García, S., Luengo, J., & Herrera, F. (2015). Data preprocessing in data mining. Springer.
- García-Laencina, P. J., Sancho-Gómez, J. L., & Figueiras-Vidal, A. R. (2010). Pattern classification with missing data: a review. Neural Computing and Applications, 19(2), 263-282.
- Gavai, A., Yadav, R., & Kaushal, R. (2019). Artificial Intelligence in Cybersecurity: A Review. *Procedia Computer Science*, 155, 47-54.
- Gavai, A., Yadav, R., & Kaushal, R. (2019). Artificial Intelligence in Cybersecurity: A Review. *Procedia Computer Science*, 155, 47-54.
- Gentry, C. (2009). A fully homomorphic encryption scheme. Stanford University.
- Gomez-Uribe, C. A., & Hunt, N. (2016). The Netflix recommender system: Algorithms, business value, and innovation. *ACM Transactions on Management Information Systems (TMIS),7(4), 13.
- Goodfellow, I., Bengio, Y., & Courville, A. (2016). Deep Learning. MIT Press.
- Goodfellow, I., Bengio, Y., Courville, A., & Bengio, Y. (2016). *Deep Learning* (Vol. 1). MIT press Cambridge.
- Goodman, B., & Flaxman, S. (2017). European Union regulations on algorithmic decision-making and a "right to explanation". AI Magazine, 38(3), 50-57.
- Goodman, B., & Flaxman, S. (2017). European Union regulations on algorithmic decision-making and a "right to explanation". *AI Magazine, 38*(3), 50-57.
- Greenleaf, G. W. (2017). Data Minimization and the Role of Data Protection Principles in Big Data. In *Law, Privacy and Surveillance in a Post-Snowden World* (pp. 193-208). Springer.
- Greenleaf, G. W., & Cottier, B. M. (2019). The European Union's Emerging GDPR as a Limitation on Data Flows. *Journal of International Data Privacy Law*, 9(3), 259-283.

- Gruber, T. R. (1993). A translation approach to portable ontology specifications. Knowledge acquisition, 5(2), 199-220.
- Gubbi, J., Buyya, R., Marusic, S., & Palaniswami, M. (2013). Internet of Things (IoT): A Vision, Architectural Elements, and Future Directions. *Future Generation Computer Systems*, 29(7), 1645-1660.
- Gunning, D. (2017). Explainable artificial intelligence (XAI). Defense Advanced Research Projects Agency (DARPA), nd Web.
- Guo, P. J., Kim, J., & Rubin, R. (2013). How video production affects student engagement: An empirical study of MOOC videos. In *Proceedings of the first ACM conference on Learning@ scale conference* (pp. 41-50).
- Guyon, I., & Elisseeff, A. (2003). An introduction to variable and feature selection. Journal of machine learning research, 3(Mar), 1157-1182.
- Hagendorff, T. (2020). The ethics of AI ethics: An evaluation of guidelines. Minds and Machines, 30(1), 99-120.
- Hajian, S., Bonchi, F., & Castillo, C. (2016). Algorithmic Bias Detectable in Amazon Delivery Service. *arXiv preprint arXiv:1603.07043*.
- Halevy, A., Norvig, P., & Pereira, F. (2009). The unreasonable effectiveness of data. IEEE Intelligent Systems, 24(2), 8-12.
- Halevy, A., Rajaraman, A., & Ordille, J. (2006). Data integration: The teenage years. In Proceedings of the 32nd international conference on Very large data bases (pp. 9-16).
- Han, J., Pei, J., & Kamber, M. (2011). Data mining: Concepts and techniques (3rd ed.). Elsevier.
- Hardt, M., Price, E., & Srebro, N. (2016). Equality of Opportunity in Supervised Learning. In *Proceedings of the 30th International Conference on Neural Information Processing Systems* (NIPS'16), 3323-3331.

- Hashem, I. A. T., Yaqoob, I., Anuar, N. B., Mokhtar, S., Gani, A., & Khan, S. U. (2015). The rise of "big data" on cloud computing: Review and open research issues. *Information Systems, 47*, 98-115.
- Hastie, T., Tibshirani, R., & Friedman, J. (2009). *The Elements of Statistical Learning.* Springer.
- Hawkins, D. M. (2004). The problem of overfitting. Journal of Chemical Information and Computer Sciences, 44(1), 1-12.
- Hobbs, P. R., & Godwin, D. C. (2015). Crop Residue Removal for Bioenergy Production: Effects on Soils and Recommendations. *Agronomy Journal,* 107(6), 2166-2172.
- Hodge, V. J., & Austin, J. (2004). A survey of outlier detection methodologies. Artificial Intelligence Review, 22(2), 85-126.
- Hoepman, J. H. (2014). Privacy design strategies. In IFIP International Information Security Conference (pp. 446-459). Springer, Berlin, Heidelberg.
- Howard, A. G., Zhu, M., Chen, B., Kalenichenko, D., Wang, W., Weyand, T., ... & Adam, H. (2017). MobileNets: Efficient convolutional neural networks for mobile vision applications. arXiv preprint arXiv:1704.04861.
- Hsu, C. L. (2019). The Impacts of Personalization and Interaction on Consumers' Purchase Intention in the Context of Online Shopping. *International Journal of Information Management,* 44, 65-75.
- Huang, M. H., & Rust, R. T. (2018). Artificial intelligence in service. *Journal of Service Research, 21*(2), 155-172.
- Indurkhya, N., & Damerau, F. J. (2010). Handbook of Natural Language Processing (2nd ed.). CRC Press.
- Inmon, W. H. (2005). Building the Data Warehouse. John Wiley & Sons.
- Inmon, W. H., Inmon, B., & Nesavich, T. A. (2016). The Data Warehouse Toolkit: The Definitive Guide to Dimensional Modeling. *Wiley.*

- Islam, S. R., Kwak, D., Kabir, M. H., Hossain, M., & Kwak, K. S. (2015). The Internet of Things for health care: a comprehensive survey. *IEEE Access, 3,* 678-708.
- Jain, A. K., Nandakumar, K., & Ross, A. (2005). Score normalization in multimodal biometric systems. Pattern recognition, 38(12), 2270-2285.
- James, G., Witten, D., Hastie, T., & Tibshirani, R. (2013). An Introduction to Statistical Learning. Springer.
- Jardine, A. K., Lin, D., & Banjevic, D. (2006). A Review on Machinery Diagnostics and Prognostics Implementing Condition-Based Maintenance. *Mechanical Systems and Signal Processing,* 20(7), 1483-1510.
- Javornik, A. (2016). Augmented reality: Research agenda for studying the impact of its media characteristics on consumer behaviour. *Journal of Retailing and Consumer Services, 30,* 252-261.
- Jobin, A., Ienca, M., & Vayena, E. (2019). The global landscape of AI ethics guidelines. Nature Machine Intelligence, 1(9), 389-399.
- Jobin, A., Ienca, M., Vayena, E., & Fellmann, F. (2019). The Global Landscape of AI Ethics Guidelines. *Nature Machine Intelligence,* 1(9), 389-399.
- Jordan, M. I., & Mitchell, T. M. (2015). Machine learning: Trends, perspectives, and prospects. Science, 349(6245), 255-260.
- Jordan, M. I., & Mitchell, T. M. (2015). Machine learning: Trends, perspectives, and prospects. Science, 349(6245), 255-260.
- Jordan, M. I., & Mitchell, T. M. (2015). Machine learning: Trends, perspectives, and prospects. *Science, 349*(6245), 255-260.
- Jouppi, N. P., Young, C., Patil, N., Patterson, D., Agrawal, G., Bajwa, R., ... & Boyle, R. (2017). In-datacenter performance analysis of a tensor processing unit. In Proceedings of the 44th Annual International Symposium on Computer Architecture (pp. 1-12).
- Jurafsky, D., & Martin, J. H. (2014). Speech and Language Processing. Pearson.

- Kaelbling, L. P., Littman, M. L., & Moore, A. W. (1996). Reinforcement learning: A survey. Journal of Artificial Intelligence Research, 4, 237-285.
- Kamarinou, D., Millard, C., & Singh, J. (2016). Machine learning with personal data. *Queen Mary School of Law Legal Studies Research Paper, 247*.
- Kambatla, K., Kollias, G., Kumar, V., & Grama, A. (2014). Trends in big data analytics. Journal of Parallel and Distributed Computing, 74(7), 2561-2573.
- Kamiran, F., Karim, A., & Zhang, X. (2012). Decision Theory for Discrimination-aware Classification. In *2012 IEEE 12th International Conference on Data Mining* (ICDM'12), 924-929.
- Kaplan, A. M., & Haenlein, M. (2010). Users of the world, unite! The challenges and opportunities of Social Media. Business horizons, 53(1), 59-68.
- Kaplan, S., Bicen, H., & O'Connor, A. (2019). Augmented Reality in Retail: A Review of the Literature. *Information Systems and e-Business Management*, 17(2), 225-257.
- Kaushik, A. (2009). Web analytics 2.0: The art of online accountability and science of customer centricity. John Wiley & Sons.
- Keim, D., Qu, H., & Ma, K. L. (2013). Big-Data Visualization. IEEE Computer Graphics and Applications, 33(4), 20-21.
- Kelleher, J. D., Namee, B. M., & D'Arcy, A. (2015). *Fundamentals of Machine Learning for Predictive Data Analytics: Algorithms, Worked Examples, and Case Studies*. MIT press.
- Kesan, J. P., Hayes, C. M., & Bashir, M. (2013). Information privacy and data control in cloud computing: Consumers, privacy preferences, and market efficiency. Washington and Lee Law Review, 70, 341.
- Khatri, V., & Brown, C. V. (2010). Designing data governance. Communications of the ACM, 53(1), 148-152.

- Kim, W., Choi, B., Hong, E., Kim, S., & Lee, D. (2003). A taxonomy of dirty data. Data Mining and Knowledge Discovery, 7(1), 81-99.
- Kitchin, R. (2014). The Data Revolution: Big Data, Open Data, Data Infrastructures and Their Consequences. SAGE.
- Koehn, P. (2009). Statistical Machine Translation. Cambridge University Press.
- Kohavi, R. (1995). A study of cross-validation and bootstrap for accuracy estimation and model selection. In Ijcai (Vol. 14, No. 2, pp. 1137-1145).
- Konečný, J., McMahan, H. B., Ramage, D., & Richtárik, P. (2016). Federated optimization: Distributed machine learning for on-device intelligence. *arXiv preprint arXiv:1610.02527*.
- Koops, B. J. (2014). The concept of privacy in the context of data minimization. *International Data Privacy Law, 4*(2), 119-130.
- Koops, B. J. (2016). The trouble with European data protection law. International Data Privacy Law, 6(4), 259-262.
- Korpela, J., Seppälä, T., Malmberg, J., & Systä, K. (2017). How Does Artificial Intelligence Help in Optimal Decision-Making in Industry 4.0 in the Context of Logistics and Supply Chain Management? In *Proceedings of the 50th Hawaii International Conference on System Sciences.*
- Kosta, E., Dumortier, J., & Carette, J. (2017). Can Consent Enhance Privacy? Comparing Legal and Online Standards of Consent in the EU and United States. *Journal of Law, Medicine & Ethics*, 45(1_suppl), 25-38.
- Kreps, J., Narkhede, N., & Rao, J. (2011). Kafka: A distributed messaging system for log processing. In Proceedings of the NetDB.
- Krishna, R., Zhu, Y., Groth, O., Johnson, J., Hata, K., Kravitz, J., ... & Fei-Fei, L. (2016). Visual Genome: Connecting Language and Vision Using Crowdsourced Dense Image Annotations. arXiv preprint arXiv:1602.07332.

- Kroll, J. A., Huey, J., Barocas, S., Felten, E. W., Reidenberg, J. R., Robinson, D. G., & Yu, H. (2017). Accountable algorithms. University of Pennsylvania Law Review, 165(3), 633-705.
- Kumar, S., & Spafford, E. H. (2004). A Software Architecture for Building Intrusion Detection Systems. *Computer Networks*, 44(5), 585-609.
- Laney, D. (2001). 3D data management: Controlling data volume, velocity, and variety. META Group Research Note.
- Langley, P. (2020). Data governance in the digital age. Computer Law & Security Review, 36(3), 105367.
- Lary, D. J., Zewdie, G. K., Liu, X., Wu, D., Levetin, E., Allee, R. J., ... & Mussa, H. (2016). Machine learning applications for Earth observation. In Earth Observation Open Science and Innovation (pp. 165-218). Springer, Cham.
- LeCun, Y., Bengio, Y., & Hinton, G. (2015). Deep learning. Nature, 521(7553), 436-444.
- Lee, Y. W., Strong, D. M., Kahn, B. K., & Wang, R. Y. (2002). AIMQ: A Methodology for Information Quality Assessment. *Information & Management*, 40(2), 133-146.
- Lenzerini, M. (2002). Data integration: A theoretical perspective. In Proceedings of the twenty-first ACM SIGMOD-SIGACT-SIGART symposium on Principles of database systems (pp. 233-246).
- Lipton, Z. C. (2016). The Mythos of Model Interpretability. *arXiv preprint arXiv:1606.03490.*
- Lipton, Z. C. (2018). The mythos of model interpretability. Queue, 16(3), 31-57.
- Lipton, Z. C., Berkowitz, J., & Elkan, C. (2018). A Critical Review of Recurrent Neural Networks for Sequence Learning. *arXiv preprint arXiv:1506.00019.*
- Litjens, G., Kooi, T., Bejnordi, B. E., Setio, A. A. A., Ciompi, F., Ghafoorian, M., ... & Ginneken, B. (2017). A Survey on Deep

Learning in Medical Image Analysis. *Medical Image Analysis*, 42, 60-88.

- Little, R. J., & Rubin, D. B. (2002). Statistical analysis with missing data. John Wiley & Sons.
- Liu, B. (2012). Sentiment Analysis and Opinion Mining. Morgan & Claypool Publishers.
- Liu, D., Elhoseny, M., Yuan, X., Salama, A. S., & Riad, A. M. (2016). Big Data: The Next Feasible Frontier for Innovations in Information Technology. *Journal of King Saud University - Computer and Information Sciences.*
- Liu, H., Li, L., Zhang, Y., & Zhang, M. (2017). Precision Agriculture—An Opportunity for EU-China Research Collaboration. *NJAS-Wageningen Journal of Life Sciences*, 81, 2-6.
- Liu, Z., Nersessian, N. J., & Stasko, J. T. (2008). Distributed cognition as a theoretical framework for information visualization. IEEE transactions on visualization and computer graphics, 14(6), 1173-1180.
- Lo, A. W. (2017). The Gordon Gekko Effect: The Role of Culture in the Financial Industry. *Annual Review of Financial Economics*, 9, 1-26.
- Losing, V., Hammer, B., & Wersing, H. (2018). Incremental on-line learning: A review and comparison of state of the art algorithms. *Neurocomputing, 275*, 1261-1274.
- Lowenberg-DeBoer, J., Erickson, B., & Vollrath, T. (2017). Precision Agriculture and Sustainability. *Annual Review of Resource Economics*, 9, 411-429.
- Lundberg, S. M., & Lee, S. I. (2017). A Unified Approach to Interpreting Model Predictions. In *Advances in Neural Information Processing Systems 30* (NIPS'17), 4765-4774.
- Mahmood, A. N., Hu, J., & Hu, J. (2018). Cyber Security and Machine Learning as a Service: A Review. *Journal of King Saud University-Computer and Information Sciences.*

- Mandler, B., Wang, M., & Wang, J. (2016). Building a Data Catalog: An Approach to Data Management. *EDUCAUSE Review*, 51(1), 1-14.
- Manning, C. D., & Schütze, H. (1999). Foundations of Statistical Natural Language Processing. MIT Press.
- Manyika, J., Chui, M., Miremadi, M., Bughin, J., George, K., Willmott, P., & Dewhurst, M. (2017). A future that works: Automation, employment, and productivity. *McKinsey Global Institute*.
- Martin, K. (2019). Ethical implications and accountability of algorithms. Journal of Business Ethics, 160(4), 835-850.
- Marz, N., & Warren, J. (2015). Big Data: Principles and best practices of scalable real-time data systems. Manning Publications.
- Mayer-Schönberger, V., & Cukier, K. (2013). Big Data: A revolution that will transform how we live, work, and think. Houghton Mifflin Harcourt.
- McAfee, A., & Brynjolfsson, E. (2012). Big data: The management revolution. Harvard Business Review, 90(10), 60-68.
- McAfee, A., & Brynjolfsson, E. (2017). *Machine, Platform, Crowd: Harnessing Our Digital Future*. W. W. Norton & Company.
- McCarthy, J., Minsky, M. L., Rochester, N., & Shannon, C. E. (2006). A proposal for the Dartmouth summer research project on artificial intelligence, August 31, 1955. AI Magazine, 27(4), 12-14.
- Mehrabi, N., Morstatter, F., Saxena, N., Lerman, K., & Galstyan, A. (2019). A Survey on Bias and Fairness in Machine Learning. arXiv preprint arXiv:1908.09635. Retrieved from https://arxiv.org/abs/1908.09635
- Mittelstadt, B. (2016). Ethics of the health-related internet of things: A narrative review. *Ethics and Information Technology*, *18*(3), 157-175.
- Mittelstadt, B. (2019). AI ethics – Too principled to fail? arXiv preprint arXiv:1906.06668.

- Mittelstadt, B. D. (2017). Principles Alone Cannot Guarantee Ethical AI. *Nature Machine Intelligence*, 1(9), 501.
- Mittelstadt, B., Allo, P., Taddeo, M., Wachter, S., & Floridi, L. (2016). The ethics of algorithms: Mapping the debate. Big Data & Society, 3(2).
- Mnih, V., Kavukcuoglu, K., Silver, D., Rusu, A. A., Veness, J., Bellemare, M. G., ... & Petersen, S. (2015). Human-level control through deep reinforcement learning. Nature, 518(7540), 529-533.
- Molnar, C. (2020). Interpretable Machine Learning. Lulu.com.
- Monostori, L., Kádár, B., Bauernhansl, T., Kondoh, S., Kumara, S., Reinhart, G., ... & Sauer, O. (2016). Cyber-Physical Systems in Manufacturing. *CIRP Annals*, 65(2), 621-641.
- Mourtzis, D., Doukas, M., & Bernidaki, M. (2016). A Framework for Supporting Industry 4.0 Implementation in Manufacturing Companies. *Procedia CIRP*, 52, 12-17.
- Murphy, K. P. (2012). Machine Learning: A Probabilistic Perspective. MIT Press.
- Najjar, L. J., & Kanso, A. (2019). Using Big Data Analytics to Enhance Supply Chain Management: A Comprehensive Literature Review and Research Agenda. *Journal of Business Research*, 99, 129-144.
- Narayanan, A., & Shmatikov, V. (2010). Myths and fallacies of "personally identifiable information". Communications of the ACM, 53(6), 24-26.
- Ng, A., Katanforoosh, M., Mourad, S., & Dai, A. M. (2017). *Deep Learning Specialization*. Coursera.
- Obermeyer, Z., & Emanuel, E. J. (2016). Predicting the Future—Big Data, Machine Learning, and Clinical Medicine. *New England Journal of Medicine*, 375(13), 1216-1219.
- Odersky, M., Spoon, L., & Venners, B. (2004). *Programming in Scala*. Artima.

- Ohm, P. (2010). Broken Promises of Privacy: Responding to the Surprising Failure of Anonymization. *UCLA Law Review*, 57, 1701-1777.
- O'Keefe, B., & Brown, G. (2019). Machine Learning for Personalized Advertising in Connected Television. In *Proceedings of the 25th ACM SIGKDD International Conference on Knowledge Discovery & Data Mining*.
- O'Neil, C. (2016). *Weapons of Math Destruction: How Big Data Increases Inequality and Threatens Democracy*. Broadway Books.
- Osband, I., Blundell, C., Pritzel, A., & Van Roy, B. (2016). Deep exploration via bootstrapped DQN. In Advances in neural information processing systems (pp. 4026-4034).
- Otto, B. (2011). A morphology of the organisation of data governance. In 2011 International Conference on Information Quality (pp. 1-9). IEEE.
- Pagallo, U. (2018). The laws of robots: Crimes, contracts, and torts. Springer.
- Pakhira, D. S., Bandyopadhyay, S., & Maulik, U. (2018). Data Clustering: Algorithms and Applications. *CRC Press*.
- Partnership on AI. (2017). Tenets. Retrieved from https://www.partnershiponai.org/tenets/.
- Partnoy, F., & Rasmussen, R. K. (2019). Regulating AI. *California Law Review*, 107(6), 1683-1764.
- Pipino, L. L., Lee, Y. W., & Wang, R. Y. (2002). Data quality assessment. Communications of the ACM, 45(4), 211-218.
- Provost, F., & Fawcett, T. (2013). Data science for business: What you need to know about data mining and data-analytic thinking. O'Reilly Media.
- Rahm, E., & Do, H. H. (2000). Data Cleaning: Problems and Current Approaches. *IEEE Data Engineering Bulletin*, 23(4), 3-13.
- Ray, P. P. (2016). A survey on Internet of Things architectures. Journal of King Saud University-Computer and Information Sciences, 30(3), 291-319.

- Redman, T. C. (2008). Data Governance: The Practice of Managing Data as an Asset. *DM Review Magazine*, 18(1), 12-14.
- Ribeiro, M. T., Singh, S., & Guestrin, C. (2016). "Why Should I Trust You?" Explaining the Predictions of Any Classifier. In *Proceedings of the 22nd ACM SIGKDD International Conference on Knowledge Discovery and Data Mining* (KDD'16), 1135-1144.
- Ricci, F., Rokach, L., & Shapira, B. (2015). Introduction to Recommender Systems Handbook. In *Recommender Systems Handbook* (pp. 1-35). Springer.
- Rocher, L., Hendrickx, J. M., & de Montjoye, Y. A. (2019). Estimating the success of re-identifications in incomplete datasets using generative models. Nature Communications, 10(1), 1-9.
- Romanosky, S.(2016). Examining the costs and causes of cyber incidents. Journal of Cybersecurity, 2(2), 121-135.
- Rubinstein, I. S., & Hartzog, W. (2016). Anonymization and risk. Washington Law Review, 91, 703.
- Russell, S. J., & Norvig, P. (2016). Artificial Intelligence: A modern approach (3rd ed.). Pearson.
- Russell, S. J., & Norvig, P. (2020). *Artificial Intelligence: A Modern Approach* (4th ed.). Pearson.
- Russell, S. J., & Norvig, P. (2021). *Artificial Intelligence: A Modern Approach*. Pearson.
- Russell, S., Dewey, D., & Tegmark, M. (2015). Research priorities for robust and beneficial artificial intelligence. AI Magazine, 36(4), 105-114.
- Russell, S., Dewey, D., & Tegmark, M. (2015). Research priorities for robust and beneficial artificial intelligence. AI Magazine, 36(4), 105-114.
- Russom, P. (2011). Big data analytics. TDWI Best Practices Report, Fourth Quarter.
- Saha, B., & Srivastava, D. K. (2014). Data quality: The other face of big data. In 2014 IEEE 30th International Conference on Data Engineering (pp. 1294-1297). IEEE.

- Sahin, C., Yildirim, P., & Eren, P. E. (2018). A Review on Retail Fraud Detection with Big Data Analytics. *Journal of Retailing and Consumer Services*, 41, 295-303.
- Sahin, C., Yildirim, P., & Eren, P. E. (2018). A Review on Retail Fraud Detection with Big Data Analytics. *Journal of Retailing and Consumer Services*, 41, 295-303.
- Sakr, S., Liu, A., Batista, D. M., & Alomari, M. (2013). A Survey of Large Scale Data Management Approaches in Cloud Environments. IEEE Communications Surveys & Tutorials, 13(3), 311-336.
- Sandhu, R. S., Coyne, E. J., Feinstein, H. L., & Youman, C. E. (1996). Role-based access control models. IEEE Computer, 29(2), 38-47.
- Scarfone, K., Souppaya, M., & Hoffman, P. (2019). Guide to Cybersecurity Incident Handling. *National Institute of Standards and Technology (NIST)*.
- Schafer, J. L., & Graham, J. W. (2002). Missing data: Our view of the state of the art. Psychological methods, 7(2), 147.
- Schneier, B. (1996). Applied Cryptography: Protocols, Algorithms, and Source Code in C. *Wiley*.
- Schuemie, M. J., van der Straaten, P., Krijn, M., & van der Mast, C. (2020). Research on Presence in Virtual Reality: A Survey. *Cyberpsychology, Behavior, and Social Networking*, 23(3), 159-173.
- Shi, W., Cao, J., Zhang, Q., Li, Y., & Xu, L. (2016). Edge computing: Vision and challenges. *IEEE Internet of Things Journal*, 3(5), 637-646.
- Shmueli, G., & Koppius, O. (2011). Predictive analytics in information systems research. MIS Quarterly, 35(3), 553-572.
- Siciliano, B., Sciavicco, L., Villani, L., & Oriolo, G. (2016). *Robotics: Modelling, Planning and Control*. Springer.

- Sivarajah, U., Kamal, M. M., Irani, Z., & Weerakkody, V. (2017). Critical analysis of Big Data challenges and analytical methods. Journal of Business Research, 70, 263-286.
- Smith, B., & Linden, G. (2017). Two decades of recommender systems at Amazon.com. IEEE Internet Computing, 21(3), 12-18.
- Stonebraker, M., Çetintemel, U., & Zdonik, S. (2010). The 8 requirements of real-time stream processing. ACM Sigmod Record, 34(4), 42-47.
- Strubell, E., Ganesh, A., & McCallum, A. (2019). Energy and policy considerations for deep learning in NLP. In Proceedings of the 57th Annual Meeting of the Association for Computational Linguistics (pp. 3645-3650).
- Sutton, R. S., & Barto, A. G. (2018). Reinforcement Learning: An Introduction. MIT Press.
- Swan, M. (2013). The quantified self: Fundamental disruption in big data science and biological discovery. Big Data, 1(2), 85-99.
- Sweeney, L. (2002). k-anonymity: A model for protecting privacy. International Journal of Uncertainty, Fuzziness and Knowledge-Based Systems, 10(05), 557-570.
- Taddeo, M., & Floridi, L. (2018). Regulate artificial intelligence to avert cyber arms race. Nature, 556(7701), 296-298.
- Taylor, L., Floridi, L., & van der Sloot, B. (2017). Group Privacy: New Challenges of Data Technologies. Philosophical Transactions of the Royal Society A: Mathematical, Physical and Engineering Sciences, 376(2128), 20170339. https://doi.org/10.1098/rsta.2017.0339
- Tene, O., & Polonetsky, J. (2012). Privacy in the Age of Big Data: A Time for Big Decisions. Stanford Law Review Online, 64, 63-69.
- Thomas, J. J., & Cook, K. A. (2005). Illuminating the Path: The Research and Development Agenda for Visual Analytics. IEEE.
- Thusoo, A., Sarma, J. S., Jain, N., Shao, Z., Chakka, P., Zhang, N., ... & Murthy, R. (2010). Hive - A petabyte scale data warehouse

using Hadoop. In 2010 IEEE 26th International Conference on Data Engineering (ICDE 2010) (pp. 996-1005). IEEE.

- Tibshirani, R. (1996). Regression shrinkage and selection via the lasso. Journal of the Royal Statistical Society: Series B (Methodological), 58(1), 267-288.

- Topol, E. (2019). Deep Medicine: How Artificial Intelligence Can Make Healthcare Human Again. *Basic Books.*

- Tufte, E. R. (2001). *The Visual Display of Quantitative Information.* Graphics Press.

- Turilli, M., & Floridi, L. (2009). The ethics of information transparency. *Ethics and Information Technology, 11*(2), 105-112.

- Vall, A., Asensio-Cubero, J., & Llorens, J. (2017). Music Recommender Systems: Challenges and Opportunities in the Digital Era. *Frontiers in Artificial Intelligence,* 1, 3.

- VanderPlas, J. (2016). *Python Data Science Handbook: Essential Tools for Working with Data.* O'Reilly Media, Inc.

- Vasudevan, V., & Zadeh, R. B. (2018). Data Integration in Big Data: Challenges and Opportunities. *Procedia Computer Science,* 132, 611-617.

- Verhoef, P. C., Kannan, P. K., & Inman, J. J. (2017). From Multi-Channel Retailing to Omni-Channel Retailing: Introduction to the Special Issue on Multi-Channel Retailing. *Journal of Retailing,* 93(1), 1-5.

- Voigt, P., & Von dem Bussche, A. (2017). The EU General Data Protection Regulation (GDPR). A Practical Guide, 1st Ed., Cham: Springer International Publishing.

- Wachter, S., Mittelstadt, B., & Floridi, L. (2017). Transparent, explainable, and accountable AI for robotics. Science Robotics, 2(6).

- Wang, R. Y., & Strong, D. M. (1996). Beyond Accuracy: What Data Quality Means to Data Consumers. *Journal of Management Information Systems,* 12(4), 5-33.

- Wani, S., Pararath, A., & Shah, J. (2020). The Role of Telemedicine in the Healthcare Delivery Model: A Comprehensive Assessment of Demand, Access, Quality, and Cost. *Telemedicine and e-Health*, 26(4), 369-375.
- Weber, K. (2017). Data governance in the digital age. Computer Law & Security Review, 33(2), 291-306.
- Weber, R. H. (2010). Internet of Things – New security and privacy challenges. *Computer Law & Security Review, 26*(1), 23-30.
- White, T. (2012). Hadoop: The Definitive Guide. O'Reilly Media, Inc.
- Whittlestone, J., Nyrup, R., Alexandrova, A., Dihal, K., & Cave, S. (2019). Ethical and societal implications of algorithms, data, and artificial intelligence: a roadmap for research. London: Nuffield Foundation.
- Wickham, H. (2016). *ggplot2: Elegant Graphics for Data Analysis.* Springer.
- Wright, D., & De Hert, P. (2012). Privacy impact assessment. Springer Science & Business Media.
- Xia, J., Yuan, L., & Zhang, Y. (2017). Crop Disease Recognition Using Two-Stage CNN Transfer Learning. *Computers and Electronics in Agriculture*, 142, 126-134.
- Yannakakis, G. N., Spronck, P., & Loiacono, D. (2018). Player Modeling. In *Artificial Intelligence in the Age of Neural Networks and Brain Computing* (pp. 303-324). Elsevier.
- Zafar, M. B., Valera, I., Gomez Rodriguez, M., & Gummadi, K. P. (2017). Fairness Beyond Disparate Treatment & Disparate Impact: Learning Classification without Disparate Mistreatment. In *Proceedings of the 26th International Conference on World Wide Web* (WWW'17), 1171-1180.
- Zaharia, M., Chowdhury, M., Das, T., Dave, A., Ma, J., McCauley, M., ... & Stoica, I. (2013). Resilient distributed datasets: A fault-tolerant abstraction for in-memory cluster computing. In Proceedings of the 9th USENIX conference on Networked

Systems Design and Implementation (pp. 2-2). USENIX Association.

- Zaharia, M., Chowdhury, M., Das, T., Dave, A., Ma, J., McCauley, M., ... & Stoica, I. (2010). Resilient Distributed Datasets: A Fault-Tolerant Abstraction for In-Memory Cluster Computing. In *Proceedings of the 9th USENIX Conference on Networked Systems Design and Implementation* (pp. 2-2).
- Zaharia, M., Chowdhury, M., Franklin, M. J., Shenker, S., & Stoica, I. (2010). Spark: Cluster computing with working sets. HotCloud, 10(10-10), 95.
- Zaharia, M., Chowdhury, M., Franklin, M. J., Shenker, S., & Stoica, I. (2016). Apache Hadoop: Fast and scalable data processing and its application to genomics. *Syst. Biol.*, 61(1), 51-59.
- Zaharia, M., Das, T., Li, H., Hunter, T., Shenker, S., & Stoica, I. (2013). Discretized streams: An efficient and fault-tolerant model for stream processing on large clusters. *Proceedings of the 4th USENIX conference on Hot Topics in Cloud Ccomputing*, 10-10.
- Zanella, A., Bui, N., Castellani, A., Vangelista, L., & Zorzi, M. (2014). Internet of things for smart cities. *IEEE Internet of Things Journal, 1*(1), 22-32.
- Zarsky, T. Z. (2016). Incompatible: The GDPR in the age of big data. *Seton Hall Law Review, 47*, 995-1020.
- Zhang, C., Bengio, S., Hardt, M., Recht, B., & Vinyals, O. (2016). Understanding deep learning requires rethinking generalization. arXiv preprint arXiv:1611.03530.
- Zhang, J., Xiao, X., & Xie, Y. (2016). Efficient distributed differential privacy with improved utility. In Proceedings of the 2016 ACM SIGMOD International Conference on Management of Data (pp. 1155-1170).
- Zheng, B., Huang, Y., Bian, J., Zhao, L., & Gong, L. (2018). The Landscape of Research on Massive Open Online Courses (MOOCs) in Computers in Education. *Computers & Education*, 122, 28-43.

- Zheng, G., Zhang, F., Zheng, Z., Xiang, Y., Yuan, N. J., Xie, X., & Li, Z. (2018). DRN: A deep reinforcement learning framework for news recommendation. In Proceedings of the 2018 World Wide Web Conference (pp. 167-176).
- Zheng, P., Yuan, S., Wu, X., Li, J., & Lu, A. (2018). Federated Predictive Analytics with Heterogeneous Data. In 2018 IEEE International Conference on Big Data (Big Data) (pp. 2513-2520). IEEE.
- Zheng, X., Cai, Z., Li, J., & Wang, J. (2014). Big data for social transportation. IEEE Transactions on Intelligent Transportation Systems, 17(3), 620-630.
- Zheng, Y., Zhang, Z., & Lyu, M. R. (2015). A Comprehensive Survey of Cloud Computing Security Management. *ACM Computing Surveys (CSUR)*, 47(4), 1-58.
- Zhong, R. Y., Xu, X., & Klotz, E. (2016). Blockchain-Based Supply Chain Financing in Agri-food Supply Chain. *Supply Chain Management: An International Journal*, 21(1), 18-31.
- Zhou, J., Cui, L., & Deng, X. (2018). A Survey of Machine Learning for Big Data Processing. *ACM Computing Surveys (CSUR)*, 51(7), 1-36.
- Zou, J., & Schiebinger, L. (2018). AI can be sexist and racist — it's time to make it fair. Nature, 559(7714), 324-326. https://doi.org/10.1038/d41586-018-05707-8

www.ingramcontent.com/pod-product-compliance
Lightning Source LLC
Chambersburg PA
CBHW050318160726
48002CB00001B/87